Beati

Xandria Williams began ⟨...⟩ a geochemist involved in mineral explo⟨...⟩ but soon turned to biochemistry and the study of nutrition, naturopathy, homeoopathy and botanic medicine. She then extended her studies to Neurolinguistic Programming, Time-Line Therapy, Voice Dialogue and many other methods of helping people with emotional, personal and psychological problems.

She has lectured extensively at many natural therapies colleges and conferences and holds classes and seminars on a range of aspects of physical, mental and emotional health care. She has written several hundred articles, has often been heard on radio and television and is the author of *Living with Allergies*, *What's in your Food*, *Osteoporosis*, *Choosing Health Intentionally*, *Choosing Weight Intentionally* and *Stress – Recognise and Resolve*.

Xandria Williams has evolved her unique and highly effective approach to tackling life's problems over two decades of research into helping people at her clinics in Sydney and London, in her seminars and through her books and articles.

Also by Xandria Williams

Living with Allergies
What's in your Food
Osteoporosis
Choosing Health Intentionally
Choosing Weight Intentionally
Stress – Recognise and Resolve

XANDRIA WILLIAMS

Beating the Blues

CEDAR

A Mandarin Paperback
BEATING THE BLUES

First published in Great Britain 1995
as a Cedar original
by Mandarin Paperbacks
an imprint of Reed Consumer Books Ltd
Michelin House, 81 Fulham Road, London SW3 6RB
and Auckland, Melbourne, Singapore and Toronto

A CIP catalogue record for this title
is available from the British Library
ISBN 0 7493 1955 0

Printed and bound in Great Britain
by BPC Paperbacks Ltd
A member of The British Printing Company Ltd

Contents

Introduction

When I was a research scientist, doing my first post-graduate degree, I started out with the naïve idea that I was going to make some great scientific discovery. It would be entirely new and would all be based on my own brilliant research.

Impressed with my own goal, and wanting also to impress my professor, I told him this when he asked me what I wanted to do for my thesis. He was kind enough to smile gently at me before pointing out that all research was based on the work and knowledge that had gone before and that if I produced a thesis that was 95 per cent existing ideas and five per cent my own, I would add significantly to the body of scientific knowledge.

We discussed this further and he pointed out that even the greatest discoveries, the breakthroughs of people such as Archimedes, Newton and Einstein, were based on all the work that had gone before. These men had simply taken a bigger leap into the future than others.

Since then I've had many reasons to recognise the truth of his comments. They are true for most of what I do in my practice, cover in my lectures and write in books and articles, and this book is no exception. Ideas come from somewhere, they are developed, metamorphosed and then applied.

Over the years and to an increasing extent, more and more is being learned about the way the human mind works. Psychologists, psychiatrists and other conventionally trained people are doing research; so are many people from very different disciplines. Many new techniques have been developed that allow us to work more creatively with thoughts and emotions. Some of the techniques have well recognised names like transactional analysis, cognitive therapy, trance and hypnosis, Neurolinguistic Programming (NLP) and Voice Dialogue, and others don't. Some are major and some are minor.

Several Neurolinguistic Programming techniques are included in this book. Neurolinguistic Programming, often abbreviated to NLP, is becoming more popular as a method of therapy and of creating change in people's lives. In part it is a study of how the mind works and how this working can be changed when required. It is also concerned with communications and rapport building and how these can be improved. NLP involves specific procedures for making changes in the way you deal with situations, and some of these are described and incorporated into Part II.

I have a passion for knowledge and read and study voraciously in the fields that interest me and, wherever and whenever possible, incorporate the ideas I have read and learned about into my own clinical practice. At the same time I have, inevitably, developed and used some of my own ideas, often changing them or blending them with others until the boundaries have become unrecognisable. There is no intent here to claim all the ideas in this book as my own: many of them are not. However, I have worked with, modified and developed most of the techniques and ideas that I describe, sometimes on the 95 per cent to five per cent ratio originally mentioned by my first professor, but often with a greater input of my ideas. I make this disclaimer as I have no wish to claim originality for ideas I have received from others. Of one thing you can be sure: all the ideas and methods here have been well tried in practice, by my patients and clients, and have been found to be of value and help to most, if not all, of the people that have used or experienced them.

As readers of my previous books on related topics will know*, I feel it is most important to recognise that in all that you do, and in all that happens to you, you do have choices. It is also important to claim and recognise your own responsibility for, and control over, your thoughts, feelings and what occurs in your life. When these concepts are combined with such techniques as Running a Phrase, Regression, NLP, working with your time line (or memory line), techniques for creating futures, and others, you can create a powerful way of lifting depression and changing other unwanted moods such as shame, guilt and jealousy.

There are two essential components that underlie much of what follows. First, it seems obvious to me – as part of my personal experience, belief system and philosophy – that you are in charge of your own life. Second, even if there are times when this may seem doubtful and you may feel unsure about this, it is the most useful belief to have.

It is certainly true that the opposite belief, that you do not have any control over your life, rests on very shaky grounds and is impossible to prove. Working along these lines with clients has shown the power of this approach in helping people to improve their lives. The major concepts that we will be working with are given here:

a) You create your own beliefs and experiences.

You do this by making your own interpretation of the events which occur around you. No two people in the same situation describe or experience it in exactly the same way. This is demonstrated repeatedly and you will have discovered it for yourself. As a result of the interpretations and assumptions you make, from the moment you are born you create your own experience and your own moods and emotions. Sometimes you do this consciously, more often you do it unconsciously and unwittingly, falling into well worn and automatic patterns.

b) You can, therefore, change mood and behaviour patterns and create others.

A logical extension of the first concept is the recognition that since you have created your beliefs, moods and emotions, you have the power to change them and create others and thus create whatever you want both in the present and in the future. This is possible provided your desire for the changes is strong enough to effect the change. Thus you can have, or bring into your life, objects or possessions and create the situations and experiences you want. Further, and possibly most importantly, you can change your state of mind and your emotions if you don't like the mood you are in at the moment.

If this is true, and if you are sufficiently determined, you can change your depression, lift it, and create other moods in its place. Stop. Before you throw the book down in disgust, claiming that if it were so easy you would have done it long ago, read on. Lifting depression will not happen in an instant and it may not be easy. However, I have found in my practice that it is often simple, surprisingly simple, and by the end of this book, if you read it thoroughly and, most importantly, if you put into practice the ideas and techniques in it, you will be surprised at some of the results you can achieve for yourself.

c) Work with the most useful belief, if the less useful ones can't be proved.
Some people have trouble accepting the first two concepts so we will consider them further. We will also consider the ramifications of believing them and not believing them.

If you chose to deny the above concepts, then you are probably assuming that you are at the mercy of your fate. You are not in control, you cannot dictate your life, you cannot decide what you will and will not do, what will occur and what won't, how you will feel, how you will live. Instead, you are like a cork tossed on the sea of life. If you currently feel depressed, then you may as well get used to it if you are going to assume you cannot change it.

If, on the other hand, you choose to believe the above concepts then, axiomatically, you are in control of your life. You can decide how you will live, how you will interpret events and happenings and how you will respond. If you are feeling depressed right now, you can decide to make the necessary moves to change this mood into another of your own choosing.

If you choose to believe that everything in your life

is of your own creating, then you can also choose to believe that you created things for a purpose and to some benefit to yourself. It is reasonable to assume that you did not intend to harm yourself, so it is reasonable to believe that everything you have created so far has been for some benefit, even if at times that benefit may seem hard to find. You may wonder why you created certain troubles and problems, yet it becomes valuable to explore the possibility that you did and to determine what possible benefit you have gained from each event and situation in your life.

Can you know for sure, with *absolute* certainty, whether you are in control, or whether your life is controlled by the fates? 'Knowing' is a personal experience. I 'know' the first two concepts to be true; they are true for me. Yet they may not be true for you, at least not yet and not fully, and it is not my business to tell you what you should believe, or to tell you what your experience is. However, I would put the following to you:

First, there is a lot of evidence to support (a) and (b). Think of your own experiences. When you know it is going to be a good day, don't you find plenty of evidence to support that experience, don't you see the times people smile and ignore the frowns? When you just know it is going to be a good day, you probably also smile yourself, and other people respond, thus you, in turn, generate the mood you expect. Of course, the alternative is also true, if you go round like a wet blanket feeling the day is going to be a miserable failure, you will probably pull the people around you down as well, so that they reinforce your mood.

I'm sure you've been in a situation involving several people where some have said it was a wonderful time and others have said it was boring. You can have as many accounts and experiences of a situation as there are people experiencing the situation. It is all in how you choose to assess it and interpret it. You also have a hand in the creating.

Second, consider the possibilities. Either (a) and (b) above are true or they are not.

1. If they are and you believe them, then come with me through this book and let's create a better future for you.

2. If they are not and you don't believe them, consider the following points.

3. If they are *not* true and you choose to believe them, you may be living in a fool's paradise, but you can have a lot of fun doing it. At least you will improve your subjective experience.

4. If they *are* true and you chose *not* to believe them, you will, conversely, be living in a fool's hell. You would be choosing to stay depressed, to remain unhappy, and to continue to suffer at the hands of a fate you could so easily, with a change of mind-set, control.

If you cannot be absolutely sure which is the truth, (a) and (b) above or their opposites, then what will you choose to believe, since you can't sit on the fence? 'The most useful belief' is that they are true. Choosing to believe you can control your life leaves you in a position of power. It gives you the means to make positive changes if things are not the way you want them to be. This is mentally and emotionally healthy. There is also much clinical evidence to demonstrate that a postive mental attitude improves your physical health, and that negative emotions adversely affect your physical health and can lead to serious illnesses as well as much unhappinesss.

d) You always have choices.
If you work with the above ideas, then you come to realise that you always have choices. You may not always like the options that are open to you, but choice is always there, to be exercised either actively or by default. If you have good choices you can choose the best option. If you are in a tight spot you can choose the least bad option. Whatever you do, keep in mind that you did and do have choices: it is up to you to exercise them and take control. If you don't do this, and if you let someone else or fate take over, that is still your choice: you choose to give your power away.

e) Working with your mind and emotions can be as logical, structured and predictable as working with molecules in a chemical laboratory.
This may seem hard, empirical or mechanical and may seem to reduce the wonders of the mind, thoughts and emotions to a mere set of mechanisms. That is not what I mean. What I do mean is that your state of mind – past, present or future – is not based on a swirling mass of emotions with no structure and over which you have no control. Work with clients has shown that you can follow a particular technique or method to bring about change – to help a person get over guilt, for instance, or to eliminate the fear associated with an event in the past – and that, time after time, with client after client, the change will occur, the situation will be resolved, albeit with a wonderful array of individual variations in detail.

As one client described it, 'It is almost as if what

you have just done has been to take my mind along a specific route, along certain logically chosen roads, to get me to my chosen destination. When you did the second exercise, I could almost sense that we were heading in the same direction, by a slightly different set of roads, and could sense that I was about to arrive at exactly the same destination, and that is indeed what happened.'

The same client continued, 'I could also see the various crossroads at which I would normally, left to myself, have taken the old wrong turnings, the ones that would have taken me to the old destination (or state of mind) that I want to avoid. And I could see that the old turnings I might have taken were all similar and based on similar choices or senses of (wrong) direction each time. The new turnings that have led me, each time we've done these different processes, to a better state of mind, also have certain things in common and they each get me to the same positive outcome. And the whole thing has been so simple, whereas I thought I would need hours and months of therapy to put my life back on track. Amazing.'

The thing that is amazing and exciting for me, is that there is no need for people to spend hours focusing on their past, no need to dig deep into the old emotions, re-experience them, even, some might say, wallow in them. You don't have to get in touch with all the old traumas, angers and depressions, discuss them, analyse them or slowly come to understand them. You don't have to scream or weep it all out or push through the old fears.

I am reminded of an experience at a recent dinner

party. The man on my right was silent through much of the first course and it was only when the person on my left was distracted that I made an effort to draw him into conversation. It turned out that his wife had recently had a nervous breakdown and he could focus on little else.

'Years,' he said, 'for years she's been seeing her shrink, every single week. She's talked it all out with him, endlessly. She's done her best, and so's he, I suppose, but she still wakes up depressed every morning. He's supposed to be good and, goodness knows, he's seen her often enough and it's cost a fortune, but it's made no difference. Depression is a dreadful thing. Maybe this place she's in now will help her. I don't understand it myself. She's got so much to live for: we're well off, the kids are happily married, our marriage is good, or at least it was. I don't know how much more of this I can stand. I can be happy, I don't understand why she's so depressed. The sad thing,' he continued, 'is that the whole process of analysis that she's been in seems to have made her very self-centred. All she seems to think about is the emotions she is experiencing, how they have derived from her past, and what she will say to the man next time she sees him.'

O dear, I thought, so much of this could have been avoided with the new therapies that are available. So often I have seen clients who are willing to take control of their lives resolve major issues in just a few short sessions. They had no need to spend endless hours and amounts of money.

Your emotions are not amorphous forces that run you. You are totally capable of running them and doing so simply, logically and intentionally. Furthermore, this can be done, not by a major act of will-power or discipline, but simply by recognising that: (a) you were heading to a place you didn't want to reach and (b) that, by a simple change of route, you can avoid all the traffic jams and snarl-ups on the first route as well as the poor destination.

Another analogy I have used is to ask: who continues to climb whole mountain ranges to reach the valley beyond once they have been shown a simple pass through which they can walk to reach the valley?

In this book you are about to learn the short cuts and the simple passes. You are about to find cause for celebration. You will rejoice at the lifting of unwanted depression and the discovery of how to have as much joy, happiness and contentment in your life as you would like. Join me and let's find out.

A word of warning: having found out how to do and achieve all these things, it is up to you to put the methods into practice. Nothing written in a book will work or will bring about changes in your life unless you truly want it to and believe the changes will occur. There is a huge difference between knowing in your head and knowing in your heart or in your guts.

I was once faced with a situation where I had to make this difference real to a group of several hundred people. I was to be the second out of four speakers and each of us was to give a two-hour talk. The audience was made up of people with cancer and their partners, whether that was a spouse, parent, family member or close friend. The first speaker had given countless and very convincing figures showing that, in a huge number of medical studies, it had been demonstrated, in a wide variety of ways, that the more positively you felt about your health and the outcome of the current situation the better that outcome would be. The audience clearly enjoyed and appreciated the talk. It was also clear, during the break, that many of them had already read a number of books on the power of thought to affect physical health.

What was I planning to talk about? Just that. I was going to tell them that their thoughts would affect their health and the outcome of their situation. Yawn, yawn, boring. I could just imagine them sitting there thinking they'd heard it all before, so I had to come up with something to grab their attention. This is what I said.

'Wasn't that last talk marvellous?'

This brought a large round of clapping, so I asked, 'Who thinks that what the speaker said – that your thoughts can change your health – is true? Just put your hands up. Look around you.'

The entire audience, with the exception of four nurses who seemed somewhat uncertain, had their hands up and everyone else could see this.

My next question was, 'Whose life is perfect right now, just the way they want it to be?'

Now, given that they all had or were close to someone who had cancer, this was a challenging question. I asked them again to put their hands up and look around. Not surprisingly no hands went up, though again the four nurses waved somewhat uncertainly.

I let a few seconds go by and then said, 'You are all lying.'

Now this is not normally something you say to an audience of a few hundred people to whom you are going to be talking for the next two hours, but I had a purpose. I let a silence grow as what I said sank in.

Either they didn't fully believe that they had control of their lives or else they were getting some benefit from having cancer and were choosing to have it, at least for the moment. If they believed, truly believed, in their hearts and their guts, that their thoughts and their attitudes could affect their health, then they had to accept that they need not have cancer and that, since they did have it, there must be some possible benefit to having it, much as they might, with their conscious mind, resist this idea.

> **I am not suggesting here that these people were at fault or to blame for having cancer. I am suggesting that a useful belief to have is that they, at some unconscious level, have chosen to have it as the safest way of getting their emotional needs met. In this regard they did the best they knew. There should be no concept of blame, rather the empowering concept and re-cognition that they have within themselves the power to make alternative choices now. [See *Choosing Health Intentionally* for amplification of this concept.]**

This is a challenging concept, I know, but I deemed it one with which the audience needed to come to terms in order to get the most out of the rest of the day, and it certainly had the desired effect. You could almost hear the people thinking, and the questions that came along with the talks for the rest of the day were wonderfully perceptive and probing.

It is very important that you DO, as well as READ, this book. If you feel you have read or heard of some or all of these ideas before and yet you still feel depressed, then it is time to start doing, to start making the changes for yourself. It is bootstrap stuff. But you can do it.

* *Choosing Health Intentionally*, Xandria K. Williams. Simon and Schuster (Aust) and Charles Letts (Holdings) Ltd (UK), 1992. *Choosing Weight Intentionally*, Xandria K. Williams. Simon and Schuster (Aust) and Charles Letts (Holdings) Ltd (UK), 1992. *Stress – Recognise and Resolve*, Xandria K. Williams. Charles Letts (Holdings) Ltd (UK), 1993.

PART I

Creating Depression

In this first section of the book we will be looking at the background to depression, the reason why it is becoming more common and some of the underlying assumptions and belief systems you may be using. We will look at the concept that you create your moods, are in control of your moods and so can change your moods. You can do this as and when you choose, but the process is more complex than a simple change of mind and needs to involve your unconscious mind. This means that it is important for you to unearth your underlying and often unconscious beliefs.

Some people are inherently more prone to depression than others and we will look at this and at the differences between optimists and pessimists. We will also consider the controversial idea that there are actually benefits to being depressed. Finally, for those who feel that this life is not all there is, we will take a look at depression within the broader context of the whole of the individual's existence.

Chapter One

Why Is Depression So Common?

Depression is nothing new. People have always suffered from it and talked about it. However, depression appears to be becoming much more common. Certainly, it is being spoken about more, but there is also real evidence that shows it to be on the increase. There have even been comments that, if it were a physical illness, it would be considered an epidemic. We will be looking at possible causes of this increase in this chapter.

First, however, let's look, without getting too technical, at the two types of depression: reactive depression and endogenous depression. The first one, reactive depression, occurs when the depression, sadness or unhappiness, call it what you will, is triggered off by a specific event or situation. You are simply reacting to this situation. You may be reacting to someone you know or love being hurt, getting sick or even dying. You may be reacting to losing something you value, failing to be able to do something you want to do or to getting hurt by someone or something. All of these situations, and others like them, can make you unhappy. There is a cause, and there is a result.

This, at one level, is perfectly natural. Yet, at the same time, these things will depress some people much more than others, and more and more it seems that smaller and smaller things are getting people down. It seems that the natural resilience to depression, natural optimism, is diminishing in some people. Whatever the situation, I'm sure you would rather be in the group which feels minimally depressed than in the group which experiences major depression every time something, even something small, goes wrong in their lives. Achieving this outcome is a major aim of this book.

The second type of depression, endogenous depression, is experienced even when there is no specific trigger. If you suffer from endogenous depression, you may feel depressed even when, on the face of it, everything in your life is rosy. Even when all is well, you may be worrying about the things that *could* go wrong and feeling depressed about them. Or you may simply feel there is a black cloud hanging over you, for no apparent reason. You may even wish to throw it off but not know how to. Life in general may seem purposeless and pointless. Or you may simply feel that it is your own life that has little point to it. Perhaps you think you are in a hopeless situation and there is no way out; perhaps you have decided to struggle on with little hope that things will get better. Or perhaps it is not that bad, you may just feel that, although nothing is particularly bad, there is nothing much that is good or fun either and that life is all rather pointless and grey.

Endogenous depression is the type more often dealt with by medicinal drugs. In many ways it is harder to deal with than reactive depression since there may seem to be no apparent specific causal event or situation to be worked on. However, huge strides can often still be made with the ideas and techniques discussed here. It has been interesting to find how often, in clients, even endogenous depression is based on some deeply buried beliefs formed earlier in life and affecting the person's interpretation of the present.

You can also, of course, suffer from a combination of these two types of depression. You may feel depressed much of the time and even more so when there are specific triggers. It seems that both types of depression are on the increase. More people than ever before are experiencing depression both more often and more deeply than in the past. Some of the reasons for this are discussed below:

Breakdown of Social Structures

People used to define themselves by their role in the social structure. They used to know who they were and feel secure as part of the social group to which they belonged. This social structure defined the appropriate way for an individual to behave and the appropriate goals to have in life. It acknowledged the individual for the achievement of these goals and for correct behaviour within his or her group, and it gave support in times of doubt or crisis.

Not so long ago there were many such groups defining, or giving a context for, an individual's identity. These included a person's nation or county, their subsection of that country, be it country or area, their city or town, their local community, their extended family and, finally, the nuclear family or their partner.

Think back, if you are old enough, to the Second World War. With very few exceptions, people were not happy to be fighting the war, yet there was a sense of doing what was right for your country, of comradeship and of mutual support. The pain and suffering were worth it if your country survived. Most people felt proud of their nationality, proud of their country and willing to make sacrifices for it. They may have had, and indeed often did have, a rough time, but, because of the value systems operating in those days, few people sat around thinking they were depressed. They got on with what had to be done, stiff-upper-lipped, and were well regarded and acknowledged by the system within which they operated.

People were also part of a community. If the season was bad and the crops were damaged, you were not a lone farmer battling the elements and competing with the farmers around you and the impersonal trading relationships with other countries and markets. You were part of a community that worked together. You helped your neighbours, they helped you, and you were part of an established pattern. Things had been done the same way for centuries and few people sat down and asked themselves if they were living fulfilling lives. It was enough that you were doing the right thing, were part of a family. You were bringing up your children and were almost certainly hoping for better things for them than you had. You had your job and you knew who you were. There was an established social order and a sense of continuity.

In the post-war period, the village square, the town markets and other such gatherings became less common, families became more and more isolated in their own homes and social life became dominated by television, with little interactive participation. Yet you could still draw strength from your family. There was still a sense of stability. Couples stayed together, children expected to have the same parents all through their growing years, and if you were in the dumps there were people around who cared. This family group consisted not only of parents and children but of aunts, uncles, cousins, grandparents and so forth. It was quite likely that several members of the wider family group would live together in one house and there was a wider choice as to whom you could turn to for support than there is today. If you didn't get on with your father, there was always an uncle or grandad who lived with you or very close by.

This concept of 'close by' is also important. In general, people grew up and lived in the one area all their lives. Even marriages tended to be within a town or village. The result of this was that you had around you people who had known you since childhood. The easiest time to make friends is in childhood and by the time you are an adult you know which of your school friends you can relate well to, which you trust, which you feel comfortable with and who you can turn to when things get tough and you feel a bit down in the dumps. If you stay put, your circle of friends and acquaintances will be quite extensive.

Over the last few decades these structures have progressively broken down. The extended family has become the nuclear family, an average of 4.3 people. You marry in hope, but divorce is becoming more common. Instead of assuming that marriage is for life and is something you work at, it has become an option. Is it good enough? Are you happy? Are you depressed? If it isn't right, should you get out while you can and have another try?

Nowadays, it is common to find that people don't even bother to get married. They hold back from commitment. This may provide greater freedom, but it fails to provide stability and security. Being insecure is a sure way to become depressed.

When marriages were relationships of convenience you could hardly feel depressed if it wasn't blissfully happy. Rather you would be relieved that it was comfortable and thrilled if it was more. Many of today's novels and mazagines have bred the idea that marriages are, or should be, made in heaven, and if yours is not always fulfilling and wonderful you are missing out on something and have every right to feel depressed.

One of the common but new situations I see that causes depression comes about as a result of this sexual and social freedom. It is so easy to live together that many couples drift into it in almost the same way they fall into other arrangements for sharing accommodation. You go out with someone for a short while and then decide you quite like each other and you might as well live together: after all, if it doesn't work out you can always split up. However, it is more difficult and usually more traumatic to split up with someone with whom you have been living than to stop seeing someone you have been going out with for a while. In the latter case you can simply drift apart or stop seeing each other and start making new friends without too much pain. If you are living together, then when you split up someone also has to lose their home and move elsewhere. It is a more public statement of failure and can be depressing as a consequence.

I also see many couples who are reluctant to face the trauma of splitting because they feel the relationship, which was somewhat casual to start with, isn't really that bad, and yet they don't particularly want to stay together either and they are depressed with their life as a result. This can be further compounded by the fact that they are denied many chances of a new relationship simply because they are so obviously, or apparently, a couple.

Furthermore, if you have a few boyfriends or girl-friends and the relationships fail, you probably don't feel too bad. If, on the other hand, you have lived with a few different people and the relationships have failed, you may start to feel a failure, since the statement is more public, both to other people and in your own mind.

All in all, this changing social structure, from being part of a nation down to being an individual on your own, has contributed significantly to making people feel depressed.

Even within apparent groups, people are now feeling or recognising that, at the deepest level, they are still on their own. More and more, people are becoming aware of their own isolation and recognising that the association with a group is, at best, vulnerable to breakdown under certain circumstances. Even a full sense of being a part of a couple is found less often and people are becoming increasingly aware of being alone and on their own.

Changing Religious Beliefs

Other changes have lead to the increased incidence of depression and one of these is the loss of religious beliefs and the security and comfort of a watchful god. When people held a firm belief in god and the promise of receiving their just rewards in heaven, it was possible to bear the stumbles and pains of this life without too much depression. Now that this automatic assumption is not there, at least for most people, there is a greater onus on making this life a reward in itself. If it is not, you may well feel depressed.

When you were sure there was a watchful god noting all your good deeds it mattered less if others did not acknowledge you. When you felt that your bad deeds were being watched by a benevolent god it was possibly easier to forgive yourself than today when people seem to be riddled by guilt, self-blame, self-doubt and self-condemnation.

Breakdown of Established Behaviour Patterns

There used to be codes of behaviour imposed by society, as well as by religion, and fully accepted by the individual. If you followed these, if you did the right thing, you could feel safe and fulfilled, happy that you had achieved success in life. You may not have been totally happy, but you had done what was expected of you by society, and you could feel good about it. Nowadays, society's rules are there for the breaking and it often seems as if the only sin is to get caught. Even those who conform may feel they've let themselves down by not having tried something they 'might have got away with'.

Much of the moral and ethical codes of the past came from religion. With the diminishing authority of religion, it becomes harder for many individuals to decide what is right and wrong for them. Much depression comes from worry about this, worrying if you have behaved appropriately when there are no set standards. It was tough enough trying to do the right thing by the standards of one, relatively consistent, god. Now, for many people, it seems that it is important to do the right thing by many different people's standards and that to achieve that goal is impossible, and failure and the resulting depression are inevitable.

This was exemplified in my office one day by Mrs Harrington. She kept insisting that she tried so hard, but that whatever she did and however hard she tried she always seemed to do something wrong and she was getting so depressed as a result.

She had recently married for the second time and her husband expected her to be full of fun and an exciting companion. He didn't like it when she blushed at risqué jokes or couldn't hold her end up at a dinner party when racy comments were flying. He got annoyed with her when she insisted on keeping some money in the bank 'for a rainy day', and furious when she insisted on declaring their holiday purchases as they came through customs.

'He keeps saying people will never find out and I must stop spoiling our fun by my stiff-necked attitudes. I do try, and in fact I'm changing quite a bit, but we still have rows and I'm getting so depressed.'

I asked her how she felt about changing her behaviour and whether or not she wanted to change faster.

'Well in some ways I wouldn't mind,' she said in response. 'Not that I'd be willing to break the law mind you, but I could loosen up a lot more and it might even be fun.'

'So what's the problem?' I asked.

'Oh, that's simple. The problem is my parents. When I do things my husband's way for a while and then go to visit them I feel so ashamed, as if I'm letting them down. After all, they brought me up and they taught me what was right and wrong. I guess they were pretty strict but they did give me a good home. When I go back home after visiting them I feel depressed at the sort of person I have become.'

Further discussion showed the problem to be even more complex. She felt she had let down her science teachers by not sticking to her career, the women's group she was part of by opting to be a full-time wife rather than spending time searching for intellectual fulfilment, and her children because she worried that she was either doing too much of their homework for them or, when she did less, that she was not giving them sufficient help.

Pleasing one god would have been much easier.

Individualism and Expectations

People are now measured as individuals and for many this is scary. 'Who am I?' and 'What is the point of it all?' are commonly asked questions. It is no longer sufficient or appropriate to create a family and endeavour to provide your children with a better life.

Nowadays an individual is supposed to 'experience' themselves, to 'fulfil their potential', to 'create their own destiny' and follow many other such ideals. For many people living ordinary or humdrum lives, with which they would otherwise be content, not doing this may indicate failure and lead to depression.

Being happy has become our principal goal. It used to be sufficient to do your duty, live appropriately, do the right thing by your community and family. Books, magazines, films and television now exhort individuals to be happy and fulfilled or to question why they are not or do not endeavour to become so.

Certainly, all these things are possible, but only if you work on them. Being told you haven't reached a goal while at the same time having no idea how to get there can be very depressing.

Global Issues

Economically, recessions and depressions have played their role in the increase in people suffering from depression. The economic situation in many Western countries is now such that millions of people are out of work. Some have lost jobs as they approach the peak of their careers. Some have lost them in their forties and fifties with no hope of getting back into the workforce again. Some people have never had a job, having been on the dole since they left school, and some of these face a future in which they may never have a job. Apart from the financial constraints this imposes, this rejection by society of what an individual has to offer can be devastating.

The world environment is enough to depress many people. Ever since the first atom bomb the world has become seriously unsafe. Since then threats to global peace and to the environment have shaken people's belief in the security of the planet itself.

The Way We Talk About and Deal With Depression

People's attitude to depression has changed: for many it is no longer something to be hidden and the shame that used to be associated with it does not exist today. There are still others, however, who prefer not to discuss the problem or to acknowledge it overtly, either out of shyness, inhibitions or a feeling that they should pull themselves together and get on with their lives.

But we have come a long way from telling people to cheer up and pull themselves together, or else, in serious cases, locking them up. We have had, and still do have, a number of anti-depressant drugs, though may of these have unwanted side-effects and are not the ideal way of dealing with the situation. More importantly, we have many new tools that have been developed in a variety of branches of psychotherapy and which help the individual deal with and overcome their depression. We will be learning about some of these tools in later chapters.

Chapter Two

Have You Assumed You Are Helpless?

People who experience depression often feel they are helpless. There is an underlying belief that life happens to them, that there is little point in trying because the forces 'out there' will overwhelm them, at any time and without notice. They may assume that, no matter what they do, something will go wrong. They may also feel that when things go wrong it is their own fault; thus they add guilt to depression. They choose to be victims, sometimes consciously, often unconsciously. They may draw strength from suffering at many levels. Socially there is the 'you'll never guess what happened to me' syndrome as people top each other's stories of failing to get a parking space, having been cheated, of experiencing rudeness and so forth. Many people seem to thrive on sympathy rather than love, yet this so easily leads to depression rather than happiness.

Taking control of your life is part of the solution. As I said in the Introduction, you can either assume you are in control of your life, in which case you can get up and do something about any situation or emotion that is not pleasing to you, or you can assume you are a cork tossed on the unsympathetic sea of life. The latter will leave you where you are; depressed, unhappy and discontented with your life.

Susan was a prime example of the assumed victim status. As a child she had been unhappy at home. Her parents divorced when she was eight and she lived with a mother who had no time for her, too busy living a whirlwind social life in an effort to get over the failure of her past marriage and a fruitless search for a future one. Her sixty-five-year-old grandmother insisted the child was too much of a handful for her. Susan was, therefore, bundled off to boarding school, not sure which was worse – the misery of being an unwanted nuisance or the embarrassment of the evenings she woke to hear her mother staggering in drunk or with some nameless, and usually short-term, new 'stepfather'. Not only that but, as a result of her mother's peripatetic search for a new beginning, fluctuating finances and insistence that they were much too good for anything less than the best they could afford at that moment, one boarding school turned into a bewildering succession of boarding schools whose standards were a direct expression of the family's financial state.

As a result Susan had little time to make friends, even had she had the confidence to try. The one thing she had learned was that the teachers were kind when she was upset. If she looked content or happy, they left her alone, assuming she was mixing with her peers. As a result she spent much of her time trying to engineer situations, real or imagined, whereby she had reason to be miserable and seek comfort. It was not long after the war and sweets were still rationed. She found ways to leave her daily allotted three unguarded, and when they, predictably, disappeared she was able to seek solace. She endeavoured to find ways, that varied from losing a sock to just missing the school walk to the village, that led to tears which earned her special comfort from a passing teacher.

While she thought up many of the ploys consciously, and dreamed of many others that didn't happen, she did not spell out to herself verbally exactly what she was doing. Few people in her situation do. All she knew was that this was her one way of getting comfort, attention or affection in an otherwise painful world. She was always the one for whom things went wrong. Sadly, this did little to earn her the friendship of her own age group and she became more and more introverted and withdrew into a world of daydreams and fantasy.

Susan came to see me as an adult, telling me that her life was a mess: all she wanted to do was marry and be happy, yet she had few friends and no one understood her. Each relationship that ended she blamed on her sad childhood and her reluctance to trust people. Every criticism hurt and she insisted that that was because no one understood what a tough time she had had and how unwanted she felt when people made adverse comments. Her past was painful enough to earn the sympathy of the countless people to whom she explained it, but that did not attract lasting friends or help her find a husband.

I settled down to ask her a few questions.

'Are you happy with your life at the moment?'

'No, of course not, or I wouldn't be here.'

'Are you achieving what you want by what you are doing? Does it generate positive friendships?'

'No, I've already told you that. No one seems to understand what I have gone through and the trouble I have making friends. If they'd just make allowances and be more kind, things would be better.'

'Is what you are doing now achieving that end?'

'No.'

'So what could you do that's different?'

'Nothing. I don't know. I need help.'

'Okay, are you willing to change?'

'I don't know, yes, I suppose so.'

Human beings are funny things. They do something, it doesn't get the result they want, yet they go on doing it, insisting the other person is wrong for not responding in the way they intended. I wrote in *Stress – Recognise and Resolve** of the woman who got angry every Tuesday morning when she washed the kitchen floor and the family routinely forgot and walked in all over it. She insisted she shouldn't *have* to remind them or lock the door. She kept washing the floor, without reminding them or closing the door, and they kept walking on her clean floor and she kept feeling stressed.

If you are upset and miserable and people, as a result, think you're not much fun and so exclude you from their invitations, you can insist all you like that they should be kind and invite you, but they won't change. And if, occasionally, they do it will be for the wrong

reasons, out of pity and not out of the friendship you really want. It is important to realise that it is you who is suffering if things are not happening the way you want them to and so it is you who must change. This is fortunate since, in real terms, and providing you are willing to change, it is much easier to change yourself than to force others to change.

I explained this to Susan and asked her what she was willing to do to change.

'There's nothing I can do. I'm just fed up and depressed. I hate being alone. I want some sympathetic friends, people I can relax with and who understand me.'

Here again was her hidden agenda, a desire for a friendship based on sympathy for her and stemming from her past sad history. She had yet to learn that people might like her for herself, hardly surprising given her family background and the way in which she had responded to it, yet a necessary lesson if she was to get out of her present misery.

There were several ways out. The one I chose was first to show her that her childhood hadn't been all bad, that in fact there had been great benefits in it, then to encourage her to stop talking about it and be willing to start afresh with the recognition that from then on she could choose to create her life the way she wanted it.

The first step was the most difficult.

'What benefits did you get out of your childhood?'

'None. I've already told you, it was a rotten,

miserable childhood. No one loved me, no one wanted me, mother was a permanent embarrassment and I had no friends. Even if I had made friends at school, I'd have been too embarrassed to take them home. I never knew who else might be there or what mood mother would be in.'

It was some time before Susan could see any view other than this. In time, however, she recognised that she had developed greater independence than any of her contemporaries, that she'd had more time to herself and so had studied well and built herself a good career, albeit as a research librarian, in a field with little people contact.

Her thinking was helped when I asked her what childhood horrors had *not* happened to her. Not having a father had been sad, but equally she had had less discipline and more freedom at home than many other children. She had not been molested, had not been beaten. They had had money and she had not had to go without for lack of finances. She had not suffered from health problems, grown up in a country at war or been an abandoned orphan.

Whenever people are sad or feel badly done by, it is common to find that they are comparing themselves and their circumstances, past and present, with the best that they see around them, never with the worst. Yet for all of us, however bad things are, they could be so much worse.

Not only did Susan gradually come to appreciate this, she also came to understand her mother better and to sympathise with her. She read a number of books like this one, and, not being one to do anything by halves, she suddenly got the point that she *could* indeed change the way she felt, she *could* create each day and make it either better or worse than it might have been, and that she did have a measure of control.

'That being the case,' she announced at our next session, 'why would I tell people I created a rotten childhood for myself? I would rather tell them what a terrific childhood I'd created. I used not to mind them feeling sorry for me, but I'm blowed if I want them to think me silly.'

That, for Susan, was the beginning of the journey from depression to contentment. I haven't seen her become an exuberant and happy optimist; perhaps that amount of change is beyond her, maybe she doesn't want it. I have seen her become quietly happy and content with a life in which her depression is a thing of the past and which now includes a small circle of good friends.

Listen to what is being said around you next time you are in a gathering of people. How many times do people talk about the problems they have had?

'I thought I'd never get here, the traffic was dreadful; all the traffic lights were against us; I couldn't find a place to park; the baby-sitter was late; the shop tried to cheat me of my change; the goods were shoddy; I got conned; my secretary was slow finishing her work; you can't find decent staff these days; my kids never do what I ask; people are so uncooperative; I'm no good at doing these things . . .' The list goes on and on. I suggest this to you as an exercise: examine each sentence you hear and decide if it is a positive comment or a negative one. You will be surprised at how many negative ones you hear. Even people who think of themselves as optimists find they make a surprising number of negative comments, many of them being of the variety that demands some sort of sympathy from the listener.

> **Recognise your own responsibilities. Recognise that you can choose to tell the world either that you have created a happy and positive life for yourself or an unhappy and negative one. Recognise that you can choose to focus your attention on the good things in your life or the bad. Recognise that people, by and large, prefer to be around happy people rather than people who are perpetually unhappy. Above all, recognise that it is more fun to be liked for yourself than to be pitied. All this can go a long way towards turning you from depression to a positive frame of mind.**

This is not a case of bottling up your depression and putting a brave but superficial face on it. Be sure you are really making profound changes and that you fully believe in them and recognise their power. Recognise that you did have and do continue to have control over your life and your moods. Focus on the fact that the glass is indeed half full of water rather than on the fact that it is half empty.

If you assume that you are helpless in the face of what befalls you, you will be. The sad thing is that so many lives are spoilt simply because people choose to lie down under what happens rather than take control. If you are, like me, an inveterate watcher of domestic and wild animal shows on television, you will have seen situations in which an animal has its prey at its mercy. It will play with its prey, it may even leave it alone to see what it will do, or get bored and move away; yet the victim still lies there, having given up hope. Unlike animals, we have the ability to go beyond this and to make conscious choices.

You are not helpless, there is always something you can do. It is that simple, yet that which is simple is not always easy.

You may, at this point, be arguing that this is an unsympathetic and hard approach to take, but ask yourself, did sympathy ever make you happy? Obviously, sympathy has its place. It is wonderful to have sympathetic friends in times of need. Yet if they sympathise for too long it can keep you in the helpless and victim state of mind. Assume instead that you can decide to take a positive approach to life, and then do so.

I ran into a patient recently whom I hadn't seen for a number of years, and asked her how she was. She had come to see me initially to find out if there was anything she could do to help her husband who had had a stroke and needed constant care. In the course of chatting, I learned that he had died after three years of round-the-clock nursing on her part, that their money had run out and after the funeral she had had to move to a tiny flat, and that her son had been killed in a car crash. Far from being depressed, however, she was full of gratitude for the suggestions I had previously made to her regarding ways to alleviate her own depression and the stress she had been under. She talked enthusiastically about the positive books she had read since we had last met, and of her new-found ability to focus on what she had. Instead of bemoaning the rough hand life had dealt her,

she was full of the news that her son-in-law was
sending her the money to visit her grandchild, born
overseas. It is all too easy to imagine the litany of woes
another person might have poured out at that time. I
could only marvel at the change she had created in
herself.

> **You are not helpless. You do have control. It
> is time to grasp this and move on.**

* *Stress – Recognise and Resolve*, Xandria K. Williams. Charles
  Letts (Holdings) Ltd (UK), 1993.

Chapter Three

What Are Your Belief Systems?

The interpretation you put on events and situations will affect your mood. So will the assumptions you make. Gaining control over these two aspects of your life and using this control to your advantage is almost enough to banish the blues for ever.

Let's start with assumptions. Very often you do not really know if people like you or not, but you do make assumptions about this, as about many things. And, once the assumption is made, you garner endorsing evidence and thus strengthen and justify it. If you assume you are unpopular, you will almost certainly feel depressed. If you assume you are popular, you are much less likely to feel this way. It is often difficult to be sure if you are popular or not. You may be invited to a party: how do you know whether you have been invited because the hosts really like you, or because they feel they owe you an invitation, or because they want to be included in your group of friends, or because they think having you will impress one of their other guests, or to make up the numbers, or because they want to introduce you to someone, or because they want to get involved in some activity of yours, or because they think you will be able to help them later?

Before you leap up and down and say this is a cold, hard, cynical viewpoint, think about yourself. Haven't you ever invited people for some of these reasons? Almost certainly you have. Much social intercourse is based on just such considerations.

Now, does the invitation make you happy? If you believe you are popular and have been invited because the hosts really like you and want you there, it probably will – provided that you like them in the first place. If, on the other hand, you assume that you are not popular and that there must be some hidden reason for their invitation, it is unlikely to fill you with cheer. In this case there is much less chance of your having a good time and you are more likely to feel depressed. Notice that your mood depends much more on the assumptions you make than on the actual truth, which, in any case, you are unlikely to discover.

It goes further than this, however. If you assume you are popular, you will probably arrive at the party with a flourish, looking forward to the occasion and willing to smile, be happy and assume everyone else will feel good. As a result, you are likely to be a cheery focal point, people will be drawn to you simply because you radiate warmth and this will increase your feelings of being popular, further strengthening the underlying assumption, and lead you to have a good time and feel happy.

If you assume you are unpopular, you will tend to be quiet, withdrawn and feel uncomfortable. You will pass this feeling on to others who are less likely to want to be near you or to talk with you. You may even move away from groups, assuming you are not wanted. Feeling yourself on your own, you will use this as further proof of your unpopularity and become depressed, or more depressed.

Notice that not only does the assumption itself lead to the mood, it also changes the course of events in such a way that not only is the resultant mood emphasised but it appears to add evidence to your original assumption and strengthen it further.

The problem continues. If you believe you are unpopular, you are unlikely to be happy unless people are continuously backing you up, telling you how much they like you, phoning you frequently and so forth. And even that may not be enough. If you are determined to assume your unpopularity, you will find reaons for their actions. You may decide to believe that they are acting out of kindness, or pity, or duty. People being people, they are not likely to have their focus on you all the time, and any apparent slight or neglect, almost always due to some cause entirely unrelated to you, will immediately bolster your fears. Given sufficient determination, you can pull anything apart and make it fit into your preconceived ideas. And the really big problem is that you will be absolutely convinced of the rightness of your assumptions, regardless of the attempts of other people to convince you otherwise. Finally, your insecurity and obvious need for their approval can drive some of your friends away and thus worsen the situation.

If you convince yourself that your partner's unexpected absence is an indication of infidelity, you will be worried and depressed when he or she is not with you. If, on the other hand, you assume they have been out doing something neutral – having a good time, earning some bonus income or buying you a present – you will be relaxed and happy waiting for their return. Again, your assumption creates the basis for your mood and can affect the course of events: if you assume infidelity and get jealous, you may drive your partner to infidelity.

Interpretation is another trap people often fall into. If you are given a present and interpret this as an expression of affection you will probably be happy. If you understand it as hiding a guilty conscience, you may make yourself depressed. If you interpret someone's frown as a criticism of you and their smile as a laugh at your expense, you are likely to feel depressed. Conversely if you interpret their frown as worries of their own and a smile as an expression of their joy at seeing you, you will feel happier.

Stop and think about this for a while. Everything you do in life and all the emotions you feel are based on beliefs, assumptions and interpretations. Even when you think you are certain, you may be wrong: it is very difficult to get to absolute truths. Jonathan was convinced his marriage was happy and a success. His wife Ruth gave him a wonderful welcome home each night and they enjoyed their relationship. He was confident his life was going perfectly and was staggered when she left him for another man, who was, in fact, the cause of her happy smiling demeanour. Denis was convinced his company was going to the wall and that his best staff knew this and were planning to leave. He became more sure of this when he found huddles of them that kept breaking up in embarrassment, with sheepish grins, when he approached. Imagine his surprise when he found they had created a rescue situation in which the entire staff took over and bought shares, so great was their confidence in him.

No matter how certain you are that your assumptions

and interpretations are correct, you may be wrong. We discussed earlier the wisdom of assuming the most useful belief, in situations where you cannot know the truth for sure (always assuming that there is an absolute truth, of course, and this is doubtul). If you want to be happy and avoid depression it is *more useful* to make assumptions that will enable you to feel happy than ones that will lead to depression. It is *more useful* to apply positive and beneficial interpretations than ones that cause you pain. It comes back to this: since you cannot know with absolute certainty, it is better to opt for the positive belief system and risk living in a fool's paradise than to opt for a negative belief system and risk living in a fool's hell.

> **Belief systems and assumptions are learned. As such they can be unlearned and changed. For this to happen they first have to be identified and recognised for what they are.**

When you feel depressed, you need to discover the underlying belief systems and assumptions that are behind your depression or that are contributing to it. To do this the technique called 'Running a Phrase' is useful. This is a simple way to get to the unconscious cause of the problem and is described here sufficiently fully for you to use it with ease and benefit.

Running a Phrase

This process is designed to get to information held in the unconscious part of your mind. For this reason you do not ask yourself questions: if you did, your conscious, analytical mind would take over and work out logical answers, and in doing this, it would automatically assess and filter in the way it has learned to do, leaving you with a contrived answer that is of little help in unravelling the unconscious roots of your problem. Instead, you start with a phrase – this keeps the conscious mind busy – and then leave a gap for the unconscious mind to fill in the rest. There are in-built assumptions in the phrase that encourage the unconscious root causes to pop up. Let's take an example:

> Jennifer had been feeling depressed on and off for many years, but it had become a real problem in the past four months or so. So I started her off with the following phrase.
> 'I'm feeling depressed because I'm assuming . . .'
> This already contains the in-built acknowledgement that the depression is due to some assumption she has made. This takes the unconscious mind through several steps right away. It does not have to debate the possibility of assumptions – they are taken for granted; it does not have to presume that these are the basis of the depression – that is taken for granted; it does not have to ask if it knows the answer – that too is taken for granted; and since you have assumed it will be able to complete the phrase, it does. Now, of course, you *can* block the process, but don't if you want to get rid of your depression. If you find yourself blocking after the first one or two attempts you might run the phrase 'a benefit I get from remaining depressed is . . .', or even 'a benefit I get from not completing this phrase is . . .'
> Back to Jennifer. Her first completion to the

phrase 'I'm feeling depressed because I'm assuming . . .' was 'I'll lose my job'. We then ran it again and repeated that a number of times. The results were interesting.

'I'm also feeling depressed because I'm assuming . . . that I won't be able to get another one.'

'Another assumption I'm making that is keeping me depressed is . . . that I'm not good enough to interest another employer.'

'Another assumption I'm making that is keeping me depressed is . . . that if I don't have a job my friends will think I'm a failure and I will lose them.'

'Another assumption I'm making that is keeping me depressed is . . . without friends I won't find another boyfriend and won't get married.'

With assumptions like that, no wonder she was depressed! The solution, now that she had learned the unconscious process, was to change it. She did this by working backwards. First, she checked the list of people she knew who were on the dole and still had friends who thought well of them, and she thought of people she knew who were not working who had a better social life, since they had more time. She also faced the fact that she was good at what she did and could probably get another job. Further, she recognised that she hadn't yet been sacked. At this point I asked her to run a second, different, phrase.

'A reason I'm assuming I'll lose my job, is . . . because other people in the company are getting the sack.'

'Another reason I'm assuming I'll lose my job is . . . my boss keeps frowning and looking worried every time he sees me.'

'Another reason I'm assuming I'll lose my job is
. . . the other secretaries are being less friendly
than usual: they must know something.'

The next phrase was:

'Another explanation for "that" is . . .', where I
specified 'that' as being the completions in the
phrases above.

This led to some interesting results. When 'that'
was 'other people getting the sack', she got completions that included, 'they are less good at their
jobs than I am', 'the others are new on the staff,
whereas I have been with the company a long
time'.

'My boss keeps frowning when he looks at me',
produced, 'he is saddened that he has had to sack
them', and 'he knows he would find things difficult
if he had to do without me', and 'he is trying to
work out ways to keep me on'.

Finally, 'Another explanation of the fact that the
other secretaries are being less friendly than usual
is . . .' was completed with, '. . . they must realise
my job is safe and be feeling jealous, inadequate or
a failure'.

By the time we had completed the process Jennifer had learned many things. She'd understood
that she was causing her own depression. She
realised she was building a house of hidden bogies.
She had also clearly articulated to herself that she
had been with the company a long time, she was
good at her job, her boss valued her and would do
all he could to keep her on, and that there were
many other explanations for the looks of her colleagues and the other bosses. In the end she had to
laugh at herself.

'Goodness, I have been building mountains out of imagined molehills. While I've been feeling so depressed, I've become such a wet blanket I could hardly blame the boss for sacking me just for that reason. I will focus on the positive aspect of what I have learned and I am sure my job will be even more secure as a result. If not, you have made me realise that I could indeed get another one. Though you know, having thought this far, perhaps I would take that opportunity, if it arose, to change my work all together: I've always wanted to go into business for myself, perhaps this would be the time. I'd like to run a domestic agency, helping mothers to get part-time work.'

As she left, she was already formulating plans. Certainly, she was a lot less depressed. It remained to be seen what the eventual outcome would be. You may be amazed at how many in-built assumptions were unearthed and the possible alternative interpretations that Jennifer found. Yet, if you do the same process on something about which you feel depressed, in all likelihood you will come up with as many or even more.

Unhelpful beliefs are often based, at least in part, on generalisations, deletions and distortions. These have been discussed more fully elsewhere.* But, in brief, generalisations are conclusions you come to based on only a small amount of input. You say the wrong thing once or twice and then start thinking you *always* say the wrong thing. People pay you compliments but you delete them and only hear the criticisms. Or someone gives you flowers and you distort this, wondering what they want from you.

Many times we find that people are depressed because they assume that the future will be bad, that things will stay as bad as they are or will get worse. If life is happy at the moment, they get depressed because they convince themselve something is bound to go wrong. If they are lonely, they expect they will stay that way. If they are failing their exams they presume this will always happen and that they will never understand the work and also that there is no better alternative for them. When you start assuming that you are out of options, that there is no way out, that there is nothing more you can do, then it is hard to shake your depression. Learn about the assumptions you are making, change them to more positive assumptions and you will be surprised at the changes you can make. One powerful way of doing this, called 'scripting', is described in Chapter 26.

Plan

- Every time you feel depressed, run a phrase, as described earlier, and discover the hidden assumptions and interpretations.
- Then analyse these assumptions. Decide whether or not it is in your interest to keep them and consider, if appropriate, what ways they could be changed.
- List alternative interpretations that you could make.
- Remember, since you cannot know for *sure* which assumptions and interpretations are correct, to use the ones which are most helpful, and which allow you to get rid of the depression.

* *Choosing Health Intentionally*, Xandria K. Williams, Charles Letts (Holdings) Ltd (UK), 1992.

Chapter Four

Are You Happy With The Mood You Have Chosen To Create?

Inherent in this book is the concept of proactivity versus reactivity. Reactive people allow the rest of the world to dictate their mood. If the weather is gloomy, they get depressed. If it is sunny, they may be happy, but if it is too hot they may get depressed again. If someone is rude, reactive people will be rude back, or get hurt and keep quiet. If someone smiles at them, they may feel happy. If someone frowns, they may get anxious. Reactive people's moods are a direct result of the world around them, to which they react somewhat like well-trained Pavlovian dogs. Proactive people decide on their own moods; they remain in control of their lives and their moods.

Reactive People

From discussions with patients and clients I hear such remarks as, 'I can't help it, every time he does . . . I . . .', or, 'It's not my fault. My husband buys the biscuits and when they're there I eat them', or 'I couldn't help it, Peter whispered to me in class and I had to answer him', or, 'I didn't mean to be late, the children were slow', or, 'I'd like to be happy but when she complains, I just get upset', and many more. There is one thing that all these phrases have in common. There is the underlying assumption that the speaker is not in control. These people are reactive. They are reacting, without thinking and without conscious control, to the world round them and letting other people and events jerk their strings. If *you* do not decide what you do and say, who does?

> Mrs Benson had spent nearly an hour with me complaining of the problems she had and the troubles in her marriage. Her husband was so busy he had no time for her; she had to deal with the children from his previous marriage; her own children were at boarding school and she hardly ever saw them; there wasn't enough money; she'd like to get a job but couldn't because . . . And so the litany went on. Yet at the same time she really wanted to make changes.
>
> 'I'm tired of feeling so put upon,' was the way she explained herself. 'I wish my life could be different. I really don't want to be nagging all day long and then be so tired when my husband gets home. I just don't know what to do.'
>
> 'Choose,' I said.
>
> 'What do you mean "choose"?'
>
> 'It is up to you to make the choices. You can choose to nag or not. You can choose to have a job or not. You can choose whether or not your own children go to boarding school.'
>
> She thought about this for a while and after a few minutes of further discussion she left.

The next week she came back looking like a different person.

'You're right,' she said. 'All I have to do is choose. That one word made all the difference. I went away and thought about what you said and realised I actually could make choices and that if I did, then I would be taking control of the situation and could be a lot happier. And you know a funny thing? I've started doing that, just in small ways so far, around the house, and everything is a lot calmer and more peaceful. Funnily, I also feel less depressed, though I've got a long way to go yet and it will take time.'

'Only if you think so.'

She gazed at me. 'What do you mean?'

'You've got used to the idea of choices now, haven't you?'

'Yes. And, you know, it was funny. Just that one word did it. I'm sure if you'd said that at the start I'd have had the answer in minutes.'

I wasn't so sure of that. The clinching phrase had come at the end of a long discussion about proactivity and reactivity in general, but I let that one lie as she continued, 'But I don't see how I can change everything overnight.'

'If you decide that you can't, then you can't. But go back to your recognition of the real meaning of choices. If you choose to think it will take you a long time to change things in your life, then it probably will. If, on the other hand, you choose to think that you can bring the changes about in a week, or even a day, simply by changing the way you deal with the world around you, then you can.'

This was clearly a new concept to her and one she would have to digest, but even as I spoke I could see her mind covering all the possibilities it invoked.

For Mrs Benson, ultimately, one word was enough: *choose*. You make the choices. If you are a reactive person you *choose* to let what other people say and do create your mood, you *choose* to let their behaviour affect your life in adverse ways.

The reactive person takes comfort, often cold comfort, from the knowledge that they can always blame other people for the events in their lives. 'It is your fault I am unhappy, you have been mean to me.' Not at all, the choice was yours, you simply chose to give them control of your mood.

Proactive People

Being proactive means that you recognise that, no matter what occurs around you, you can choose what you do. Your choices may, at times, seem to be limited, but you do always have choices. You don't have to argue just because the other person does. You don't have to shout when they do. You don't have to get anxious when they frown, go out because they want to, go to work because the world thinks you should, or smile sweetly because it is the done thing. If you are proactive, you act from a position of personal strength, a mental, emotional and moral 'straight spine'. We've probably all come across such people. No matter what you say or do, you know you cannot sway them, unless they choose to change their mind, nor can you manipulate their mood. No form of emotional bribery, such as 'what will people think?' or 'I'll like you more if you do', will influence them.

Proactive people are not to be confused with the stubborn mule who makes an impulsive decision and sticks with it no matter what. Stubborn people are themselves reactive. They make initial reactive responses and then, no matter what they think, if indeed they give the matter much thought at all, they won't be swayed.

Proactive people automatically and instinctively come to their own conclusions and decisions and act upon them. If, in time, they decide that some other course of action or response is appropriate, they will change; but this change will come from within, once they have analysed the situation, not in direct response to something from outside.

Once you fully grasp this concept and put it into practice, then your mood is within your control. You can choose to feel depressed or you can choose to feel happy. 'Whoa,' I can hear you saying, 'when I'm depressed I'm depressed and there's nothing I can do about it.' Not if you think like that. But I challenge you to do the following. What mood are you in right now? Are you happy, bursting with life, fun and enthusiasm? Probably not, or you would not be reading this book. So, assuming you are feeling less than one hundred per cent happy, do this.

- Consider your present mood. Become aware of it.
- Now smile. That's it, plaster a silly grin on your face.
- Put your shoulders back, head up.
- Think about the good things in your life.
- Think about the bad things that are not in your life.

- Make a full, honest attempt to increase your level of cheer.
- Run a little voice inside your head saying, 'I'm happy, life is good, I feel fantastic. The world's wonderful.'

How do you feel? If you have put a hundred per cent of energy into this, it is almost impossible that your mood has not changed. In the next chapter we will go into this more fully.

What's happened now? You've relaxed. Have you slipped back to feel more depressed again? Is that what you want? Yes, of course it takes effort, at least at the start. But once you recognise that you have control of your moods and once you put the ideas in this book into practice, you will realise that you are choosing your moods – and who wants to choose to be depressed?

How to Become More Proactive

There are many ways to become more proactive.

The first is to realise, truly realise, deep down in your guts, that you *are* responsible for your life. You are in control, and all you have to do is to recognise that and take control. Lip service, however, will not do: you have to believe this one hundred per cent. Many clients who come to see me are wishing their lives would change, hoping someone will come and make a difference, waiting for the fairytale prince or princess, praying they will be offered a better job, crossing their fingers that their children will get opportunities, and so forth. The time is now. Grasp the nettle. Create your own life and thus your own mood.

Are there things you want to do but have been

shelving? Perhaps you would like to holiday on the Greek islands but are waiting for the perfect companion. Don't wait, plan the holiday and then ask around for someone to go with you. Would you like to redecorate your home? Then plan it, go and choose the colours, things have a way of happening if you act as if they will.

Be aware of your internal dialogue. Do you find yourself saying, 'If only . . .'? 'If only I were slimmer I would feel better. If only I had more money I could get out and do the things I want. If only someone did something or something else happened, then I'd be happy.' Isn't that the underlying assumption?

Catch all your 'If onlys' and make them happen.

You can create anything you want in your life if you truly want it badly enough and if you are willing to do what it takes to make it happen. If you don't want it badly enough to make it happen then realise this and stop 'if only-ing'. If you make one thing that you want conditional on another thing happening, over which you have little or no control, then you are in trouble. You can choose to feel better before you become slim. Go out and do things for which you don't need money and set about making money so you can do the things you want to do. Once you grasp this concept, you realise that you can and do create your mood and that, unless you are enjoying being depressed, you can remove the depression.

The process of changing your mood may not be easy, but it is simple. You are the only person who can do it. If you doubt that, think of the

people you know who are miserable even when things are going well and when those around them are being cheerful *and* trying to cheer them up.

There is another powerful way of being proactive and that is by creating your future 'from the future'. This process is called writing your script, or scripting, and is described in Chapter 25.

Chapter Five

Creating and Eliminating Depression

There are three ways of creating or eliminating your mood or depression: you create your moods physiologically, with your body; you create them mentally, with your mind, via the types of visual images and sounds that you compose, and you also create them with labels – labels embedded in the language you use, labels you apply to yourself and that other people apply to you.

If You're Depressed – Move

Your body reflects your mood. When your mood changes, so do your posture and expression. Conversely, changing your posture can change your moods. You probably know this already, at least in part, but you may be surprised at the full power of your body to change your mood.

If you are depressed – move! You cannot stay depressed if you put your shoulders back, look at the ceiling and make your face into a smile.

Let's consider this more closely.

What happens to your body when you feel depressed? How do other people look when they feel depressed? If you look at someone who is saying nothing, how do you know whether they are depressed or happy? It's all there in their body language, isn't it?

Typically, when you're depressed you hang your head down, you slump your shoulders, you curve your spine forward and you look at the ground. You change your facial features, your mouth turns down, you get those sad creases between the eye and your eyebrows form a particular shape.

Let's try a little experiment. We will assume you are sitting down. The first step is to bend your shoulders forward and down. Let them sag downwards and then bend them over so your body is hunched and you are leaning slightly forward, your arms hanging inwards. Hang your head down and forward. Take a good look at the ground just in front of you, or better still, at your lap or your navel. Hug yourself by putting each hand under the opposite elbow, almost as if you're trying to hold yourself together. Let all your muscles relax and droop. Let your stomach sag. Shiver a bit, even if it is a hot day you can focus on a shivery feeling.

Now let your mouth droop. Consciously turn the corners down, pout a little bit, let your lips go slack. Pucker your chin, make it quiver. Get those little creases between your eyes, those vertical creases that tell the world the way you feel. Don't frown, you're not trying to look angry or confused. Let your upper eyelids fall a bit to hood your eyes. Pretty upsetting, isn't it? But hang in there, you've more to do yet.

Slow your breathing down and make it shallow. Instead of breathing normally just take half breaths.

Now talk to someone. If you are on your own, talk to yourself, do it out loud, only not too loud. In fact, you will get the best result if you talk just above a whisper, and not too fast. Talk slowly and put some hesitation in your voice, as if it is almost too much trouble to make the effort to speak at all. Put a few stops in each sentence, as if you are about to break into tears and are having trouble controlling your emotions.

How do you feel? Pretty terrible, huh? Do you feel depressed? Of course you do. You may not feel suicidal, although that is possible, but you will certainly feel more depressed than when you started the exercise. If you habitually feel depressed then this exercise is likely to have heightened the feeling. If you normally feel happy and are reading this book perhaps to know how to help someone who is depressed, you may not have induced the full feeling of total depression in yourself, but you will feel a lot less happy that you did before.

Don't move. Stay in that slumped position. Your next challenge, without moving a single muscle, is to feel happy. Try it. No, don't smile, don't laugh, don't move your shoulders or your facial muscles, don't change your breathing. Don't even twitch the tiniest muscle. *Don't move.* Don't change a thing. Now, feel happy. Pretty difficult, isn't it? If you have improved your mood, you will almost certainly also have changed your body in some way, however slight. Check it out. Check every part of your body. Has anything changed? What about those tiny muscles round your mouth and eyes, have they moved? Go back to feeling depressed, really sink back into that feeling. Check your body again. Has it slumped back down? Has anything changed in the last few seconds? If you managed to feel happier, you almost certainly moved, even if it was only a tiny bit.

It is very difficult to feel happy when you have put your body in the position associated with depression.

Move. You want to shake that dreadful mood off, don't you? So, stand up, shake yourself, get rid of that depressed feeling.

Now we are going to try the opposite. Stand up straight, throw your shoulders back, stiffen your spine. Throw your arms around in a way that makes you feel really good. Breathe deeply and really expand your chest. Tip your head back and look at the ceiling. Put a huge grin on your face. Open your eyes wide. Keep looking at the ceiling. Walk around. How do you feel? Smile. You're probably feeling pretty good about yourself, certainly better than you were a few minutes ago. You might even be feeling happier, more positive, more capable, more in control.

Your next task is to feel depressed again. *Don't move.* Concentrate all you can on feeling depressed but keep that smile in place. Keep your spine straight, your head back, your breathing strong. Now try to feel depressed . . . keep smiling. I'll bet your smile slipped as you tried to feel sad, keep it in place.

It's pretty hard to do, isn't it? The moment you try to feel depressed, you also start to move your body instinctively into the posture that you associate with depression.

Now, who has control of your body? You do, of course. This means that if you simply make the conscious decision to maintain a positive and happy posture and expression, it is pretty difficult to feel depressed. Conversely, if you let your body droop into the posture and actions associated with depression, it is difficult to feel happy. *It's your body. You're in control. It's up to you.*

It is quicker and easier to change your posture than your mood, if you try to change your mood without changing your posture, you will be putting a major obstacle in your way.

You may argue that the above is all very well, but that you do not feel happy, you do feel depressed and you can't pretend otherwise. The truth is you can. Depression is just a feeling. It can be altered. Remember, one person will feel depressed in a situation where another will feel happy. Since depression in a given situation is not an absolute, is not set in concrete, but is something you choose and thus something you can change, if you truly want to stop feeling depressed, you can change your body and thus your emotions. Try it. You'll soon find that if you control your body for a whole day, including your smile, it is pretty difficult to maintain your depression and it becomes a lot easier to take a happier and more positive view of life.

You may insist that the depression came first and the body movements followed, and that being the case you should find out why you're depressed, deal with that and let the body movements come second. Fine, if you can do it quickly and easily, but think about what we have just done. Which was easier? Was it easier to change the position of your body and let your mood change as you did so, or to change your mood in spite of maintaining the old body position? It was easier to move your muscles and improve your mood than to change your mood whilst staying in the old position, wasn't it? After all, you move your muscles every day. From the moment you get out of bed until you return to it, you are consciously and unconsciously moving your body. Why not decide to move it in the way that will improve your mood?

Think back to a time when you were totally happy. No matter how depressed you feel now, there will almost certainly be some time in your life when you felt truly happy, positive, optimistic and full of joy. If there really isn't such a time then think of someone you have seen in that mood. Think about your happiest friend or a character in a film who was totally happy and seemed, looked and sounded as if he or she felt the way you would like to feel. Do this exercise with this person in mind. However, if you try hard enough, I'm sure you'll find a happy time that involves you. Once you have this time fully in mind, and have adopted every detail of the happy posture, then fix or anchor this feeling. We will talk about anchoring later and in more detail (see Chapter 12), but right now pick a gesture or a sound and associate that with this good feeling. You may choose to snap your fingers, thump your fist or say 'Yeeeesss'. If you do this often enough you will soon find that initiating the action or sound will help you to recreate the good mood. It may help you to do this exercise with a friend and articulate your findings. You can also experiment together, in the way I did with John.

> John was depressed and so I did this exercise with him and asked him to describe his posture to me.
>
> 'Tell me what to do,' I told him. 'Assume I am an actor auditioning for a part, and the part I am to play is you being as depressed as you can possibly be.'
>
> He looked a bit uncertain but was willing to go along with the experiment.

'OK, well, I'm slumped over aren't I, my head is down and on one side.'

'What happens if you straighten your head?'

John tried it and said, 'No, it must be on the side. That way I'm confused, uncertain and insecure and that adds to the depression.'

'Okay, good. Now what about the legs, I notice yours are tucked under your chair and are crossed at the ankles which are extended so the tops of your feet are on the floor. What happens if you bring your legs out in front of you?'

'No, that won't do.' John was clearly getting into the swing of things. 'I feel a lot more confident.'

'What about your hands, they are turned palm up and one is inside the other. What happens if you separate them or turn them over?'

John moved his hands, putting each one palm down on his thighs. 'That changes my mood too. I now feel much more ready to act, as if I'm about to get up and do something and that gives me a sort of positive feeling, so it's not so easy to feel depressed.'

'Notice that your top lip is tucked in, what are you doing there?'

'I've got it between my teeth.'

'What happens if you leave it outside your teeth, just tuck it below your bottom lip for instance?'

'It feels kind of silly, but not so depressing.'

'Good. Now what happens when you let your lips just touch together – don't smile.'

'That feels better, more serious though, not really happy, at least not until I smile,' he said as he did so.

When you do this with a friend, you may find that some things which add to their feeling of depression do not have the same effect on you. For instance, as I was copying John, I found that laying my hands one over the other, palm up, created a sense of peace, but that putting them face to face and then clasping them between my thighs added to the depression. Find out what works for you and then do the opposite when you want to create the opposite mood.

Your Mental Pictures and Sounds

Go back to a time when you felt depressed. Mentally, what did you do to create this mood, what thoughts did you have, what did you say to yourself, what pictures did you make in your mind, what feelings did you create, what did you anticipate? What would someone else have to do to recreate this mood in themselves? What would an actor have to do? In a sense, this is like the experiment with John, only this time you are focusing not on your body but on what is going on inside your head.

Now recall a time when you felt your happiest and do the same thing. Find out what you are saying to yourself, what pictures you are forming and so forth. You can apply these techniques at times when you feel depressed and want to change your mood to one of happiness.

To amplify this process it is valuable to recognise that there are three main ways in which you process information in your brain. You create pictures, you make sounds and you experience emotions. In most people one of these modalities is dominant, although it is probable that you will also use the others. If you are going to change your mood it is particularly important that you work with your dominant sense. This means that if you are visually dominant you will want to use pictures as the main way of changing your mood internally, but you will probably also want to hear the appropriate words or sounds. If you are aurally dominant you will benefit from getting all the sounds inside your head, verbal and non-verbal, in line with the mood you want to create, but it will probably help to create the pictures you associate with the mood as well. If you are a kinesthetic person (used in NLP terms as relating to your feelings) and simply experience the emotions then you will have to make the effort to work with the pictures and sounds as well to help you make the desired changes.

If you are a visual person and feel depressed, you probably create depressing pictures in your mind. If you try to feel good and tell yourself you're happy while still picturing how bad things are, then you're unlikely to have much impact on your depression. If you are aurally dominant, then no matter how good a picture you paint or how much you would like to feel good, unless you can say the appropriate things to yourself you will continue to feel depressed.

To find out about yourself, ask yourself what is going on in your mind right now. Are you creating visual images of what we are doing, are you seeing things in colour, are there shapes, is there movement? Are you repeating the words again, inside your head, are the sounds loud or soft, what is the pitch? Or do you do neither of these but simply experience the feelings?

What these questions are doing is helping you to discover your mental strategies and understand how you create the feelings of depression or happiness. For some people to feel happy they have to have wonderful images in their minds, others have to hear wonderful sounds and others simply have to feel good.

Another way of deciding which way you do things is to consider the words you use in daily conversation. Are they visual words and phrases such as 'image', 'picture', 'see', 'that's clear', 'I'll focus on that'? Or are they aural words and phrases such as, 'sounds good', 'rings true', 'clear as a bell'?

So think back again to a time when you felt truly happy. How did you do it? What is the first thing you are conscious of when you think back to that time? Now imagine yourself in a situation where you felt depressed, as depressed as possible, so we can get maximum information, and let's find out how you maintained that state. Ask yourself what is going on.

Again I spoke to John and asked him to recall a time when he did feel happy.

'What are you seeing or saying to maintain this state? What are you picturing in your mind, what are you seeing, either in the world around you or in the pictures you are creating in your mind? What thoughts are in your head, what are you hearing or saying to yourself?'

'I don't see much but I know I'm happy. I'm telling myself I am and it sounds good.'

'What else?'

'I keep hearing music, nothing specific, just sort of jingles, but happy jingles. And there's more. It's hard to describe really, just sort of joyous sounds, even laughter. They're not really there, it's like they're floating in the wind.'

'Are the sounds high pitched or are they in deeper tones?'

'High pitched, like people giggling, yet not exactly.'

'Great. Now what would I have to do if I wanted to create depression in the way you do it? Could I use these same sounds or do I have to change them? Think back now to a time when you felt very depressed, what do you hear?'

'That's odd, the sounds are all deep, and they are sort of fuzzy, like I'm not properly tuned in to the station. And they're slow sounds and dull, like you hear in a thick fog.'

'Excellent. Now what I want you to do is to keep thinking about the time you felt depressed but change the sounds, don't change your mood, just the sounds. I want you to continue to feel as depressed as before. Get rid of the fog, make the sounds you hear clearer, raise their pitch, add some light music, change all the sounds to the way they are when you are happy. What is happening to your mood? Remember to stay depressed.'

John laughed, 'I can't. You knew I wouldn't be able to, didn't you? Just in the way that it was difficult to stay depressed when I changed my posture.'

And John was right. I did know he would find it difficult to remain depressed when he changed the nature of the sounds. I then did the same thing with his visual images for, although he thought he didn't have any, when fully questioned he did.

Sara was a very visual person and when we did this exercise she found that to feel cheerful she had to have the right colours. I wasn't surprised since when I had asked her what the problem was, she had said, 'I feel rotten, I'm depressed and nothing seems to be going right in my life. Everything is so *drab* and *dull*, I just can't *see* how it can get better. I've nothing to *look* forward to.'

It is hard to be happy, as a visual person, if you cannot create an appealing picture of the future. Sara described her life as drab and dull, adjectives which usually apply to the look of a thing, rather than to the sound or feel of it.

When I asked Sara to go back to a time when she felt truly happy and then to tell me what was in her mind, not only did she have a very clear picture of the scene but she saw the picture in bright colours and bathed in a glowing light. When I asked her to change the colours in her mind from bright to pale, then to dull and then to black and white and out of focus she said the fun had gone out of the memory and she was feeling depressed again rather than cheerful.

Sara was then asked to form a mental image of her life at that moment and sure enough the image was consistent with her negative emotions. She was picturing it in black and white, as if, she told me, there were a grey cloud hanging over it. She was then asked to take the picture she had of her life at present and, mentally, to erase any of the grey from it, bring it into sharp focus and change the drab black and white picture to a brightly coloured one and bathe it in light. I said nothing about trying to change her mood, yet quickly her expression changed as she sat up and smiled. When I asked her to keep the brightly coloured image of the present, yet to go back to feeling depressed about it, she had difficulties.

We spoke in the first section of this chapter about the way in which the position of your body and your facial expression can affect your mood and vice versa. Here we have your mental picture and sounds affecting you physically and emotionally.

Posture and expression <—> mood
Mental pictures/sounds <—> mood

Exercise

This is a simple way for you to find out how you create your mood of depression and then how to change it. You can do this on your own, or you can do it with a friend, which is probably better:

Imagine you are trying to teach the other person to feel depressed. You will have to articulate all the details to them. Pretend they are an actor or an actress and they are going to play the role of you, the depressed person. Once you know just how you create your moods, both the unwanted depressions and the desired happy states, you will know exactly how to change your moods.

Another excellent way to discover how you create the feeling of depression is to ask yourself the question, 'How do I know I'm depressed?' Identifying the answer to this question will usually show you just how you creat the mood and what you can do to dispel it.

I posed the question to Rodney. He had trouble explaining the way he felt and looked somewhat surprised.

'I just know I am. You know when you feel depressed. You just, well, you feel depressed. You know what I mean.'

'No, I don't actually. I rarely feel depressed, and I'm not sure I can empathise with the way you feel. I wonder if you would mind explaining it to me and telling me how you know when you're depressed, then I may be able to help you better.'

He looked as if he thought I was a bit strange but at least it got him talking.

'It's as if there's a heavy blanket, it comes down and drapes over me, it's heavy.'

'Good, what else?'

'Everything looks grey, there's no more colour.'

'How do you know you're happy, do these things change?'

'Yes, I guess they do.'

I had him access a time when he was happy and describe how he knew he was happy and compare that to how he felt when he knew he was depressed. You don't always have to do this, but I wanted to be sure as he had such trouble coming up with the information. Usually it is enough simply to specify how you know you are depressed. Then all you have to do, as I asked him to do, is change the things that you associate with and label as depression.

The moment I asked Rodney to imagine the blanket becoming lighter and floating way up into the sky, and to add colour to the black and white, he began to feel his mood lifting.

The question is the key. How do you know you are depressed? The answer will tell you what you have to do to change the mood and lift yourself out of the depression.

Labels

Labels can create reality. Once someone gets into a pattern of saying 'I'm depressed,' it is likely that they will dwell on this thought and may think or say it out of habit, even when they are not, in fact, feeling particularly depressed. When someone repeats such phrases as 'I'm depressed', 'I'm sad', 'I'm unhappy', 'Nothing good ever happens to me' or 'There's nothing to look forward to, life isn't worth living', it is all too easy for these to become labels, self-fulfilling prophecies. These then develop a power of their own.

Another common and counter-productive thought pattern falls into the category of 'I'm the sort of person who . . .' Someone may say 'I'm the sort of person who gets depressed easily', or 'I'm the sort of person who keeps getting the raw end of the deal', or it may change to 'I always seem to recognise the problems that could occur, I'm that sort of person', or 'I couldn't just think of the good things, that isn't me.'

This type of generalisation extends the assumptions through time and means you then tend to live up to them. When you make those statements aloud, as is commonly done, you also create that expectation in other people's minds and, knowing this, you may then feel you have to live up to what you have said and the way you have labelled yourself, since they expect it of you.

> **Labels can be used to justify your actions. They then become your master. The solution is to recognise them and then break free.**

Mrs Hannaway walked slowly into my office and sat down on the chair indicated. It was a few years since I had seen her. I asked how she was and sat quietly waiting for her to say something, a process that often unnerves a client but equally often gets to the heart to the of the problem faster than a lot of polite chatter. Eventually she said:

'I'm depressed.' This was not a difficult thing for the observer to recognise since she was slumped over, her mouth drooped and she was talking in a dull monotone.

I then took a liberty based on the nature of our previous relationship and the work we had done together in the past.

'Oh, really,' I said, 'I thought you were Mrs Hannaway.'

'No, no, of course I am, you know what I mean: I feel depressed.' Now that, I thought, is a very different thing.

'I see, and how long have you been feeling depressed?'

'I'm always depressed.'

'Always?' I asked, with a heavy emphasis.

'Yes, well, no. That is, not always, but most of the time.'

Because she and I had already worked together, she knew what I was getting at. Even if she had not, this simple bit of conversation in itself could have been sufficient to startle her out from under some of her unconscious labels. Three things had already happened. First, I had jolted her out of her usual state. Second, I had separated her, the person, from the mood she was experiencing, in the process of which she had recognised the label she was using. Third, she had had to recognise that she was not always depressed and that since this was true it meant that she did experience other, and probably more positive, moods.

I asked her to say 'I'm depressed' and notice exactly how she felt inside. Then I asked her to say 'I'm Mrs Hannaway and I am currently feeling depressed, but at other times I feel differently' and notice how she felt. It was clear from her expression that this made a difference. As she said, the problem was less overwhelming when she made those changes.

Do this for yourself now. Think of some of the generalisations that you make: You may say 'I'm depressed', you may also say such things as 'I'm no good', 'I'm a failure', 'I'm a mess', 'I'm lonely' and more. None of these statements is true, yet by a quirk of the English language they are considered to be grammatically correct. You are *not* these things, although you may currently be feeling them.

You may be feeling depressed, that you are no good, a failure, a mess and lonely, but you are not those labels. Furthermore, the initial statement, 'I'm depressed', implies a state of permanence, at least to your subconscious mind. If you want to be more accurate – and if you don't you will have to ask yourself why not – you can add a time frame to it by saying, 'I am feeling depressed at the moment'. I'm sure you will find that by doing this you have already reduced the problem to more manageable proportions.

As a society we are excellent at creating labels for ourselves and for other people and then believing that the label is the truth.

The question 'Who are you?' may receive a variety of

replies, such as 'I'm a dancer', 'I'm Mrs Jamisons's son', 'I'm the town clerk', 'I'm just a housewife', 'I'm an architect', 'I'm a member of this or that church or society'. In these examples the label relates to the person's job or to their relationship to someone or something known to the questioner.

At the emotional level you might answer this question, 'I'm an optimist', 'I'm a pessimist', 'I'm a shy person', 'I'm a success', 'I'm a failure'.

These are all labels. Yet it is sad to find how often we believe the labels we invent and then try to live by them, giving them a life of their own, and thereby fulfilling them.

When we say to a child 'You are bad' instead of 'You're a wonderful child and I love you dearly, but what you have just done is very bad indeed' (we might even add '. . . and not up to your usual standard'), we are labelling the child. To say 'You are bad' is to make the whole of the child bad and not just the misdeed. Once the child accepts this label, they are likely to believe that they are indeed a bad child and to continue to fulfil this role. They come to feel that the label is an absolute truth and not something they can control or alter.

In the same way, when Mrs Hannaway said 'I'm depressed' she labelled herself and created for herself a persona and a self-perpetuating mood designed to validate the label.

It can sometimes be difficult to change a label since it is closely associated with the identity of the whole person. On the other hand once Mrs Hannaway recognised that she had been feeling depressed not for ever but only for a period, whilst almost certainly feeling a lot of other things too, it was easier to find ways to change her state of mind.

Exercise

> *Once you have worked out your own mission statement, your own statement as to who you are and what you stand for, a process discussed in Part III, it is much easier to separate your 'self' from the way you are feeling. I charge you now with this. Every time you find yourself saying 'I am . . .', change it to 'I am (your chosen self-description) who is currently feeling . . .'*

David carried out this exercise. He was a well dressed businessman in his early forties but with a deeply lined face and greying hair more typical of a man in his late fifties. He had arrived to see me saying he was depressed and that nothing he could do seemed to make any difference.

'It's no good, I just have to accept that I'm a failure. My business is failing, it has been for years, and now my marriage is on the rocks. I seem to be a failure all round. It's no wonder I'm depressed.'

After talking to him, I learned that he had been a very successful businessman for twenty years, first working for a large company and then, about twelve years prior to our meeting, buying a small retail business and turning it into a successful franchise operation. For ten years he had been married to a woman ten years younger than himself and they had been very happy, at least until two years prior to his visit to me. I decided to put him through the following sequence:

'First, David, I would like you to think of some

of the statements you commonly think to yourself, about yourself. What are they?'

We soon had a list that included 'I'm a failure', 'I'm no good as a husband', 'I'm no good in business' and 'I'm depressed'.

'Now,' I continued, 'I would like you to take each statement one at a time, and concentrate on it. What happens to you internally? How do you feel? Be aware of what is happening to you, physically, mentally and emotionally as you make these statements.'

Since he had been experiencing these moods for many months, it didn't take long for him to sink down into the deepest of the depressions with which he had been living.

'OK,' I said, 'now please take each statement, one at a time, and change it. Instead of 'I'm no good as a businessman', I would like you to change the statement to cover not just the immediate past and present, but the whole of your life, or as much as is appropriate.'

We worked on this together and eventually he came up with 'I'm a businessman who has been successful for the past twenty years but in the last two years has had some business problems, in part at least related to the current recession.'

'Fine. Now repeat that sentence over and over. Later on I will ask you to tell me how you feel.'

He hardly had to tell me. His posture and expression gave him away. His shoulders lifted and his frown lessened. Rather than letting him comment immediately, I kept him focused on the task at hand. I said, 'The next phrase is "I'm no good as a husband". I would like you to change this one, too, again taking into account the larger context.'

David's alternative phrase to this was, 'I've been a good husband for the past ten years, I've had a good marriage with my wife, provided well for her and been faithful. We've had a lot of good times. Currently we're going through a rough patch because of my worries at work.'

David's third statement had been 'I'm a failure', and he changed this into 'I'm currently having problems in my life but there are many things at which I have succeeded. I've been a good son, and have created a happy and loving family. I have many skills including being able to read, write, drive well, balance the family budget, entertain my friends well, create new ideas, inspire my staff and be a good father. Currently, along with many other people, I am not dealing with the recessionary business climate as well as I would like, but I'm doing my best.'

I made a couple of suggestions for the last part. First, I suggested that he delete reference to other people. He had to feel happy with himself. It didn't really matter what other people did or how well they were doing. Second, I suggested that he change 'I'm doing my best' to 'I know I have or can develop the skills necessary to do this as soon as I choose.'

This meant that his statement became 'I'm currently having problems in my life but there are many things at which I have succeeded. I've been a good son, and have created a happy and loving family. I have many skills including being able to read, write, drive well, balance the family budget, entertain my friends well, create new ideas, inspire my staff and be a good father. I am not dealing with the current recessionary business climate as well as I would like but I know I have or can develop the skills necessary to do this as soon as I choose.'

When David had created each statement and then thought each part of it through, I asked him how he felt.

'That's remarkable. Nothing has actually changed but I feel totally different. It's as if I can see a light at the end of the tunnel, and what's more I know I can reach it.'

He was right and he was wrong. Nothing had changed and everything had changed. His outward circumstances had not changed, not in the time he'd been with me. But outward circumstances, as we have seen before, are only the background against which you create your own internal reality. David's internal reality had certainly changed, and this is the reality that is ultimately important to each of us. No matter what is going on, you have total control over your internal experience and can change it as you wish.

Not only had these verbal changes led to a different internal experience for David, they had also changed the way he felt about the future and given him improved resources for dealing with the situation. As he put it, 'By making those changes I am forced to keep in mind the larger perspective, the times I have succeeded, the skills I do have, the record of what I have already achieved and, as a result, I can sense that I could succeed again, as soon as I figure out how to do so. It is no longer a case of feeling helpless, but rather of having the drive to use the skills I have to pull out of this and recognising that I have the capacity to do so. It's still going to be tough . . .'

'Only if you think so,' was my nearly automatic interjection.

'. . . but I now know I will be able to do it and I feel much more powerful and capable.'

Later, David told me of the discussion he'd had with his wife following our meeting. She had said that she felt that she was being excluded from him and his business during the current crisis. She had believed that he thought her too young and immature to help. As a result, she was tense and snappy. When they talked it all over and shared what was happening, they were able to pull their marriage back together again and to work together as a couple on the business, in her case in a very necessary supporting role.

Labels, labels, labels. They have a lot to answer for. Search out the labels you use and decide which ones you want to keep and which ones you want to get rid of. Keep in mind that you are yourself, you are not the label. You decide who you are, what you want to be and what you stand for. You can then comment on the way you are feeling at any moment in the context of that moment within the whole of your existence.

Chapter Six

You Talk To Yourself Anyway,
So Do It Constructively

In Transactional Analysis a person is seen to have three major 'parts' that can create different behaviour patterns in them. These 'parts' are the Child, the Adult and the Parent. You have probably experienced these three yourself. Sometimes you feel like an adult, making your own decisions, interacting with other adults and so forth. At other times you may feel as if you're being a mother or a father to everyone. You may be taking care of the boss, your parents, your friends and so forth and playing a parent role to them all. At other times you may feel like a child, either kicking up your heels and having fun or going to other people as if they were your parent or mentor and depending on their advice and guidance rather than making decisions of your own.

Subsequent research into Transactional Analysis has shown the value of working with other 'parts' such as the Critic, the Driver, the Victim and so forth. On this basis it can be assumed that there is a 'part' that creates depression. This 'part' can then be talked to and questioned as to its purpose. In this way much valuable information can be acquired. Further, it is possible to negotiate with the 'part' and get its agreement to use a different method to achieve the same result.

Ideally, this procedure is done by someone trained in its use. However, it is possible for you to learn the rudiments of the technique from this chapter and then to practise it. There are also books that have been written on the subject. The dialogue work involved can be done with a friend or it can even, with a little practice, be done by the individual, although this is more difficult. You can also have a '"parts" party' in which you can create a mental scene of your different 'parts' discussing what they do, what they would like to do, and how things can be changed for the benefit of you as a whole.

The procedure is relatively simple, as the following example shows:

> I was working with Peter. He had been feeling depressed for a while and had come in for advice. I had explained to him about the different parts that could be considered to be components of a person's make-up and he had agreed to work this way, so I said, 'Peter, could I talk to your Depression part?'
>
> When he agreed I motioned him over to sit in a different chair. He had already been told that when he was in that chair he was to talk to me as if he were solely the Depression part, leaving 'Peter' as a whole person metaphorically behind in the first chair.
>
> Once he was comfortable in the second chair I continued, 'Hello, I believe you are Peter's,' and looked over at the empty chair and nodded my head at it, 'Depression part?'

'Yes.'

'Good, so is it all right if we have a chat?'

'Yes.'

'OK, can you tell me a bit about yourself, why do you choose to make Peter feel depressed?'

'Oh, it's better that way.'

'Really, does he like being depressed?'

'No, I suppose not, but it's useful.'

'Now that's really interesting. Why is it useful?'

'Well, he has this problem with his marriage. He's afraid his wife doesn't love him any more, certainly she doesn't want to make love to him. Actually he's afraid that she may be having an affair.'

'And how does your work help him?'

'Oh, that's easy. I make him depressed. When she realises how depressed he is, she is more affectionate.'

'Excellent, well done. Do you have any idea why she behaves that way?'

'Not really, but perhaps she feels a bit sorry for him.'

'So you do a good job for him do you, getting him what he wants?'

All the time we were talking I kept nodding in the direction of the empty chair when I mentioned Peter's name. I was also making a point of seeing the situation from the point of view of the Depression part. If you argue with or criticise a part, it will probably stop talking to you.

'Does that mean he gets more sex?'

'No. At least, not usually, well, sometimes it does. But he is less scared that she'll leave. In fact I

think she feels pretty guilty when I make him
depressed.'

'Excellent, and thank you for talking to me, that's
been most helpful. Perhaps you would like to go
back and join Peter.'

With that I waved Peter back to the original chair.
I sat quietly for a while, letting Peter digest what
had occurred.

'Goodness, that's amazing. You know I guess I
do put it on a bit. I feel pretty sure that she still
cares for me, at least in an affectionate sort of way.
The trouble is I still love her very much. I guess I
am afraid of her leaving me, though I've probaby
been burying that thought. But I do know she is
more affectionate when she thinks I need cheering
up. There have been so many problems at work
that it's been easy for me to blame them for my
moods.'

Dialogue work is a very simple, yet surprisingly
powerful, way of learning more about yourself. As long
as the questioner is sympathetic to the 'part' and
respectful of the information gleaned, there is little
harm you can do with this. There is one proviso. Since
it is possible, by focusing on this concept of having
many 'parts' that new 'parts' may actually be created, it
is important at the end that the questioner sends the
'part' back to integrate into the person as I did in the
above example. You may also want to comment on the
fact that the 'part' is just that: a part of the fully
integrated person. Otherwise, simply act as if the
person is the 'part' and find out as much as you can.
The more you know about the reasons behind your

depression the better able you are to change the situation.

Working with parts can also be used to resolve internal conflicts and this is described in chapter 16.

Much more has been written about this in books on Transactional Analysis and Voice Dialogue. There are also practitioners who can help you explore further. However, this little sample may be all you need to have some fun with the idea and produce some helpful information.

Chapter Seven

The Melancholic Temperament

The ancient Greeks loved to divide the different aspects of their world into four sub-categories. They considered the physical world to be made up of four elements: air, earth, fire and water; the year was divided into four seasons; and they believed that the health of the human body depended on the proper balance of the four fluids or humours. They also divided personality into four temperaments – Choleric, Sanguine, Phlegmatic and Melancholic. They considered each person to be made up of a blend of these four parts and the most balanced person to be a blend of an equal amount of each component. The interesting thing from our point of view is that these basic personality traits, known by the same names, are still considered by psychologists today to be a useful representation of the four major character types.

While the Greeks divided the personality into four temperaments there was no suggestion that people in general were 100 per cent one temperament or 100 per cent another. It was recognised that people are generally a blend of all the temperaments but in widely varying proportions. Usually two or perhaps three of these temperaments are clearly evident in a person, although one temperament may be dominant. The ratios can also vary with time and circumstance but the general mix remains specific to that person.

The ideal personality may contain an equal blend of all four temperaments, all developed from the first, immature stage through to the third and final stage, but that is rarely seen and if it were the world would be a dull place. Instead, you may have a dominantly Choleric person who can, from time to time, sink into Melancholia, or a dominantly Phlegmatic person who can throw off their routine and become optimistically Sanguine.

For our purposes we will not consider the first three temperaments in any detail. However, for the sake of perspective, and before we focus totally on the Melancholic temperament, it is worth giving a thumbnail sketch of the other three. To do this we will consider each as if the person who displays the temperament is one hundred per cent this temperament. What follows is necessarily only a *very* brief description and, like a caricature cartoon, not really a representation.

Choleric

The Choleric type is usually short and stocky, striding through life assuming the role of leader and expecting others to do his bidding. He or she may throw tantrums if they don't get their own way; they may leave others to do the detailed work once they have conquered the territory. In general Cholerics are too busy ruling and leading the world, being strong, even aggressive, expecting others to fit in with them and either controlling or giving vent to their temper to have much time to be depressed. They may be a demanding tyrant, a Napoleon or a Hitler, a strong and stirring leader such as Churchill, shining in times of war. They may develop into benign leaders, using their strength to care, tolerant of others' mistakes and pleased to be able to provide for those who depend on them. Cholerics usually see the wider picture, know what they want and then go for it by the most direct route possible, although if a new goal becomes desirable, they are capable of changing direction as they deem appropriate. The true Choleric is rarely depressed and certainly not for long.

Sanguine

Sanguine people are the happy optimists. They are usually tall, slender and beautiful. They are exciting to be with, they dance through life bringing fun and laughter into parties and gatherings. They have multiple interests, darting from one intriguing idea to another with the rapidity of a butterfly, but often have little staying capacity and rarely see things through to completion, unless they become very mature and self-disciplined. Whilst they are often widely read and stimulating to others, they can also be Jack- (or Jill-) of-all-trades and proficient in none. Wonderful lovers, they can be economical with the truth, are rarely faithful, though they are convinced that their affairs in no way affect their marriages. This may be hard for their partners to understand yet Sanguine characters are such fun to be with, it is easy to forgive them. The Sanguine is one of the happiest personalities: if they are depressed it lasts but a short time and they are soon up and laughing again, at themselves and at the world.

Phlegmatic

The Phlegmatics are the steady plodders. They walk straight ahead but mainly because it is too much trouble to make a decision and change direction. They are well organised, love routine and make excellent and reliable assistants. They fail to see the wider picture but are wonderful at detailed work. No matter how monotonous or routine the job they are never bored. They are the treasured guests who will almost certainly do the washing up for you and leave the place neat and tidy. They are usually unsure and lacking in confidence, especially when it comes to making choices or decisions and for this they rely heavily on others, preferring to copy someone they know, or know of, and respect, rather than rely on themselves and their own judgement. They can become depressed but usually make little fuss and keep doing what is expected of them without protest.

Melancholic

Unlike the other three character types, the Melancholic, as the name implies, is often down and will let you know it. The more of the Melancholic temperament you have in your make-up, the more likely you are to be depressed. For this reason we will consider this temperament in some detail, paying particular attention as to how you can help a Melancholic person change his or her nature to a point where their depression is reduced and the wonderful, understanding and caring side of their nature can blossom.

Not surprisingly, in view of what we have already said about mood being reflected in physiology and vice versa, the movements and gestures of the archetypal 100 per cent Melancholic temperament are all downwards. They tend to droop from the shoulders and their major movements and emphasis are downwards such as letting the arms fall. Facial lines are vertical, leaving sad grooves between the eyebrows; the mouth tends to turn down at the corners, perhaps revealing a bitter expression and the eyes show pain and suffering. They tend to walk with their heads down, looking at the pavement or the ground, and to be lost in introspective thought, slumping along carrying the burden of the world, and, more importantly, of themselves, on their shoulders. They clearly demonstrate, visually, the melancholia for which they are named.

Clothes too can reveal the Melancholic temperament. People who are dominantly Melancholic often choose sombre colours and inconspicuous styles, none of which does anything very positive to show off their figures or looks. They are likely to look older than their years and seem old long before their time, unlike youthful Sanguines.

All this, of course, applies to the person who is 100 per cent Melancholic. Keep in mind that few people are all one temperament, though many people are dominantly one with only small amounts of the others. However, these clues may help you to recognise yourself or someone you care about and are trying to help. The description here fits the most extreme of the Melancholic type.

We'll move on now to consider the mental and emotional make-up and development of the Melancholic type.

Melancholics know that the world is a dark and gloomy place, they are sure that dreadful things are about to happen and that catastrophes are the norm. They also know that the good times are the most dangerous of all because then there is the most scope for disaster. The Melancholic becomes tense and uptight when things are going well, and is much more able to relax in disaster, since disaster is the normal state of the world. In a sense they could even be said to enjoy suffering. One strongly Melancholic client told me that he felt guilty when things were going well, as if he had no right to happiness when there was so much suffering in the world.

Melancholics are pessimists, always seeing the worst side of things and anticipating the worst possible outcome. They are also introverted, wanting to have a lot of attention paid to them and their problems, and are inclined to dwell in the past. They are verbally articulate, speaking their minds freely and all too willing to tell you their problems and the problems of the world. If you ask the Melancholic a simple question such as 'How are you?', they will answer in infinite detail, down to the last ache, twitch and worry.

At the slightest sign of illness Melancholics will take time off work, wrap themselves in blankets, surround themselves with medications and await the worst, which they are sure will occur. Melancholics do not want to be cheered up. The worst thing I, as a counsellor, could do to a Melancholic is to tell them their problem is minor and that they will soon be cured. They would immediately go off and find another practitioner, one who understood just how serious their problem was.

Melancholics long to have someone truly understand them, yet they are so locked within themselves that this is difficult. They are in fact extremely selfish yet they would be amazed if you told them so. They are not interested in other people, not even in other Melancholics and will vie with them as each tries to prove that their lot is the harder and their own life is the more difficult.

If you are a Melancholic, or have a lot of the Melancholic temperament in your make-up, you may recognise some of these characteristics in yourself. You may even recognise a few of these characteristics yet try to deny them. I haven't yet met a Melancholic who was pleased to be one. In fact, in seminars I run in which we cover this topic, without fail each person who has proved to be a Melancholic has asked to do the questionnaires again, sure that this time they will answer the questions differently and show that they are actually of some other temperament. This is sad, for the Melancholic has a lot to offer once he or she matures.

Metamorphosis and Development of the Melancholic

While it is true that the Melancholic usually sees the worst side of any situation, it is also true that they understand the suffering other people are going through. If there is a Melancholic child in the school, that is the child to intoduce to the new boy or girl who is homesick. The Melancholic child will understand the suffering of the new boy or girl. Melancholics understand the woes of others and can empathise with them. Thus they can be the best of companions when the going gets tough, particularly if they are mature. They make wonderful carers of the long-term ill, they work well in hospices, they are wonderful companions for the dying. However, all this happens only when the Melancholic matures, so let's consider now how you can help yourself or some other Melancholic to mature:

- Do not try to cheer Melancholics up as that will only confirm to them that you don't understand the full intensity and seriousness of all the problems and worries they have. When they tell you how terrible the weather is, agree with them. When they tell you how bad the news is, agree with them. When they tell you about something awful that happened to them, sympathise. In this way they will realise that you fully understand them and empathise with them and that you truly know what a difficult place the world is. When they realise this and when they run out of things to complain or be depressed about, they are free to begin to think of some slightly positive things and to take tentative steps into mild optimism.

  If you are trying to help a Melancholic, try to offer them these resources, but do not let them take charge of the situation, for if you do you will lose your power over them and thus your ability to help them and they will relapse back into their old ways.

- A good way to lead a Melancholic out of their melancholia is to ask brief, punchy questions. Give them only a short time in which to answer – otherwise you will simply get a long monologue full of more of their problems – and then ask another question, and another, and another. In this way you keep moving the Melancholic's mind from topic to topic and they cannot drown in any one of them. You can allow them to talk themselves dry, until they feel that every possible negative situation has been covered.

- The next stage in helping a Melancholic is to find someone who will arouse their sympathy and who needs them. This need, on the part of the other person, must be genuine. The Melancholic will quickly detect any pretence in this regard; after all, they know true suffering when they see it. Try to find someone who really needs them and who values their sympathy and support. It doesn't matter if this person makes demands on the Melancholic in terms of time. In fact, one way to help the Melancholic mature is to *make demands on them* and create situations where they will be asked to make a personal sacrifice, in time, effort, possessions or whatever is appropriate. At the end, be sure to show your appreciation for what the Melancholic has done and acknowledge what they have suffered by doing it.

If you are the Melancholic person and are willing to work on yourself, the above insights should help you. You may also choose to get a friend to help, although I know you may find it painful to let them have these insights into your nature. Keep in mind that with a heavy slice of this make-up in you, you have a lot to offer other people and a lot of strengths, once you have developed them.

> **To help yourself you might choose to focus your attention on people in distress or in need of comfort. You have a great capacity for empathising with people in distress and can give them valuable support and solace, lifting your own mood in the process.**

Melancholics who have matured to a point where they have come out of their total self-absorption are wonderful in difficult situations, provided they are asked to help others and not given time to dwell on their own problems.

Once you come to understand your nature you can use it to maximum benefit. You can learn to overcome the depression and develop your understanding and sympathy in such a way that it can bring you great satisfaction.

Chapter Eight

Optimists and Pessimists

We do love dividing people into categories. Think of the questionnaires in magazines and so forth, the quizzes such as: 'Find out if you're an Extrovert or an Introvert', 'Learn your Body Type', 'Discover the type of partner that's right for you', 'Which Temperament are you?'. These, and countless other such quizzes, are often the first page people turn to. This may be harmless fun, but it may also be a useful tool for enabling you to assess and then change and improve your life. A lot depends on how you treat the process.

In the last chapter we looked at the four temperaments. In this chapter we are going to look at the division of people into two groups, depending upon the way they view the world: whether they inherently take the positive and optimistic view or whether they inherently take the negative and pessimistic view.

I'm sure you've been in a situation when two people have reported on an event and its meaning and they have come up with totally conflicting and opposing conclusions. Perhaps the skies have greyed: one will be convinced that rain is about to set in for a long period and that their weekend will be ruined; the other will see this as a sure sign that it will rain now and be fine when they want to go out. Perhaps two people set out to find a missing object, lost on a country walk. One refuses to give up hope, confident that they will eventually find it; the other is convinced that the search is useless. A friend may sound vague and distracted when invited to a party: the would-be host may conclude that the friend does not want to come and thinks the party will be boring, or they may assume that the friend has something on their mind at the time that is worrying them.

What is it, in people, that determines whether they take an optimistic or a pessimistic view of life? Is one view better than the other? Are there times when it is beneficial to be a pessimist and other times when it is beneficial to be an optimist? It is these, and other related questions, that we will be exploring in this chapter.

What makes you an optimist or a pessimist? Without going into detail at this point, we can generalise and say the following: pessimists believe that life is tough and that things that can go wrong will go wrong; optimists believe that life is a ball and everything will work out fine. They both feel that they are the ones who are being realistic.

Pessimists believe that optimists are irresponsible and foolish and are heading for an inevitable fall. They believe that optimists live in this airy-fairy world where they simply don't understand what is going on. In some cases that may be true. So if you are a pessimist and if you are planning to make a change, let's not aim for blind, foolhardy optimism, but rather a practical level of optimism that can serve you well. Only you can determine what that level will be.

Certainly, there is little benefit in being such an optimist that you fail to take proper care. If, when you fly your plane, you happily assume someone else has checked it over and fail to run the security checks, that is foolhardy. If you drive home from a party and optimistically assume there will be no police cars on the road and that you will get there safely, even if drunk, that is irresponsible. If you decide you don't need insurance or to plan for a rainy day, or for your retirement, because, as an optimist, you assume either that nothing bad will happen to you or, in the case of your retirement, some external force will take care of things and provide for you, then you could be in for some nasty shocks.

What are you? Some people are certain they are pessimists, others are certain they are optimists, many are not sure or may oscillate between the two. Perhaps you are not sure. It is not always easy to tell which you are: you may even think you are one and discover you are the other. Does it matter? After all, you may say, whatever you are is whatever you are and you have to live with it. Not at all. Recent and current research is showing that you do not have to live with your attitudes and beliefs. They are attitudes and beliefs that you have created by yourself and for yourself and that you are free to change. If they are not serving you, if they are leading to problems in your life, then you can change them.

It is the optimists who tend to lose their money in wild-cat ventures, assume the tax department will ignore them, arrive late at work reckoning the boss won't notice, lend money without security, and take other unnecessary risks. There are times when it is helpful to be a careful pessimist.

There are certain jobs where it is better to be or to hire a pessimist than a optimist. These include jobs involved with safety, security, record-keeping and the care of others. Pessimists make good accountants, litigant lawyers, proof-readers, and the like. It should be a pessimist rather than an optimist who designs and checks the safety features on your car, on aircraft and supertankers, and the levels of toxic chemicals allowed into the food chain. Pessimists are likely to be more understanding and tolerant than optimists when dealing with people who are in trouble and in need.

So there are many times when it is useful and valuable to be pessimistic. There are activities that you would rather have performed by a pessimist than by an optimist, there are occasions when you will feel better being with a pessimist than with an optimist and there are situations when you yourself will be safer acting as a pessimist than as an optimist. However, the opposite is also true and at other times you will feel better being an optimist and being in the company of optimists. One thing is clear, there is convincing evidence that pessimists suffer from depression far more often than optimists do.

Few people like being depressed. Wouldn't it be wonderful if you could follow a few simple steps and change from being a pessimist to being an optimist? Better still, wouldn't it be wonderful to be able to change from being one to the other and back again at will? This would then mean you could get the best of both worlds. If you could alternate at will you could reduce your chance of suffering depression, and even, if you wished, eliminate depression from your life entirely.

How to Tell Whether You are an Optimist or a Pessimist

It is possible to distinguish between optimists and pessimists by looking at the way people explain the events in their lives to themselves. They will give events different weights of SIGNIFICANCE, project onto them different TIMESCALES (so one mishap could over-shadow a lifetime) and entertain varying views on their own level of RESPONSIBILITY for events.

A closer examination of this idea will reveal how differently optimists and pessimists view these three aspects of their life's events:

Scope/Significance

If you are an optimist, you will view a set-back as a limited situation without further implications. If you forget to do something, you may assume that it is simply that you forgot to do that one particular thing. If you are a pessimist, you will probably extrapolate from this one event and assume that it means you have a rotten memory and are stupid into the bargain. If you are a pessimist, you will do the reverse with positive situations. Here are some of the things pessimists and optimists may each say in a particular situation

	Pessimist	**Optimist**
In a negative situation	It's hard to study.	That was a difficult book to understand.
	Shops don't have clothes that suit me.	That shop doesn't carry my styles.
	I'll bet it's gone for good.	I can't find it for the moment.
	I'm stupid.	I'm good at some subjects, bad at others.

	No one likes me.	A few people don't like me.
	You don't like me.	Over this matter I'm out of favour with you.
In a positive situation	This paper had easy questions.	I cope well with exams.
	I'm at ease with a few close friends.	I'm at ease with people.
	Just this once, things went my way.	I'm always lucky.
	A few people like me.	I'm popular.

Here you can see how the pessimist assumes something negative is an example of a bigger truth and something good is an isolated instance. The optimist, on the other hand, chooses to believe that something negative is an isolated example and that something good is, in general, true.

Timescale

If you are an optimist, you probably believe that positive situations will last for a long time and troubles will be short-lived. If you are a pessimist, you are more likely to assume that negative situations will last for a long time and that positive and happy times are bound to be brief.

If a pessimist is trying to lose weight, has a binge at a friend's wedding and gains half-a-kilo, he or she will say, 'I can *never* lose weight'; the optimist will say, 'I can lose weight if I stick to my diet but not if I overeat'. If a pessimist gets lost he or she will say, 'I *always* get lost'; the optimist will say, 'I can get lost when I go somewhere new if I don't consult the map carefully'.

Optimists and pessimists will make differrent assumptions and different statements to themselves to describe situations. Here are some of the things they say to themselves that relate to time and duration.

	Pessimist	*Optimist*
In a negative situation	Diets never work.	I can lose weight when I stick to the diet.
	I always blow it.	I made a mistake this time.
	Nobody will ever want me.	Right now I'm on my own.
	You never talk to me.	We haven't talked properly for a while.
	It always rains when I plan a picnic.	This time I chose a rainy day for the picnic!
	People always ignore me.	No one noticed me today.
	I always say something silly.	I put my foot in it today.
In a positive situation	That was a rare fluke.	I'm always lucky.
	I made the grade but it won't last.	I've done it once, I can keep doing it.
	I was invited this time: they must have been short of guests.	They always include me.

| I got it right for once. | I'm usually successful. |
| This time it's not raining. | I'm always lucky with the weather. |

Notice how the pessimist assumes bad situations are long-lasting and permanent and good ones only temporary. The optimist does the reverse and assumes that bad times are passing episodes but the good times are here to stay.

Responsibility

If you are an optimist, you probably accept that the good things that happen in your life are of your own creating but that the bad things are someone else's doing or part of a bigger picture, and thus not your fault or responsibility. This way of explaining things means that your self-esteem and confidence remain high and you are usually happy.

If, on the other hand, you are a pessimist, you probably think that all the bad things that happen in your life are of your own doing and thus you have low self-esteem and self-confidence, and are riddled with self-blame and guilt. Good things, you probably believe, happen by chance and are not something that you can control and certainly not something you can take credit for creating. With these attitudes and beliefs, depression can occur all too easily.

The examples below of what optimists and pessimists might say when confronted with positive and negative events demonstrate the level of acceptance of responsibility they are each willing to take for the good and bad things that occur in their lives:

	Pessimist	**Optimist**
In a negative situation	It was all my fault.	It was not my fault.
	I make stupid decisions.	I was badly advised.
	I let the side down.	The team did poorly.
In a positive situation	We won because they made up for my mistakes.	My input was crucial to our success.
	I was just lucky.	I seized the opportunity.
	I had good cards.	I played the hand well.

Notice the way pessimists think that the problems they experience are their own fault and responsibility, but that the good things that happen were brought about by others. In contrast, the optimist is clearly assuming that the problems are caused by other people and that the good situations are of their own creating.

By now you should have a pretty good idea as to whether you are dominantly an optimist or a pessimist.

The exceptions to this generalisation are those rare people who are already willing and able to take total responsibility, without blame, for all that happens in their life, and who can do so while maintaining a high level of self-esteem. In this case depression does not result, even when they acknowledge creating a situation that did not turn out the way they wanted. Merely by gaining the knowledge that you are in control can prevent depression.

Your Beliefs and Attitudes

Optimists are optimists because they assume things are and will be good. Pessimists are pessimists because they assume things are and will be bad. Both optimists and pessimist create self-fulfilling expectations and so bring about the very situations and emotions they are anticipating. They do this in two ways: by creating an inner belief system based on their subjective view of events in their lives and the interpretations they choose to put on them; and by the effect their emotions and their attitudes have on outside events.

Optimists tend to create positive experiences and to be happy, whereas pessimists tend to create negative experiences and to be depressed. If you are depressed and want this to change, the obvious answer would seem to be to change your beliefs and attitudes from those of a pessimist to those of an optimist. Is it that easy?

Your attitudes may seem to be deep-rooted and permanent, yet it is possible to change them. You may have stopped trying to change and decided to accept that you are the eternal pessimist, that depression is part of your nature and that it is your lot in life to wake up depressed or to get upset easily by any misfortune. You may even, at one time, have been willing to believe you could change, you may have tried to change already, possibly by adopting a positive mien. Maybe you smiled, whistled, or planned and said positive things. Did it work? Probably not, since the underlying beliefs and attitudes had not been changed. Perhaps you have attempted making affirmations, formed a variety of positive statements and tried to believe they were true. Did this work? It may have done, but the chances are it didn't, not unless you not only said them but visualised them and felt them so deeply they became a truth for you – something few people doing positive affirmations really achieve. Have you tried focusing on all the good things in your life, only to go into depression anyway, possibly realising that you could lose them?

Don't despair, there is more that you can do. In fact there are a number of constructive and specific steps you can take to turn from being even a hardened pessimist into a functioning optimist, thereby eliminating, or at least reducing, depression. We will discuss some of these steps in this chapter, others are covered throughout this book.

Moving from Depression to Optimism

It almost goes without saying that the optimist will generally be happier than the pessimist. However it is also true that, by and large, optimists will be more successful, healthier and live longer than pessimists. The aim here is to help you to cure or avoid depression by changing from pessimism to reasonable optimism. The fact that this can also lead to greater success, better health and a longer life should be an added incentive for you to make the effort to accomplish the changes.

One way to change from being a pessimist to being an optimist is to change the way you explain situations and events to yourself.

No situation is intrinsically depressing, nor is it inherently exciting and positive. Everything depends on the interpretation you, as an individual, place on it.

Rain is neither good nor bad. The way you feel about it depends on whether you focus on the good it will do the garden or the harm it will do the washing on the line. You can be happy being rich or worried by the responsibility. Red traffic lights can delay you or give you time to think. A big city can be full of interest or frighteningly violent. It all depends on your interpretation. You can take this further. To see some extreme examples, consider the following:

You would normally be sad at a funeral and happy at a party. However,

(a) it is possible to be relatively happy at a funeral if you assume that the turnout is a wonderful demonstration of how many people care.

(b) it is possible to be miserable and depressed at the height of the party if you assume that people are only pretending to like you to be polite.

A funeral is not going to be a happy time, but you can focus on all the pain and loss you are experiencing and make the situation even more painful. Alternatively, you can concentrate on the large number of well-wishers and their caring attitude, and perhaps on the pain and suffering that is over for the deceased person. You cannot change the fact that they have died. You can change your own inner experience. You do not love and care less for focusing on the positive. You do not demonstrate greater love by focusing on the pain and increasing your depression.

At a party you can either have fun or feel like a failure, depending on the assumptions you make. You will actually never know what someone else is thinking. You may think you do, you may get close, but you will never know for sure. You cannot get inside their head and experience their thoughts and emotions. What you receive is, inevitably, filtered both by the way they choose to express themselves and by the interpretation you put on this outward expression. So, why assume others are only being polite and thereby create a bad time for yourself? Why not choose to believe that they think you are a great asset and that they love having you and so let yourself enjoy the party. Maybe you are saying that that would be like living in a fool's paradise. That's possible. But since you can never know for sure what they are thinking, why not risk being wrong in a way that leads you to assume that they like you and thus live in a possible fool's paradise, rather than believe they don't like you and live in a possible fool's hell?

Again, I repeat, it is your interpretations and what you say to yourself that will dictate your mood and thus whether or not you are easily or often depressed. Change the focus of your thoughts and the interpretation you put on a situation and you can change and improve your mood.

Exercise

> *The following method will show you one way to change your interpretation of an event. This process may be all that you need to get out of depression. On the other hand, it may be just one step in the many you will take to change your mood. It is possible, with this method, to make quite major changes in your life. It depends to a large extent on how diligent you are in following these next steps.*
>
> *As you go through the steps, keep in mind the distinctions we have made about the explanations accepted by pessimists and those accepted by optimists. Keep in mind, too, that there is no absolute reality, only*

the one you create within your own head by the way you view, filter and interpret what happens in your life. Your old belief is neither more nor less true than the new one you are attempting to put in its place. Neither the old nor the new is inherently true or false, they are each your self-created experience. Since this is the way of things then why not choose the belief that is the most useful?

Here are the five steps that will help you out of depression:

1. Identify the situation or event that makes you feel depressed.

2. Verbalise clearly the belief that you have about this situation or event.

3. Become fully aware of the specific consequences of this belief.

4. Be your own devil's advocate and argue for different beliefs or conclusions, ones that empower you and are more useful than your present belief in enabling you to feel good about the situation.

5. Commit to a total focus on the chosen new belief.

For example:

1. The Event

You go out with someone a few times and decide that they are pleasant company and that you would like to develop a closer relationship with them. Suddenly, without warning, they stop phoning. When you eventually talk to them, they are stiff and distant.

2. The Belief

Your usual response may be to believe that something you have said or done has put them off. You may assume that they found you lacking, that they didn't like you when they got to know you better, that if you had behaved

*differently you could have had a good relationship, that it
is all your fault that the two of you have broken up. You
may tell yourself 'I'm no good at relationships'.*

3. *The Consequence*

*As a result you chastise yourself, berate yourself and feel
depressed at the loss of a relationship that might have
been, if only you had been different. You assume that any
future relationships will turn out this way too, and get
even more depressed.*

4. *Other Possible Beliefs and Interpretations*

*When you look for other beliefs and interpretations you
may choose to believe that something else, about which you
could know nothing, cropped up in the other person's life.
Perhaps an ex-lover has returned, perhaps they are in
trouble at work and cannot focus on a new relationship,
perhaps there has been a crisis in their life that is fully
occupying their attention. Whatever it is, you can assume
that it had nothing to do with anything you said or did.*

*Alternatively you may decide that they have shown
you the sort of person they really are. You may come to
the conclusion that they are rude and unreliable and that
it is fortunate that you have discovered this early on,
rather than later when you might have been more
involved and could have been more deeply hurt. You
could choose to recognise that they are not good enough
for you and do not meet the standards of loyalty you
want in a close friend. You may conclude that you are
better off without them and that it is lucky you will be
free when someone more suitable turns up.*

5. *Focus on the New Beliefs*

*Every time you find yourself thinking about that person,
quieten the negative voices, run the above process from
beginning to end and focus on the empowering beliefs.*

After you have practised this process for a while, in

relation to a specific problem you may find that you are able to go directly to step four whenever you find yourself beginning to get depressed about it.

NB: The above process sounds straightforward and it is certainly simple. However the simple is not always easy and you may need some further assistance. Here it is:

Ask questions. *Ask questions of yourself, but make sure they are helpful questions, not unhelpful questions. Here are some examples of both:*

Unhelpful questions about a situation or event:
  Why does this always happen to me?
  Why do things keep going wrong?
  How come I always get the raw deal?

Helpful questions about a situation or event:
  What's good about this?
  How can I turn this to my advantage?
  What could this mean that would work in my favour?
  How can I enjoy or find satisfaction in this situation?
  What can I learn from this?
  What am I able to do to improve the situation?

Helpful questions about your life in general:
  What's good about my life?
  What am I happy about?
  What am I grateful for?
  Who loves me?
  Who are my friends?

Martin had been seeing me for a month about depression in general when he came in particularly depressed one afternoon. I asked what was bothering him and he told me he was having trouble at work, he couldn't seem to do anything right and he was afraid he was about to lose his job. As a result he had spent the past week worrying that he wouldn't get another one, fretting about how he could manage to provide for his wife and the new baby if he didn't, and feeling thoroughly miserable about the effect this would have on his marriage.

This is what happened as we went through the five steps:

1. The Event

It turned out that his boss, who normally smiled at him when their paths crossed, had been abrupt and aloof one day and then had been, according to Martin, either avoiding him ever since or critical of anything he did.

2. The Belief

As a result Martin had become afraid of losing his job.

3. The Consequence

As a consequence he had become tense and nervy. His work, he was sure, had deteriorated as a result. As Martin said:

'I've been so worried about the situation that I can't seem to concentrate properly and then I find I have done something wrong. Who knows what other mistakes I must have made and missed?'

4. Other Possible Beliefs and Interpretations

This is the critical step, and this is where Martin had trouble. He simply couldn't think of any reason why his boss, who had been smiling and pleasant for the six months he had had the job, should suddenly change his behaviour. He sat there thinking about it and all he could focus on was the possible dreadful things he had done and the possible consequences. So I started asking him questions:

'What other explanation is there?'

This brought unconvincing suggestions that his boss might have problems in other areas of his life but, as Martin was quick to say, 'He's always been good tempered before, even when I know he has had problems.'

'What's good about this?'

Martin's first response was 'Nothing', but on further thought he suggested that he could take the opportunity to relate better to his colleagues and ask them, rather than his boss, for advice when he needed it.

'How can you turn this to your advantage?'

'Well,' he said, 'I guess I could use the time to show that I can work well on my own and be more independent.'

'What could this mean that would work in your favour?'

This one took him a long time but in the end Martin did suggest that it was possibly another worker who was causing his boss problems and maybe he could be in line for promotion or a good transfer rather than the sack.

'How can you enjoy or find satisfaction in this situation?'

He felt it was wrong to get benefit from a situation where his boss was obviously not happy, but when pushed he did suggest that he could try to enjoy showing what he could do when working on his own.

'What can you learn from this?'

'Nothing, at least at this stage,' was Martin's vehement response, so we moved on to another question.

'What can you do to improve the situation?'

Martin decided to be as pleasant as possible, regardless of his boss's mood.

5. Focus on the New Beliefs

Martin then agreed to do his best to focus on these new beliefs.

The following week Martin reported that nothing much had changed, that the boss was still curt and withdrawn, but that he had changed his own attitude. As a result he had done his own work faster and had the time to offer to do a job that had been pending for a while.

He was still worried about losing his job so we went through the five-step process again. The results were similar except that he had heard a rumour of problems in another section of the office, so he was slightly more inclined to believe that the problem lay elsewhere, rather than with his own work.

The next week Martin came in looking much happier. He said he'd decided to smile at the boss anyway and to be as cheerful as he used to be and to ignore the bad moods. Nothing much had changed except that Martin said he himself was feeling somewhat less depressed.

'It's OK as long as I keep focusing on those five steps,' he said.

The following week brought the answer.

'The boss was all smiles on Monday morning, it was amazing, back to his old self, slapped me on the back when I arrived and suggested we got stuck into some changes he wanted to make, based on that extra job I did for him when I'd had some spare time. He even complimented me on getting that done and thanked me for my good humour and support during the past month. Support, can you believe it?

'And you know what it was? I heard it from one of the girls who is friends with his secretary. It was nothing to do with work at all, not even the problem in the other section. His girlfriend had left him. It seems it took her a month to think it over but they got back together again last weekend. And to think I thought I was going to lose my job. Wasn't that absurd? If only I'd known all along then I needn't have felt depressed at all.'

I decided this was the time to bring up the question he had skipped at the start.

'So what can you learn from this?' I asked.

'Well, I guess,' he said after some hesitation, 'that the process works for a start.' And he smiled. 'You're right in what you say, too. You might as well assume the best mightn't you? After all, if I'd done that I could have avoided a lot of worry. But at least some good things came out of it. He says I was the one person who put up with his moods and he's sure I'll do well with the company.'

Had Martin been an optimist at the start, instead of a pessimist, he might well have made some of the positive assumptions from the beginning. He might well have assumed that the problem had nothing to do with him. He would probably have used the opportunity straight away to try to cheer the other man up, offer positive help and make the best of the situation.

By going through the five steps and asking the appropriate questions, Martin was able to back away from automatic pessimism towards a more optimistic view of this and other future situations.

You can use this five-step technique for minor causes of depression or for major ones. You can use it when you feel down about something minor, such as not being invited out, a letter not arriving, or the shop being out of your favourite brand, or you can use it for major worries in your life.

The larger the problem and its cause, the more energy and determination you may need to make the necessary changes in your interpretation of it, and to focus on these alternative positive explanations.

If you have trouble focusing on and committing to the new beliefs (step five) you might need the help of someone experienced in this way of thinking. You will also find helpful ideas elsewhere in this book. But at least now you have added another way to your arsenal of tools to lighten your depression.

'Reality'

Before we leave this topic, it is worth getting back to the question of reality, or the supposed objective reality that people talk about when they are reluctant to change their views.

You may still be arguing that by making these changes you are fooling yourself, losing touch with reality and entering a fool's paradise. Keep in mind that the only reality is inside your head. If you can do this, you can view your life, past, present and future, in an positive framework, and so be better prepared to create a happy future for yourself.

In the above example, Martin could not know what the other person was thinking, so there was no advantage to his dragging himself down and disempowering himself with a negative belief when he could improve his state of mind and increase his resources to deal with the situation by taking a more positive belief.

I recall many years ago telling a friend what a wonderful year I had had and how lucky I was. She gazed at me in startled amazement and pointed out that in the previous few months my business had been burned down, that the few things I had been able to salvage had been stolen, that I had had to move the clinic and set up a temporary one and that although I was now back in business, things were not going well and we were still running at a loss.

My optimism had been instinctive, so I had had to think hard before I could refute her point of view. Finally, I argued that I had had a chance to get rid of, by burning, a lot of old rubbish that had been accumulating and that I now had brand-new premises. I'd discovered how many helpful friends I had when they'd rallied round and I was positive that things were now on the up-and-up and would soon be better than ever. This assumption turned out to be true, no doubt fuelled by my optimism. The pessimistic view could have seen me in desperate straits.

Put the above ideas into practice and you could be rid of depression for ever. You may start simply by lightening your depression or you may surprise yourself and have a major impact right at the start. The result is, ultimately, up to you and to the amount of changes you are able and willing to make. Whatever you do, do not make slow progress a reason for blaming yourself and getting even more depressed.

If you do need some outside help, find a good practitioner who can reinforce this technique and work with the other ideas in this book.

Chapter Nine

The Benefits Of Being Depressed

This may seem an odd chapter title. The benefits of being depressed? Who wants to be depressed? What possible benefits can there be? Surely anyone would rather be happy than depressed? Maybe yes, but maybe no. For some people there are obvious benefits in being depressed, and to some extent I've alluded to this in previous chapters. For others there may be benefits but they are not immediately apparent.

Insofar as you have had a measure of control over what has happened in your life, you have also had control over your mood. Let's first of all assume that you have created your mood – after all, if you haven't, who has? And let's assume that, at some level, everything you create for yourself is to your advantage, for this seems a reasonable assumption. It then follows that there must be some advantage in your being depressed.

In the cold light of day, when analysed by the conscious, unemotional and analytical mind, the benefits of being depressed may seem to be small and not worth the price, yet at an emotional level people often hang on tightly to these perceived benefits. They are even willing to experience deep depression in order to achieve them and are unwilling or too afraid to try other methods of attaining their goals.

If being depressed is scoring some wins for you in life then you may be reluctant, at least on an unconscious level, to give these benefits away. For this reason it is important to explore the possible benefits of depression and, if you still wish to keep these benefits, to find some alternative way of achieving them.

It is often difficult to find the benefit behind being depressed. The whole concept seems strange to our usual way of thinking. For this reason you are unlikely to get very far with logical analysis and reasoning. A more useful tool is to run a phrase. This process was described in Chapter 3.

When you run the phrase 'A benefit I get from being depressed is . . .', you bypass the usual analytical or intellectual responses that come up when the phrase is posed as a question. By using the phrase as the beginning of a statement you have presupposed both benefit and that your mind can come up with an answer. If at the start your mind rebels then let it know that it doesn't matter how outrageous the completions are, and that you will accept them all. You might even pretend to be someone else at the start, and make some up. Even this has value, because you can then ponder on these completions and wonder at their significance – after all, you chose to make up those particular ones and not some other equally unlikely completions.

> I had been working with Molly for a few weeks and had begun to feel we were getting nowhere. During each session she appeared to make strides and she always went away happier than she came in and said, on her next visit that yes, she was feeling

better. Then I would ask about the depression and she would say there was no change. The situation didn't seem to perturb her and this set me to thinking. She was the eldest of three sisters and a brother. Her mother had been killed in a car crash when Molly was fourteen and the youngest child only three and she had adopted the role of mother. Her father worked long hours and she had taken over the chores and looked after the other children. She'd had few boyfriends, insisting she'd had to look after her sisters and brother, and, by the time the youngest sibling had left home, her father had decided he couldn't manage without her. However, a few years later he had suddenly married again, leaving Molly alone. That was when the depression set in.

I explained the running a phrase procedure and asked her to run the phrase 'A benefit I get from being depressed is . . .' After a few false starts she came up with the following competions:

'. . . the others come round to cheer me up.'
'. . . it reminds the others of what I did for them.'
'. . . I don't feel so silly.'

This last one was interesting so I moved on to it and asked her to run 'A reason I would feel silly if I wasn't depressed is . . .' She completed this with '. . . other people expect me to be depressed' and '. . . it would mean I'd wasted my life.'

I thught we had enough there to work with so I asked her what she meant by these remarks. She agreed they were odd but, after she had thought about it for a while, she came up with a rather interesting analysis.

'It's funny, it's as if willingly giving up my own

chances of marriage to look after the family and then them moving on and leaving me was a dumb thing to do if I did it by choice and because it was what I wanted to do. If, on the other hand, I'd had no choice, but simply had to do it, then I haven't been silly and they were the ones who were wrong for being ungrateful and leaving me and not needing me any more, especially Dad, and of course I'm depressed. If I stop being depressed then I'm stupid instead. Besides, this way they do come and see me and I like seeing their children.'

Clearly Molly had two secondary gains from her depression. It validated her past actions and it brought the nephews and nieces around. Until she could deal with these two situations she had an ongoing benefit in being depressed. We did deal with them, helping her to achieve the same benefits in other ways, but that is not part of this story.

With other clients, too, underlying benefits to depression have surfaced, I recall one client, recently bereaved, who felt guilty for things he had said and done while the other person was alive. By continuing to feel depressed, he felt he was compensating, both in his own eyes and in the eyes of other people, for the lack of care he had given while that person was alive. Another woman continued to feel depressed as a way of avoiding ackowledging that she hadn't really liked her husband or had a happy marriage.

In another case, a young man came to see me, still experiencing bouts of deep depression following a childhood incident. As a schoolboy he had been fighting with an older boy to get on the first, rather than the second, school bus. The younger boy had tricked the older bully and then felt dreadfully guilty when the second bus had crashed and the bully had been killed. We found that the young man's depression stemmed from his disgust with himself for being glad that the bully was no longer around to torment him. If he gave up the depression, he felt, it would compound his guilt.

Many people find that ultimately depression is a way of dealing with guilty feelings and of getting sympathy, attention and acknowledgement from other people. If you are getting loving care and attention because you are depressed, it may be scary to throw off the depression, become cheerful and ask for that same level of love and caring to be freely given.

There is little point, to my mind, in judging these strategies. The fact remains they exist. Everyone has to deal with life in their own way; everyone is born with a different set of attitudes, emotions, circumstances and so forth. Everyone has created the present in the best way they can. Many times the strategies people use are the safest way they know of getting their needs met.

If you are using depression for the benefits it brings you, then it is up to you to decide whether or not you wish this to continue. Do you want to go on being depressed or are you willing to find some other way of achieving those benefits? Are you brave enough to be happy and to let it show?

The important and useful thing is for you to identify the underlying situation and then make your own decisions out of conscious choice. Nine times out of ten I find that clients, once they recognise the underlying agenda, want to change, but occasionally they don't. Perhaps the time is not right for them, perhaps it never will be. If you choose to continue with your present method for getting attention you will, probably, continue to get the attention, but you will also have to go on feeling depressed, with all the consequences that go with it. It is up to you as an individual to learn as much as you can and then, with full awareness, make your own decision. The choice is yours.

Chapter Ten

The Bigger Picture

Many people believe that this life is only a part of their existence. Some believe in an after-life in some ethereal form. Others believe they return in a corporeal form and have future and past lives on earth.

In the West the majority of people tend not to believe in reincarnation, trusting that when the body dissolves, dust to dust and ashes to ashes, there is nothing left. Because you cannot see, feel or weigh the soul, it is often given little recognition. It is all too easy to forget that more than half the world believes in reincarnation in some form or another.

It is not the purpose of this book to try to change people's fundamental belief systems about the spiritual side of life. I consider these beliefs and experiences to be personal and precious and to be decided by the individual. My own personal experience is that past incarnations are realities and future ones are taken for granted, but just as no one can invalidate these for me, I would not try to enforce these beliefs on others.

Increasingly, however, in the West, there is a tendency to believe in past and future lives. Some reports claim that as much as thirty per cent of the West's population believe in reincarnation, and this chapter is for those who do. If you feel you only have one life and this is it, then you may wish to skip this chapter.

If you believe in reincarnation then this can broaden the context of current problems and difficulties and can help to ease depression by allowing for the resolution of the problem in a future life or between lives. It is possible that many of the factors that are making you feel depressed cannot be changed in this lifetime, but if you believe in a future life you can hope to resolve them later.

You may, for instance, wish you had children, or more children, but be beyond childbearing age. You may have physical disabilities or illnesses that are incurable and have handicapped your life. You may have missed opportunities or lost touch with friends. People you have loved may have died, you may have been involved in wars or famines or natural disasters. You may wish you had been born a different race, nationality or sex. All these and more are things that cannot be changed in one lifetime. If you believe in only one lifetime, you can either come to terms with these disappointments, make the most of them and find valuable and positive learning experiences in them, or you can let them get on top of you and depress you. If, on the other hand, you believe in a future existence, both between lifetimes and during a future life on earth, it can be a comfort to know that when there are things you feel cannot be corrected in this life, you can have another chance next time and that death is not the end of your relationship with those you love.

The extent to which you really believe in reincarnation is tested when you consider it part of the solution to your depression. I have known many people say they believe in reincarnation yet act as if they don't.

They act as if this lifetime is the only chance they have to achieve their goals. But there have been other interesting experiences, particularly that of Susan Morgan.

Susan was in her mid-forties and well into the menopause. She was single, a career woman, happy in her job and with her friends and normally content with her life. Recently, however, she had been feeling unsettled and depressed. She put it down to the menopause and the changes this brought about and had come to me seeking guidance. After we had talked for a while she said that maybe she was having regrets about not having a family:

'Maybe I should have had children. Maybe I am regretting that. After all, until recently I still had the option, and while I had the option I kept thinking there was plenty of time if I ever did change my mind. Now it is too late.'

'Do you really regret not having children?'

'To be honest, I'm not sure. I do regret something. I do feel depressed, really down in the dumps. Perhaps I just regret the fact that it is no longer an option. I think too, in a funny way, that I *ought* to regret not having them and feel depressed because I don't, since that makes me an odd sort of a woman.'

I mentioned the possibility of other lives and that she might have had one in which she'd had children she didn't want, but she laughed and said she doubted we had more than one life. After a few more minutes I suggested we went back into her past to find out if there was some other reason for her depression, the implication being that I expected to be dealing with this lifetime only, as indeed I was. She got comfortable and I led her into a light trance. I think we were both surprised by the result; certainly she was.

Susan suddenly said she was in a bazaar, and then fell silent, so I started to ask her questions.

'Where are you?'

'I'm not sure, I think it's North Africa, somewhere like that. It's very hot and dusty.'

'Are you in this century, or some time past?'

'Past. A few centuries ago I think.'

'What sex are you?'

'I don't know.'

'What are you doing? What are you wearing?'

All these questions helped to focus her mind and soon Susan was talking with very little prompting from me.

'I think I must be male. I'm working in a stall, selling rugs. It's my father's business and I have to do as I'm told.'

'Are you happy?'

'Yes and no. I have a lot of friends and when I can get away from selling rugs we have good times. And I like the women. But what I really want is to leave home. I'm eighteen and quite old enough to marry. I'd like to have my own wife and children. I'd like to be in business for myself and be my own boss.'

'How many children do you want?'

'About six or seven. I fancy myself as the head of a large family. Besides, they'll work for me, too. And I don't want my father or anyone else telling me what to do.'

After a little while I sugested she let that view fade, and relax more deeply. I then asked her what else she could see, not with any great expectations but waiting with an open mind to find out what would happen and what her unconscious mind would bring up as being appropriate for her at that time. Suddenly she started talking.

'I'm much older, over thirty I think. I do have children now, several of them, and it's a bore. My wife is dull. All she thinks about is the children and the house and her friends, but I'm so tied down. I have to work all day long to support the family and with so many people to feed I have to work in the bazaar for long hours. I wish I were single again. It was so much more fun then, with my friends, and with no responsibilities.'

'Do you wish you hadn't had children?'

'Definitely. If I had my life over I would stay a bachelor for ever and have fun.'

This was all said vehemently and there was more in the same vein and then Susan became quiet and I suggested she bring herself back to the present and, when she was ready, open her eyes. When she did, she sat there for a while looking somewhat startled, but also smiling.

'Wow, that was odd. If I didn't know better I'd say you planned that. But you didn't, did you? You couldn't. It was my mind that did it. Do you really think that was a past life or was I just making something up?'

'What do you think?'

'I don't know, it all seemed very real.'

'How do you feel now? Are you still depressed? How do you feel about not having children?'

'That's what's really interesting. I had such strong feelings while that was going on. I could feel myself wishing so strongly that I hadn't had children and feeling that they had limited my life, it was really powerful. It certainly explains why I haven't wanted them this time. And no, I don't think I do feel depressed. It seems to have put everything into perspective.'

We talked some more and Susan continued to wonder if it really was a past life. I of course favoured the view that it probably was. Whether or not hardly mattered: it either was a past life or it was something her subconscious mind had created or drawn up from her past. Perhaps she had read such a story as a child and resolved never to have children. What did matter was that Susan suddenly had a different perspective on her depression and she left feeling better. Two weeks later she phoned to tell me that she was much happier and that whatever had happened had had a lasting effect.

Depression and Death

If you feel there is a continuation after this lifetime and are depressed about someone dying, think about the words you use. The words 'dying' and 'death' have such final connotations. If you think instead of the other person 'leaving their body', the thought may be a lot less painful.

Martin was deeply depressed by his father's illness. They had had a close relationship and now he had to watch his father dying slowly from cancer.

'I'm torn,' he said. 'Part of me wishes he would

die, as he is in such pain, the other part wants to keep him with me for as long as possible. I don't really know how I'll cope when he's dead. He's always been there to talk to.'

I knew from earlier discussions that Martin claimed he believed in other lives, so I asked him, 'Why do you talk of him dying, why not talk of him "leaving his body"? After all, that's what you believe isn't it?'

'Yes I do, but, I don't know, I guess it's just what everyone says.'

We talked around the idea further. In the end Martin said, 'You know, if he was going on a long holiday, or to live in some other country, I'd feel sad but not devastated. If I really do believe in reincarnation this really isn't much more is it? I mean we won't be able to talk on the phone or anything, but since I know his spirit will still be there, I will still be able to feel that he is around. Perhaps I'll be able to be even closer to him, who knows?'

On his next visit, Martin reported an interesting development. He said that in some ways he had almost dreaded visiting his father because they both kept trying to pretend that he would recover. This time, Martin said, they had discussed death, and the idea that his father's spirit would still be around after he died. They had both been able to say things they had wanted to say before but couldn't, they had discussed Martin's mother and what she would do and the grandchildren's future.

'It was almost as if we were planning what would happen after Dad went overseas,' Martin said. 'It was so relaxed, and we were very close.'

'How do you feel now?'

'I still feel sad, of course, but that heavy and deadening depression has gone.'

Months later Martin phoned to say that his father had died two months after our last consultation but that during that time they'd become a lot closer and talked a great deal.

'I have the sense that we completed things,' Martin said, 'and it's wonderful not only to have had the closeness but to feel no regrets now for things I wish I had said. In many ways we were much more honest with each other in the last two months than we had been before. And I think it brought a lot of comfort to Dad too.'

Who can say for sure if death is the end? Perhaps we cannot know. Perhaps, you may be saying, Martin was wrong and his concept of the future an illusion. Maybe. The point is, he found a way of decreasing his depression and, moreover, was able to enrich the present and make the most of it. We are back to a point that I have made before. If you cannot be absolutely certain which answer is correct, then pick the one that is *the most useful*. At worst you are risking living in a fool's paradise, rather than in a fool's hell. At best you are finding a broader context within which to handle a situation or set of emotions that are having a negative effect on you at that moment.

PART II

The Way Out

In Part One we covered, mainly at a conceptual level, a wide range of attitudes underlying depression. We spoke of the fact that depression is on the increase and considered some of the possible reasons for this. You have thought, I hope, about the way you create your moods and about the fact that many people choose to believe and act as if they are helpless. We covered the concept that to have your life the way you want it, you have to become proactive and develop a clear idea of how you are going to live. We looked at personality types and the differences between optimists and pessimists, and how this information can be put to use. You were asked to become aware of your belief systems in relation to many aspects of your life, particularly those affecting your moods and your depression.

In Part Two we will change the emphasis and detail specific things you can do to change or modify your moods. You will receive guidelines enabling you to work on which aspect of your moods is causing you problems and leading to depression. You can certainly do the exercises on

your own; however, many of them may be more
effective for you if you find a friend and work
together on each other. In this way you may be
able to help them as well as have them help you.
As a result you may get even deeper insights into
yourself and be able to help yourself better than if
you worked only on yourself, even with another's
help. On the other hand, if you wish to be private
and work on your own, you can also do this. If the
problem does not resolve itself, you may want to
find a practitioner who can help by working with
you, but this may not be necessary.

When practised fully, the methods described
here will help you to make major changes in your
moods and in your life.

Chapter Eleven

Meet Your Unconscious Mind

It is not easy to change your mood, lifting it from depression into a more positive state, with your conscious mind. If it were easy, you could simply tell yourself, consciously, to become happier, and it would happen. You already know this doesn't work since you have almost certainly told yourself to cheer up many times, with little or no effect. The real changes come about at the unconscious or subconscious level. For this reason it is important at this stage for you to meet your unconscious mind and to become aware of what it does and how it behaves. By knowing about it in greater detail, you can work with it more constructively and effectively than you have in the past.

When I first talk to clients about their unconscious they often look confused. Alternatively, they may deny it exists, or they may say that if something does not seem real to them, consciously, then it does not exist. If you were asked to write down ten attributes of your unconscious mind, you would quite possibly be unable to do so, yet we will consider twenty or more in this chapter.

Whether or not you are fully aware of your unconscious mind and the power it has, you have been using it in many ways. You have certainly used it unconsciously. You may also have tried to use it consciously. You may, for instance, have tried to work with it already by doing affirmations. You may have said, over and over to yourself, something like 'I am happy, I am happy', but you may still be miserable and now feel that affirmations do not work.

Affirmations do work but you do need to know what you're doing and how to work with your unconscious mind to achieve the best results. The first step is to meet this unconscious mind and get to know it. Once you learn to recognise it, understand it and how it works, you'll be able to see that you can use it to make major changes in your life. You can then use affirmations if you want to, but we will be doing much more than this in the chapters ahead.

Your Unconscious Mind and Your Physical Body

Some people question that they even have an unconscious mind. Your unconscious mind is nothing magical, it is simply the part of your mind of which you are unconscious or unaware. Not only are you unaware of it, but more often than not you are unaware of what it is doing.

All the internal activity of your physical body is run by your unconscious rather than your conscious mind. It is your unconscious mind that beats your heart, that remembers to breathe, that activates the digestive system and moves your muscles. All these things are happening unconsciously. The decision to move your leg may be made consciously (although not always) but beyond that the process is unconscious: you couldn't possibly make the necessary conscious decisions to move each of the dozens of muscles involved the right amount, at the right time and in the right sequence.

Driving a car starts out as a very conscious activity but once the skill is mastered, it becomes unconscious. How many times have you been driving along in a daydream and then 'come to' and had to look around to find where you were? As I type into the computer the thoughts are going from my brain onto the screen but the process of hitting the correct keys is unconscious. The moment I ask my conscious mind where the next letter is, my fingers slow down and start to stumble.

Since the unconscious mind runs the internal workings of the body, it is obvious that it knows how to do this. It understands exactly how it should be run for perfect health. It is equally clear that it also knows how to deviate from this. If you feed it worrying thoughts from your conscious mind, it can create an ulcer. As you tell it how nervous you are at the thought of giving an after-dinner speech, it can create diarrhoea. As you fret over a problem you can't solve or a deadline you can't meet, it can create a headache. The exciting thing about this is that if you talk to your unconscious mind correctly, you can instruct it to improve your mood or your health, or to recreate perfect health if you have been unwell. It is all a question of finding out why your unconscious mind has chosen to make you depressed or unwell in the first place and then generating the required change. As we shall see later on, your unconscious mind has your best interests at heart and so it must have concluded that there is some point or purpose to your being depressed or unwell in the first place, and this must be dealt with before your health can improve.

Your unconscious mind has, as one of its aims, the

goal of preserving your body and keeping you alive. Your unconscious mind will pull your hand away when it accidentally touches something that could burn it, or whip the steering wheel of the car round when another car approaches you out of control. There is no time, in any of these situations, for your conscious mind to take in the details, analyse them, make a decision based on the facts, select the best course of action and then put that plan of action into operation. It is only your unconscious mind that can make these decisions and operate in split seconds. Perhaps one of the most extreme examples of this is when the unconscious mind decides to pump a mother so full of energy that she can lift a car off her baby or perform some other such seemingly miraculous feat, a feat that could not be done in cold consciousness.

Your Unconscious Mind and Your Memories

Have you ever wondered how you store and organise your memories? Once, I offered to help a friend sort his photographs of his travels but I was unable to sequence them or even sort them geographically. I did not have the key. Only he could do it, only he knew the sequence, how to file them, how to order and organise them. He needed his 'memory line' or 'time line' to know the sequence in which to place the photographs.

Without some such organising system, provided by your unconscious mind, you could not sort and store your memories logically or sequentially. They would simply be a random collection of memories. Your unconscious mind has some way of ordering them, usually along a line from the past to the present and on into anticipations of the future. As we shall see in Chapter 12, this line may go from behind you to in front of you, from left to right or in any way that your unconscious chooses, but there does have to be an organising sequence. If there were not you would not be able to link cause and effect. Think about that: you might feel pain, but if you could not be sure that the smack came first and not after, you would not know what caused the pain. You would not plant seeds because you would not be sure if the plant came before or after sowing. We will be exploring this concept of a time line or memory line in Chapter 12.

Your unconscious mind also stores the memories that do not relate to time. You may think that you have forgotten a language you learned at school or the details of maths or science, but they are there, if somewhat deeply buried and reluctant to surface. All of your skills, too, from reading to writing, from knowing about a specific subject to knowing how to learn, are stored in your unconscious mind. In fact learning takes place at the unconscious level. This is also where you store your values and your personal philosophy.

It is interesting to speculate as to exactly where, physically, these memories are stored. Some say they are stored in your mind or in your brain, but there is evidence that they are actually stored throughout your body, yet in such a way that they are not necessarily located in any one area. If you have your foot amputated, for instance, you will not lose a segment of your memory. Yet from rebirthing experiences and from various types of body-work therapy, it is clear that memories can be accessed by working on different parts of the physical body and releasing local tensions.

Another aspect of the unconscious mind relates to your habits, both physical and mental. Have you ever tried, consciously, to give up a habit? Difficult, isn't it?

Perhaps there is a phrase you use that you would like to drop, perhaps a gesture you would like to change. One client recently wanted to stop hunching up her shoulders but had great difficulty doing this. As she said, 'I just do it automatically, then suddenly I realise what I have done and have to make an effort to relax them. I must be more aware.' Being more aware is rarely the answer. If she had to focus her mind all the time on keeping her shoulders relaxed it would be hard for her to think of much else, and then when her thoughts did wander, her shoulders would hunch up again. It is much simpler to reprogramme the unconscious mind to form a new habit, the habit of relaxing the shoulders. The same is true of mental habits. If you habitually respond to situations in a certain way, then the best way to change this habit is to reprogramme the unconscious mind where that habit is stored. This is something else we are going to do in the chapters ahead.

We have already seen that the unconscious mind is where you store and organise memories. A habit is essentially a number of memories stored together. By working on these memories and reprogramming them you can delete unwanted habits, you can also acquire new and more positive ones.

By now you may be starting to realise what a power-house this unconscious mind is. Wouldn't it be wonderful if you could tap into it at will, make use of its skills and make the desired changes in your life? You can. To a considerable extent you can do this on your own and you will learn how to do this in the chapters that follow. You can also do it with the help of qualified practitioners. Whatever you do, don't underestimate your unconscious or its ability to have a wonderfully positive effect on your life once you start really communicating and working with it.

Your Unconscious and Your Emotions

Your unconscious is definitely the place where you store and generate your emotions, including depression and all those unresolved negative emotions such as fear, shame, guilt, anxiety, anger and sadness. You only have to ask yourself the extent to which you consciously create and control your emotions to realise that. So often people will say things like 'I can't (consciously) help it. I just feel so and so', as if the emotion is not of their own (conscious) creating.

The unconscious is also where you store all those things that have happened in your life that were too difficult to handle. What did you do when they occurred? You buried them, didn't you? You buried them way down in your unconscious mind. And you kept them there, for protection. If it is too painful to think about the times you have experienced rejection, then it is the job of your unconscious mind to keep the memories buried. Remember, though, that this takes energy.

From time to time your unconscious mind will bring up one or more of these memories, just to see if you are ready or able to deal with it yet. As we will see, your unconscious mind is your loyal and willing servant. It is trying at all times to please you, rather in the way a young child might. So we can be sure it is not bringing up these negative emotions to cause you pain. Rather, it is bringing them up because it thinks this could be a time for you to handle them. It is trying to be helpful, and because it realises that these emotions, stored and unresolved, are doing you no good, it gathers up its

courage from time to time and pops them up into your
conscious mind for consideration.

You may feel like saying that these negative emotions
protect you, that by being angry you keep people at
bay, for instance, or that by staying afraid and defensive
you avoid getting hurt. This is not so. It is the fight-or-
flight mechanism which protects you and that is not
removed, no matter how much growth and development you do. Negative emotions, as attempts to protect
you, can be only superficially successful. The underlying emotions and concerns remain and, in addition,
there is the danger of creating new problems with these
emotions. Anger, for instance, may seem to prevent
someone taking advantage of you, but in fact you are
probably still taken advantage of, and in addition the
anger remains to cause you ongoing trouble. When the
underlying reasons for the emotions are addressed you
will find it totally safe to do without them and to let
them go. As a result you will feel better, freer and have
a lot more energy.

It takes a lot of energy to work with negative
emotions, a lot of energy to store or suppress anger. It
is exhausting to deal with fears and worries, anxieties
and depression. If your unconscious mind is dealing
with a lot of these emotions there will be less energy
left over to run your physical body. This means that if
you are tired you might think about dealing with some
of these negative emotions in order to release energy
for the things you really want to do.

The Workings of the Unconscious Mind

Your unconscious mind is very obedient. It will, at all
times, try to follow orders as it receives them from your
conscious mind. If you keep saying to yourself 'I'm

going to be late, I'm going to be late, I just know I'm going to be late' then your unconscious mind will do all it can to obey orders, fulfil your expectations and make you late. It may do this by prompting you to do one more chore before you leave home, or by delaying the time you start to get ready, or even by making you lose concentration and so lose your way. If you keep saying 'I bet I'll fail' then your unconscious mind will try to bring this about. If, on the other hand, you make positive statements to yourself then it will try to bring these about too. This is where we get back to the affirmations we started with.

> **The unconscious mind needs repetition. If you feed it information only once it may not pay much attention. But if you repeat it many times then it gets the message.**

Affirmations will work as long as your unconscious mind is convinced about the message it's getting. If you keep saying 'I will succeed' but accompany that with mental pictures of failing and the emotions of failure, then these are the messages your unconscious mind will receive, and it won't be fooled by the verbal chatter. So if you are going to make affirmations then make them congruent. Make sure you see them, hear them, feel them and live them and totally believe in them: this is the message to pass on to your unconscious, not a silent message of disbelief.

There are two other facts to keep in mind when working with your unconscious and telling it what to do. First, it does not process negatives and, second, it has no sense of humour. If you repeatedly tell yourself you 'must not fail', all your unconscious mind will hear is 'fail'. So instead you would be wise to tell it that you 'will succeed'. You have probably seen incidents such as the following: a small toddler is carefully and confidently carrying a cup of tea to grandmother. It is only grandmother who doubts the ability of the child and says, 'Watch out or you'll fall.' What happens? The child's unconscious mind watches out and then creates the fall. Note that it works on the last thing it hears, in this case 'you'll fall'.

In the same way, you cannot think about what you don't want to think about without thinking about it. Saying 'I won't think about a cigarette' or 'I won't think about food' is hopeless. Saying 'I hope I don't make a mess of it this time – like I did last time' will result in the message 'make a mess of it'. You would be well advised to change the wording and say instead, 'this time I will succeed'.

As regards humour, have you ever joked around with friends and told them what idiots they were or said something like, 'What? Me like you? Don't be daft!' or 'No, of course I don't want to come' when you meant the opposite? At the conscious level you know this is a joke but your unconscious doesn't. You may recall times when you knew, consciously, that some such statement, when said to you, was a joke, yet deep down you still felt hurt. That was your unconscious mind responding.

Your unconscious mind will take things personally. This can be both negative and positive. It may see a barb in an innocent comment but it may also be able to see a useful parallel or moral in a story, which the conscious mind would be unwilling to accept. I once had a patient who was insisting that he didn't need to take vitamin supplements because 'you should be able to get everything you need from your food' and he wouldn't change his dreadful diet because 'all my friends eat that way and they aren't sick'. I could hardly tell him that he was crazy, and that if he didn't make changes soon he'd be an early heart attack statistic. Instead, I told him a story about someone who felt the same way as he did (without making the comparison) and I finished up by saying 'and as she continued to refuse to make any changes in her diet I said to her "You're mad. You're far too intelligent really to believe that. Anyone with half a brain can see that you have to make some changes or you will be seriously ill, and think of the effect that will have on your family."' His conscious mind and I laughed together over her stupidity. His unconscious mind processed it as if I had said the same words directly to him, something I could not have done without incurring his anger and conscious and subconscious resistance, and by the end of the consultation he was asking what changes he should make to his diet and what supplements he should take. Using quotes or reportage is a very useful way of getting your message through to people via their unconscious mind.

Since the unconscious mind takes things so personally and to heart, it is very important to take it into account when you are dealing with other people. If you assume they are wonderful, they will be. If you assume they are dishonest, they will be. What you project onto them is what their unconscious minds will accept and as a result you will get this same message fed back, simply because their unconscious mind is taking personally the messages you are sending them.

One of the problems with the unconscious mind is that it is highly moral, it thinks that if you've been bad you have to be punished. It may create your punishment by making you feel bad, by making you miss situations you would enjoy, or it may do so by making you ill. It is important to keep this in mind when working on healing physical problems.

One other thing you may have noticed about your unconscious mind is that it is never satisfied. It is programmed to continue to drive you to want more, whatever you do. When you were a poor student it thought heaven would be a full-time salary. When you got a job and a salary it just knew that double that income would make it feel good. It once created a desire in you to own a car, any car, just so long as you had a car. Then it found that wasn't enough and created the desire for a smarter, faster car.

> **There's no satisfying the unconscious mind.
> Yet isn't this wonderful? It spurs you on to do,
> be, give and achieve more and more.**

Your unconscious also works with symbols. Some of your dreams constitute wonderful symbols of a reality that your unconscious is trying to communicate to you. Such dreams and the concept of an alternative reality allow you to contemplate things in which you don't believe. You may even choose not to believe in the unconscious mind, yet you can contemplate it and recognise much of what it does. This will also allow you to consider and deal with things other people believe in, even when you don't agree with them.

Get to Know Your Unconscious Mind

Now that you have met and come to understand your unconscious mind, get to know it even better, communicate with it, trust it and use its resources. In this way you can make use of all the personal growth and development ideas that exist in books, on tape and in seminars. You can also find practitioners who can help you to reprogramme your unconscious mind to go in the directions that you want it to.

Since you now have a better idea of how your unconscious mind works and what it does, you can use affirmations successfully. You will be able to make, set and achieve goals and if you use memory-line or time-line therapy, you will be able to release a lot of negative emotions and change a number of limiting decisions you have made in the past and which are restricting you in the present and future. Understanding the power of the unconscious mind enables you to work towards new objectives using *all* your powers and therefore to be more effective in achieving them.

Have fun with your unconscious mind and work with it. In this way you can create an exciting, satisfying and rewarding future for yourself. For a start we will be using it and working with it as we go through the following chapters.

Chapter Twelve

Your Memories:
Ways To Store and Use Them

Time and the flow of time are usually taken for granted, part of the background of our lives. Few people think about time as a variable resource to be used and manipulated. Rarely do we think of how we organise and store it, how we view it and how we could make useful changes to the way we do these things. Yet, unconsciously, we do demonstrate our different uses of time. If you make this usage conscious and then take control of it, it is possible to make many valuable changes in your life, with consequent changes to your moods and emotions.

Think of some of these expressions or comments: 'she lives in the past', 'he should look to the future', 'I must put the past behind me', 'they only live for today', 'the future looks black', 'my future flashed in front of me'. These statements and many others like them bear unconscious witness to the truths we are about to explore. Some people do literally live in their past. If on your memory line, a concept we will consider shortly, the past lies behind you and the future in front of you and you spend all your time facing back to the past it is very difficult to see the future. When some people look along their memory lines into the future it appears black, whereas to other people it might glow or be brightly coloured. All these statements can be taken literally and considered in relation to the way people's minds are working.

Time is like an organising system. Think of it as a long row of slots into which you can put your memories of particular events or your anticipations (future memories) of events yet to occur. There may be large slots into which you put a day or a month. There may be small slots into which you put individual memories of minutes or even seconds. If you had no such system, cause and effect would become meaningless and you would not be able to tell whether, for example, you had felt pain before or after a fall.

Think of the people you know. You will almost certainly have some who are very organised with regard to time; they make and keep their appointments and expect others to do the same. When you are with them, you eventually become aware that their time with you is up and that they have something else they should be doing. You will also know other people who are often late but who, when they do arrive, give you their total attention for as long as you want it. Nor do they mind if you are late for an appointment with them, they are simply glad to see you when you do turn up. They live fully in the present.

If you live in the present and are depressed, it will be hard for you to envisage a happier time at some point in the future; the present will be all-encompassing. Conversely, living in the present is helpful if the present is pleasant and the future is worrying. If you live with a strong awareness of the future, you may be unable to enjoy the happy present for fear of depressing events ahead, although it could be advantageous to be able to focus on the future when the present is depressing. Being able to manipulate the way you handle time can be an advantage and later on you will learn how to do this.

The ability to change the way you view time does not depend simply on an immediate decision as to where you will put your attention. It depends on your having a full understanding of the way you view, store and arrange time and on learning techniques to enable you to change these factors at will. With this in mind, it is time to explore the concept further both in general and in relation to you in particular.

Determining How You Store Your Memories[1]

Most people have some sort of mental line, not necessarily straight, along which they store their memories, sequentially from the past, and their anticipations of the future. It may not be a straight line and indeed it often isn't. Your memory line may be similar to that of many other people or it may be highly individual. It may go through you or you may see it from a distance. It may be below you, above you, in front of or behind you, to your left or right, or any combination of these directions. It may also vary in colour, brightness, focus and many other details. Let's find out what yours is like. To do this we will gather several bits of information:

[1] The concept of time-line is an integral part of Neurolinguistic Programming (NLP), which was originally developed by John Grinder and Richard Bandler. Time-Line Therapy has been further developed by Tad James.

First, where is your past? When you think of something that occurred in your past do you mentally look to your left or your right, behind you or in front of you, underneath you or above you? There are no right or wrong answers here, simply become aware of what you do. Now think of the future. Where do you look, mentally, when you think of the future? Again, do you look to your left or right, do you look behind you or in front of you, do you look underneath you or above you? Perhaps you do none of these things, perhaps you store time internally; if so, what is the internal picture?

A common pattern is to look left for your past, with the distant past furthest to your left and the near past closest to you, and to look to the right to see your future extending into the distance. Another common pattern is to have your past in a line behind you, again with the distant past furthest from you and the recent past close to you, and the future extending out ahead of you. However, do not let yourself be influenced by this. If either of these patterns is yours, that's fine, but take time to explore and find out if this is so and if not then find out what your pattern is.

Think about things you did one year ago, five years ago, ten years ago and find out how you know which came first. Your initial reaction may be to say that you store them by geographic location. Perhaps you have lived in several different houses and, since you know when you lived in each one, you know roughly which event came first. But if this is the case confine your thoughts here to different things you did in the one house. Allow your mind to become aware of the mental location of the memories. Is one further to the left or to the right of the other, in front of or behind the other? Think of what you have done on each birthday. How do you know which came first, how do you store those memories?

We'll shorten the time span. Think of something you do regularly, like making your bed, eating meals, going to work, exercising, watching television. Make sure they are in the same setting, the same house, office or gym. You will soon be aware of a slightly different location in your mind for the times further from the present and the times closer to the present.

Now, take one example. Think, for instance, of getting dressed. Keep the location the same: don't go back to a time when you lived in a different house. Think back to one of the earliest times you got dressed there, then to a recent occasion when you did the same thing. You are now going to look for other changes within each memory that are a reflection of time, not just the relative geographic locations of the memory. What differences do you notice? You may find the earlier memory is smaller, or paler, or black and white as opposed to being in colour, it may be in or out of focus. It may be more or less detailed, it may have a frame round it whereas the recent memory may not, it may be moving or stationary. It may be lighter or darker, or different colours. There will be other differences; it is up to you to discover them.

Still bearing in mind the act of getting dressed, think of a future time when you will do it. What differences do you notice between this future memory and the past memories? Is this future memory a little less focused, a little less detailed? Is it in the same colours? Notice any differences there may be.

Finally, take the same activity in the same location and imagine doing it in the far past, the recent past, the present, the near future and the distant future. Become aware of the differences in the memories.

Don't be concerned if you get different experiences as you concentrate on memories. One client told me that when at first she thought about the past and the future in relation to her whole life, she saw it as a long line coming in from the distant past from the far left and the future going away from her both in front of her and to her right. But when she did the last part of the above exercise, the past was moving away from her in a line that went down and forward and the future went up and forward and both lines were made up of overlapping transparent images of the activity.

Another client told me that the way she stored memories depended on the timespan. She saw the present year as a circle, rather like a clock face, and she located the event in the appropriate part of the circle. If she wanted to think of what had happened in March, she moved to that part of the circle; to picture what she would do in November, she moved over to that part. On the other hand, if she was thinking of the current week she viewed it as an S-curve lying on its front like a big dipper with Monday at the top, Thursday and Friday at the bottom and the weekend making the climb up again. Her future memories fell into a straight line. For many people, however, probably for most people, the memory line is a much simpler and straighter line.

Your memory line may go through you or you may be to one side of it. You may be above or below it. Explore for yourself. You may like to do this with a friend. As you do so, be aware of what you do with your hands as you describe

your past, present and future. Where you wave
your hands will often indicate the location of
the memory. When you do this exercise with a
friend, you may find that he or she has a different memory line; this in itself is a useful experience, as you realise that other people's minds
function differently to yours, even in something
as basic as storing your memories.

Experimenting With Your Memory Line

Now that you have determined your memory line, you
can experiment with it. If your past is to your left, find
out what happens when you put it on your right and
reverse the direction. If your memory line goes through
you, step out of it; if you are normally not on the line
try stepping onto or even into it. If the past is in focus
and the future blurred, change them round. If you have
been thinking of your future as black and heavy find
out what happens if you make it transparent, coloured,
light and bright. If you have been thinking of it as an
uphill climb, find out what happens when you slope
your future line downwards. Alter the details that
define the differences.

Henry experienced the present as a steep-sided
hole, six feet deep and about three feet in diameter,
with the past up at ground level behind him and
the future at ground level in front of him. He
couldn't see either where he had been or where he
was going. The hole was narrow and dark. No
wonder he felt depressed much of the time. He
was asked to bring the present up to ground
level. He did this but said that although it was

some improvement he felt precarious, as if the ground could subside underneath him at any time. Next, I asked him to make the present a raised mound, about six feet above ground, and to build it of solid earth with the base larger than the old hole so that it both filled it in and overlapped onto solid ground all round, and to describe what that felt like. He didn't have to, the smile on his face was immediate.

'Gosh, that's amazing,' he said, 'suddenly it's light, sort of sunny, everything seems possible from up here, the past was fine and the future's a breeze.'

The total transformation did not happen overnight, but as he practised he became more and more adept at standing on top of his hummock in sunny daylight rather than being below ground level in the dark pit, and at the same time he gradually lost much of his depression. Friends noticed it first and then, as the process became more automatic for him, he became aware of it himself, not only when he practised his new way of thinking but also at times when he was not consciously doing the exercise.

Here's something else for you to do: look for breaks in your memory line. You may have a kink in it, particularly your future memory line, and this may be depressing you. One client, Jason, reported that he could see the next year as a straight line but then it dipped down and he had trouble seeing the future beyond that. Another woman found that her memory line looked like a string of sausages, each sausage representing a year. Between years she felt constricted and uncertain as to where she was going.

Here are some other examples from my own work with clients. They will help to give you perspective on the many possible variations and a context within which to view your own system. You can also try them out for yourself and discover the consequences of rearranging your memory line. When you do this you may find some memory lines you would like to adopt for yourself, at least in some situations, and others you are happy to avoid.

Deirdre's memory line had the past behind her like, as she put it, toast stacked vertically on an endless toast rack going off into the distance. Her future was the same. The difference was that events in her past were transparent while the slices of the future were solid and she couldn't see through them. No wonder she never felt she had a future and had trouble making plans and imagining how they would work out. When it was suggested to her that she make the future 'slices' transparent her mood lifted.

Many people's lines pass in front of them from left to right. Often the pictures get smaller with distance so that the far past fades into the distance and so does the distant future. Martin, who said he wasn't so much depressed as just never happy with what he was doing, found that his pictures got bigger and bigger the further he went into the future. As a result he spent much of his time living in the future which was often overwhelming, and out of touch with the, small, present. When he consciously changed the sizes round he was better able to experience and enjoy the present.

If your past is in front of you, you may have trouble seeing the future. This was so for Angela. Her memory line had the past out in front, the present to her immediate right, and the future off on a line further to her right. She'd had a particularly unhappy childhood and seemed unable to get over it. As a result she was not enjoying the present and was spoiling her new marriage. As she put it, 'It's as if I keep expecting it to go wrong and so am making it happen. I don't want to do this – he's a wonderful man and basically we're happy – it's just that I get so depressed. All I can see is the dreadful childhood I had and the way my parents fought until they divorced. I keep seeing it.'

Of course she did, it was right in front of her all the time. By putting her past behind her, literally, she was able to focus on and enjoy the present.

Is there a right or wrong memory line? Is there a best memory line? No. From my own work with clients there is a seemingly endless variety of types of memory lines. What works for one person would not necessarily work for another. What was a black hole of depression for Henry was security for Valerie. Her memory line also had a hollow in it, though not as deep as Henry's. Her past was slightly up and to the left, her future up and to the right. She said she felt secure in the present, as if she could relax there, slightly hidden from the world, before she drew breath and faced the challenge of the future.

If the future is crowding in on you and getting you down, stretch it out. If it seems too distant to have much relevance to your present mood, bring it closer: this may increase your motivation to deal with the present. If it looks dim and gloomy, shine a bright light on it or change the colours.

Do all this gently. Some changes are acceptable and easy; others will set up considerable inner turmoil. We are not looking for memory-line gymnastics as an exercise for its own sake. We are looking for ways to help you change your moods when they are not either enjoyable or beneficial.

You will almost certainly find it helpful to do these memory-line exercises with a friend, better still with several friends. This can be a lot of fun and you will get a broader perspective than when you do them on your own. You will almost certainly be surprised at the many variations you find and at the importance people put on the specific details of their own individual memories; details that may, to you, be either unimportant or non-existent. Again this will show you that this whole concept is not arbitrary but constitutes a real phenomenon.

As a further experiment, find someone whose memory line is very different to yours and discover what happens when you organise your own memories in the same way as they organise theirs. To do this, you will have to ask a lot of questions and be sure you get the full, detailed picture of the way they operate. This will help you become more clear on the details of the way you store your own memories. You will also notice that, having done this, you can relate better to the other person and that you have developed an understanding of some of their personality traits and moods.

Once you have discovered your own memory line, you can start to use it. Remember, how-

ever, to respect it. By now you will have done
some experimenting, you will have experienced
the results of making changes and so you will
know at least something of its potential power
and how the way you feel changes as a result. If
you have changed your memory line around, be
sure that you do put it back to the way it was, at
least for the time being. Do not assume that
when you have finished exploring and playing
with it, it will automatically return to the way it
was: it may not. So put everything back as you
found it until you are sure you want to make
and keep any changes. Otherwise you might be
in for some surprises.

Changing Your Memory Line

We talk of changing your memory line. How is this
done? Doubtless, you have already tried doing it, and
probably with a measure of success. However, there are
some extra hints that may be helpful and some warn-
ings and cautions that you should consider.

● **Take care and pay attention to what is appropriate
for you.** The past has already happened and is fixed,
but the future is yet to occur. When you change your
memory line, you can change your experience of
reality and even your sense of yourself, of who you
are and where you're going. So do it with care and
with respect. If the changes you make are appropriate
and right for you, it is likely that they will happen
smoothly and easily and the consequences will be
beneficial. If they are not appropriate then you may
feel disoriented and uncomfortable and the changes

may take place erratically and at random. Be aware of what is right for you. That does not mean that all beneficial changes are totally comfortable. Some changes that are helpful will also need some time for adjustment, but they will fit in with your aims and goals. They will also lead to beneficial consequences.

- **Tell yourself that any proposed changes are temporary and will remain so until your unconscious mind is sure they should become permanent**. This allows your unconscious mind to consider them without pressure. Once you have chosen the changes you want, try them out in all sorts of different situations and make sure the changes are appropriate.

  After you have made the change find out how you now feel about yourself, the present and the future. Do you feel more relaxed or pressured? Do you feel happier or more depressed? Do you have more confidence and control or do you feel out of control? Does it allow you to do what you want or does it impose restrictions?

  One client with the future compressed close to him felt oppressed by it, and that was getting him down: he felt better and more able to cope when he stretched it out. Another, Geraldine, found that when she stretched hers out she started to feel that there was heaps of time. As a result she delayed starting and doing the tasks required of her and was always running late. This depressed her so she brought it back to the way it had been.

- **If there is someone you would like to be like, to copy or emulate, find out how they store time**. Learn all the details of their memory line and then arrange yours in the same way. Find out what happens. It is unlikely that you will become a clone of the other person but you may make some positive changes in that direction.

If you are depressed and you know someone who is always happy, find out about their memory line. You may learn that it is bright where yours is dark, that it is clear and visible while yours is indistinct. There are countless possibilities: explore them and find out if they will work for you and help to lift your depression.

If you are a pessimist and worry about the future, explore the memory line of someone who is optimistic and excited by the future. If the past keeps dragging you down, work with someone who has also had a troubled past but who has not let it blight their present experience. Learn about their memory line and copy it to have a new experience yourself. If you feel comfortable with your altered memory line make the appropriate changes, if not, put things back as they were.

- **You may want to make permanent changes or you may want to make the changes temporary. You may want to make changes only in certain circumstances.** Mrs H decided, literally, to put her troubled past behind her most of the time, but when she was counselling others at work during the day, she brought it back and up to the left so she could call on it for past experiences to share.

Mr K lived in the present and could see little future. This normally kept him at work long after hours as his focus was on what he was doing, not what he should be doing next. The resulting tensions in his marriage were distressing him. He decided to change his memory line at work so that he could see his whole day at once and be more organised, but leave it alone during the weekends so that he fully experienced and enjoyed the time with his family. Not only did he have more time at home as a result, but his work was done more efficiently and his business improved.

- **Make sure the changes are desirable**. Check to discover if there are any disadvantages to the way you feel with the new memory line. In the case of Geraldine, although stretching her future out lifted a mood and enabled her to be happier, it also meant things didn't get done, so she had to find another way of lifting her mood and leave her memory line as it was.

- **If you do not believe you have a past, create one**. One person claimed that they had no past. This turned out to be not quite true. Every time I asked her about her past, she waved her left hand over her left shoulder and said no, it didn't exist: clearly her past was behind her, carefully tucked away out of sight. She had had an abused childhood with a number of other problems and clearly this was something she didn't want to have a look at. All attempts to either bring her past into view or have her turn and look at it failed. Yet she did want to have a complete memory line and said that she felt she would be less disoriented if she had one, as now her life seemed to be without roots and she didn't feel as if she belonged anywhere, which was part of the reason for her depression.

The answer, when we finally got there, was simple. I had her sort all of her memories into good and bad and put the good ones in one line and the bad ones on another, lying slightly to the side of it. Then I gave her the option of looking at either line at will or both if she wanted to. She reported later that there were times when it was useful to look at both lines, but that in general she kept the good-times line out to her left side and the bad-times line behind it and hidden. This way she felt she could preserve what she had learned from the bad times without having to go through them all again unless she chose to.

- **Make sure you have a future memory line**. Some people find that they don't have a future memory line and this in itself can be depressing. If you can see nothing in the future, you have nothing to look forward to and so the present becomes all important and is often insufficient on its own to keep you happy. Imagine, for instance, what it would be like if you worked at a job you didn't particularly enjoy and didn't have a real sense of the pay packet at the end of the week, or of the things this pay packet could provide. It would be easy to feel depressed. Or imagine doing the housekeeping, which few people enjoy for its own sake, with no sense of the lovely clean house you'll have as a result and the family coming home later. Again, it would be easy to get depressed. Not many people have no future memory line at all, but there are some who don't. Many others have either a brief and truncated line or one whose components or position make it difficult to see.

One objection you may have, when trying to create a future, was illustrated by Clare: 'How can I possibly create a future when I don't know what is going to happen?'

'Don't worry about filling in the details. Just create a line, in whatever direction you want, and see what happens when you leave slots along it into which you can place future events.'

'No, that looks empty and makes me feel even more depressed.'

'Do you have any idea of what could happen in the future?'

'No, none at all. I guess that's one of the reasons why I do feel so miserable.'

As Clare was unable to visualise a future, I suggested that instead she made a list of a number of possible futures that she could logically have, at least in theory. She was able to do this, although she didn't feel she could relate personally to any of these projections. The possible futures included staying in her job or leaving it, what might happen if she behaved in one way or another, if she treated one person well or not so well, etc. She had trouble creating them but she did agree, when presented with a number of options, that they were all possible. Then I suggested that she put them all in place, all starting at the present and branching out in slightly different directions like multiple narrow beams of light going out from a central point. Suddenly she looked more interested in the whole project.

'That's fun,' she said, 'it's like having dozens of moonbeams to choose from and I can walk out along any one I want to.'

I gave her time to explore each of her moonbeams and she suddenly began to see their potential.

'Golly,' was her comment, 'now things suddenly look good. I can decide which way I want to go and then, at this moment, do the things that will get me there.'

Clearly Clare felt, if not exactly excited and happy at the new prospect of her future, at least a lot less pessimistic and depressed. Over the next few weeks she reported that doing this regularly had had a major affect on the way she felt, especially at the times when the present wasn't all that exciting. She also said that the process was becoming automatic, which is a common response from people who have made useful changes.

• **If you have no memory line at all life will be disorganised and learning will be difficult.** This is rare, but I do recall one person with little or no memory line. She was, as might be expected, totally disorganised and scatterbrained to the point that it infuriated all her friends. They only stayed friends, I suspected, because when she finally was with you she was interesting to be with. Making plans with her, however, was impossible. It was also disorienting to talk to her as she would talk of things from her childhood as if they had happened yesterday and of things you had just said to her as if she had always known them. Her strait-laced parents had come to believe that she was a pathological liar and couldn't be trusted simply because the way she described her life and events didn't fit into their chronologically organised world. However, she wasn't aware that there was any error in this or that she wasn't telling the truth as others saw it. For instance, she would tell me that many different things had happened 'yesterday', when clearly they had happened in the preceding weeks or months.

One thing she was good at, however, was knowing what she did and did not like and want. I went through the Values Elicitation process with her (as described in Chapter 22) and by organising all the things she wanted and putting them out in the future we were able to create that part of her memory line.

You can do so much with your memory line. You can work with it to resolve almost any issues from your past and to reshape and plan your future. You can certainly use it to lift depression over past events and over what is happening now and what you think will happen in the future. If you would like to take this concept further, look for a practitioner who practises Time-Line Therapy.

Chapter Thirteen

Anchoring The Good
and Releasing The Bad

As a child at boarding school, whenever I got a letter from my grandmother the smell of her perfume would waft out and remind me of home in a way the verbal content of the letter never could. This is an anchor. Do you have a lucky outfit you wear on certain occasions, knowing it will bring you luck because it has in the past? That is an anchor. Do you and your team have a special chant or action you perform before a game? That is an anchor. All you need is a snippet of a theme tune to recall a film or a television programme. That is an anchor. A number of companies have slogans or theme sounds that they use continually. These are anchors. Watch a horror movie with the sound turned off: it is never as nerve-tingling as when you turn up the volume and hear the threatening music. That is an anchor. A couple may have a theme song, or a special restaurant where they know they will have a great time. These are anchors. The rallying cry of troops, the war dances of tribes, the school song, these are all anchors. Letterheads and logos are anchors, reminding you of what they imply. Even the tone of someone's voice can be an anchor, or a particular word or phrase they use or say in a specific way.

Do you feel worse every time you go to your doctor or therapist, at least as you approach their building? It's not surprising as this is the building or office you associate with times when you are sick. It is important to create positive anchors with such places as well. One of my aims, after a therapy session, is to avoid letting the client go back into the waiting room: I don't want the anchor to pull them back to the way they felt before the session.

Perhaps a particular tune puts you in a bad mood. Perhaps you feel nervous when you see someone in a uniform of authority. These could be examples of negative anchors, related to some unpleasant experience in the past when you heard that tune or were chastised or punished by an official.

Anchors can be positive or negative, good or bad, strong or weak. They can be sounds, sights, smells, objects, words, movements, almost anything. What they do, each time you experience them, is transport you back to the state you were in when first you experienced them.

Soon after I graduated I got a job overseas, bought myself a small car and spent the weekends touring the countryside with a friend. I would often thump the wheel in my joy and say, 'wow, this is the life'. Now, when I'm in the car, any time I may feel a bit down, all I need to do is thump the wheel and use the same words to feel my spirits lifting. This is a self-induced anchor, used consciously.

To discover your own, already existing, anchors, think of all the good times you have had in your life. What sounds, sights, sensations, activities and so forth do you associate with them? Initially you may say 'nothing', but think some more. I had never thought of my sports shoes as an anchor until one day when I was tying my tennis-shoe laces I felt my spirits lifting and realised how strongly I associated them with the joy of playing sports. Since then, when I have wanted a lift and have decided to go for a walk, I have consciously chosen to put on my tennis shoes, knowing I will feel even better as a result. Mind you, I also continue to reinforce the positive aspect of this anchor by continuing to do fun things in those shoes as well.

Take some time to list all the things that make you feel good. Keep pen and paper handy in the next few days and write them down as they occur to you. Since many of them, probably the majority, will be unconscious, you will have to do more than this: every time you feel your spirits lift, every time you suddenly feel a surge of happiness, optimism, expectancy, love, gratitude, joy or any other positive emotion . . . stop . . . consider it, find out what was the trigger for that emotion. Once you have identified it, write it down.

You can do the same with negative anchors. Consider any of the sights, sounds, objects, events etc. that make you feel bad. Write them down. Then be conscious, over the next days and weeks, of the times when you suddenly feel a drop in your spirits. Stop and investigate what happened; isolate the negative anchor.

There are many anchors that operate in your life. You will be aware of some of them, not of others. You may be using some of them consciously, others may be totally unconscious. You may currently have negative anchors that make you feel depressed. Unless they serve some other useful purpose you would be wise to identify these and get rid of them. You may already have some positive anchors and it will benefit you to identify these and to use them consciously, as and when you need them. You may also want to create new, positive anchors. Having eliminated those that you don't want, polished up the good ones and created new ones, the next thing is to use them, for by using anchors you enhance them and increase their power.

Setting Up Positive Anchors

The first thing to do is to use the anchors you already have. Identify them, strengthen them and then use them. Like all tools, they need care and attention, so, after you have used them, and when it is appropriate, recharge them. The more anchors you have, the easier it is to lift your spirits.

Exercise: Finding Existing Anchors

Think of a time when you felt really happy, one of those days when everything was perfect and you felt loved, successful, happy and fulfilled. Think about the day, in all its details. What was there that would make a suitable anchor? Perhaps you were doing or saying something distinctive, perhaps you were moving in a certain way. Perhaps there was a particular feature that you can recall that typified that positive feeling for you. Focus your mind on this as you think of the occasion. Go back in your mind to that happy time and recreate the feelings and identify the anchor. Once more, think back to the good times, recreate the mood, and recreate the anchor. Do this over and over again; each time the anchor will get stronger.

Every time you feel happy, add to this anchor, by repeating it consciously and connecting it to your present good mood. Pretty soon you will have an anchor you can *use consciously when you feel down and need a lift. Just remember to keep recharging the anchor so you can continue to use it and get a positive effect. Don't fire it off only when you feel down, use it when you are happy also as a way of topping it up.*

Exercise: Creating New Anchors

Think about something you do, or could do, easily and consciously, that would make a good anchor. If you always wear a ring, you might decide that moving it or turning it on your finger would be a good anchor. You might choose to rub your ear or thump one fist into the palm of the other hand. The latter action is one I personally like to use as an anchor but it is an obvious and overt move and might not go down well in some circumstances. Since I snap my fingers at the dog, who I love, it is easy for me to make snapping my fingers a positive anchor. You often see little children clapping their hands together in excitement. This then acts as an unconscious anchor for them and if you later watch an adult clapping you will see a smile break out on the child's face. Clapping your hands or some other similar movement is a good positive anchor and one that you reinforce each time you see a performance that you like and at which you clap in appreciation. You might choose straightening your tie, or adjusting your clothing as anchors. Watch resourceful people who are about to go into a meeting. See how some of them tidy themselves up and then stand straight and throw back their shoulders. They have set off a series of positive anchors, ones which say I look good, feel terrific and can achieve my aims.

Whatever anchor you choose to use, make it one with which you are comfortable and which will work for you. Remember that you are not limited to one anchor: you can have as many as you like, you just have to keep track of them and not fire off the wrong one at the wrong time.

One man I know uses each of his fingers as different anchors. When he wants to feel powerful and tough he pulls his thumbs; when he wants to feel strong and in control he pulls, taps or points with his index finger; when he wants to feel happy he pulls his middle finger; when he wants to feel loved and loving he pulls or links his fourth or ring finger; and when he wants to cut down on his own strength and aggression and fit in with other people he pulls the little finger.

These anchors work well for him and whenever he feels depressed he can pull himself out of it by linking his third fingers together and reminding himself of happier times and telling himself, by implication, that this present depression will soon lift.

> **Do not be half-hearted. You may have to work at setting anchors up. Create or experience the mood and fire the anchor ten, twenty, thirty times – whatever it takes. Remember also to check anchors. Let yourself be neutral, fire the anchor, and find out how you feel. If you feel the way you expected then your job is done; if not, then keep recreating the anchor until it becomes strong and effective.**

Since we are currently talking about depression, you will want to set up happy anchors. But you could also set anchors for other moods. You might want to have anchors for feeling successful, resourceful and confident. Make them strong: anchors that are weakly established will have only a minor beneficial effect. Also make sure that when you are establishing a new anchor, you don't try to anchor a new mood onto what is already an anchor for some other type of mood.

Marie had been in to see me on several occasions. The previous time we had talked about anchors and she had said she would go away and work on them.

'But it's no good,' she said when she returned. 'I decided that every time I made a fist I would feel good. I set the anchor, just like you said, but it doesn't work. Every time I make a fist and thump the table, I just feel angry.'

For some people making a fist is empowering, for others it reminds them of times when they were angry, unhappy or miserable and they thumped the table. On further discussion it became obvious that this was the case for Marie, so we changed the anchor. Had we wanted to go on using it, we would first have had to destroy the old meaning of the anchor. This is often a good thing to do, but since Marie rarely made a fist and thumped the table, I decided to leave that action as an anchor she might want in the future at the appropriate time, and instead set up a totally different one for her positive anchor.

Marie told me that at school she and her friends had drummed their feet on the floor when they felt happy and positive, as this was a move the teacher couldn't see, so I suggested she use that instead. The results were impressive.

'It's pretty funny,' was her response after we had set the anchor and she had gone away and used it for a week. 'I was in the bus the other day and not feeling too good, so I started to drum my feet on the floor, quietly like, not so's anyone would really hear, and suddenly I felt really happy. I started thinking about all my old school friends and the fun we'd had. I didn't mind doing the shopping after that. And you know what? I think I'll get back in touch with some of them; we had a lot of good times together.'

Disarming Negative Anchors

As soon as you become aware of a negative anchor, something that triggers off in you an unwanted emotion such as fear, anxiety, depression or anger, you will want to get rid of it. You can do this by using either specially created new anchors or already existing old ones to override the negative anchor. Let's say that your positive anchor is to rub one foot on the other. Next time the negative trigger occurs, immediately use this positive anchor. When it occurs again, use the positive anchor, and then again the next time it occurs. In time you will feel the power of the negative trigger diminishing. Remember, too, to keep recharging the positive anchor, for if you do not, it could become a negative one.

Veronica said that she got nervous every time the head of her department walked through the section where she worked. She badly wanted a promotion and she knew that the only way she would get it was if this man noticed her and appreciated her work. Yet she dreaded the man's arrival and whenever he did walk by she became nervous and tongue-tied.

We set up some strong confidence anchors for

Veronica. To do this, I asked her to think of the times when she had felt supremely confident in her work: the times when she had done a good job and a customer had praised her, a time when she had been able to help one of the senior staff when they had been stuck. She also called up times outside her work environment when she had felt confident. Each time she had one of these situations firmly in mind she rubbed her left wrist.

After a few weeks she reported that this had helped, but that she still felt nervous, though it wasn't as bad as before. So I tried a different tack. I asked her what promotion would mean to her.

'That's easy. For a start I'll be able to wear the new smart uniform, the one the seniors wear. And I'll get a pay rise.'

'And what will you do with that?'

'That will give me just enough to move out of home and get a flat of my own. About time too – the house is pretty crowded now the twins are growing up.'

'What else?'

'Well, I'll feel ever so proud; and my Mum, she'll be proud of me too. I can just hear her telling the neighbours.'

Clearly Veronica could imagine the situation very well. She wanted it so badly that she could almost taste it. I told her to imagine every aspect of it and then, when she was totally involved, I suggested she put the image of her boss into the scene. She gave a bit of a start but I went on to say, 'This is the man who can make all this possible, so whenever you see this man you will automatically think of how calm, positive and confident you feel with this promotion and you will want to thank him for giving it to you. Each time he comes into the department it will mean you are a step closer to achieving promotion.'

Previously the sight of her boss had meant criticism and nervousness. I was now altering, or reframing, the way she viewed him so that his appearance would now mean that she was one step closer to promotion. At the same time, I was firmly anchoring to the sight of her boss all the good feelings she would have when she received the promotion, so that the sight of him would trigger off a very resourceful and confident state in her. Within a week she was able to report that her work actually got better when her boss was around.

It is very important to keep assessing your anchors and to recharge positive anchors. An over-exercised positive anchor may become worn out and negative.

Daphne knew all about anchors, or so she thought after our session together, and she decided to make full use of them. She hated large supermarkets and frequently got a claustrophobic urge to rush out of them. This obviously made shopping difficult, yet she had to do it and the supermarkets were cheaper than her small local shop.

Daphne had three adorable grandchildren and was at her happiest when playing with them. When she was with them she felt, as she put it, 'a wonderful rush of love and pure joy, it's almost overwhelming'. To form a positive anchor, Daphne used this rush of love and joy that her grandchildren gave her. When it occurred, she would rub the back of her head to anchor the feeling. When she went shopping and her panic began Daphne then rubbed the back of her head again.

All went well to begin with. The positive mood Daphne invoked when she rubbed her head helped to dispel the panic. Then problems started: she told me she was beginning to find the grandchildren too much to handle, and that she had started getting panic attacks when they visited her.

Eventually, we pinned the problem down. Because her panic in the supermarkets was severe, she was rubbing her head a lot while she was there. Furthermore, because she could only stay in one for a short while she had formed the habit of going shopping several times a week and buying a small amount each time. On the other hand, she only saw her grandchildren about once a week. The positive anchor had become a negative anchor. Now, when she was with her grandchildren and rubbed the back of her head, instead of recharging the positive anchor she was firing off the negative anchor of her anxiety in the supermarket. The answer was to find a number of different anchors and use them sequentially in the supermarket, making sure to recharge all of them as often as possible. This did work and although Daphne didn't manage to enjoy supermarket shopping, she did, in time, manage to do it without panicking.

You can have a lot of fun with anchors. Use them with awareness and you may be surprised at the result. Create some positive and happy ones for yourself and use them to recall those moods next time you are feeling depressed.

Chapter Fourteen

No One Likes To Be Criticised

Being and feeling criticised is a great way to become depressed. Few people like being criticised. It is a rare person who receives criticism, either of themselves or of something they've done, or even of people they care about and what they have done, without feeling any negative emotions and with a neutral remark such as 'Thank you for that critical comment, that is useful information and I will consider it.' It is far more common to hear criticism, feel injured and go on the defensive.

In general, criticism hurts. Few people have sufficient self-esteem to welcome criticism. Even if the criticism is constructive and well-intended, even if you can learn positively from it, it is nearly always disconcerting. Whether or not you agree with the critic, care what the critic thinks, or want to argue with him or her about the comments, it is all too easy to feel let down and to become depressed.

There are many types of criticism. Overt criticism is easy to spot: a critical statement is made of you or your actions and you can respond accordingly. Covert criticism is often less easy to handle: you may feel people are criticising you behind your back, or you may take lack of praise as an implied criticism. If you ask someone to go to a film with you and they say no, do you feel a silent criticism of your choice of film, your company, or your temerity in assuming they would like to go with you? If you suggest that someone joins you in a venture and they turn you down, are you cast into depression, feeling criticised for wanting to be involved in the project yourself? If you are not included in an activity, a social group or a work project, do you feel criticised or in some way inadequate and depressed as a result? If someone fails to smile at you one morning, do you take it as a silent criticism, assuming you must have done something wrong, or something to displease the other person? These and many many more situations like them, whether they involve self-inflicted criticism, assumed implied criticism, behind-your-back criticism or overt criticism can all lead to depression.

In this chapter you are going to discover how to take criticism positively, and so how to avoid the depression often brought on by criticism. You will discover how to learn from criticism and how to turn it to your own advantage. You will learn how to assess and evaluate it objectively, rather than emotionally, and to decide whether or not you agree with it and want to make changes as a result, or disagree with the comments expressed and want to ignore them. Above all, you will learn how to deal with criticism without getting depressed.

Right and Wrong: Believing In Yourself And Respecting The Beliefs Of Others

Believing in Yourself

When we take on criticism and it hurts, there is, inherent in that process, the underlying assumption of being right and being wrong. If you had done the right thing, so the assumption goes, you would not have been criticised. If you are being criticised, you must have done the wrong thing. After all, if you were totally confident that what you had done was right, would you have felt criticised? Of course not. Your immediate thought would have been that the other person's comments were wrong or inappropriate or that they had different standards and values to you. This in itself could upset you, but the real cause of pain would then have been recognised and could be looked at.

A helpful first step is to do away with the idea of absolute right and wrong. If you are crying out at this stage that this is impossible, that you cannot do away with right and wrong, that they are an essential part of the fabric of our lives, our social structure and our morality, then remember that many things that are considered right in your society are considered to be wrong in some other society. In most Western societies it is 'right' for women to show their faces, to wear miniskirts, to go out alone. In many Muslim countries this is 'wrong'. In some societies it is 'wrong' to tell a lie and essential that you always tell the truth. In other cultures telling the truth is tactless and 'wrong' and it is better to save face and allow the other person to do the same. Some religions dictate that you must not eat certain foods, but in other religions totally different concepts of 'right' and 'wrong' apply. These different understandings of right and wrong go beyond societies, cultures or religions. Within a town what is the 'right' way to behave in one street will be the 'wrong' way to behave in another. The rules vary within families: not reporting your sibling's misdeeds, for instance, may be considered an act of loyalty in one family and deceitful in another.

There are few, if any, absolute rights and wrongs. However, there certainly are ways to behave that are appropriate and considered to be acceptable in one setting and other ways to behave that are considered to be appropriate in a different setting. Most of us try to live by what is acceptable in the twentieth century, in the particular country and social setting in which we operate. If you choose to behave in a way that conforms, you may have a smoother path in life than if you choose to behave in a way that your peers consider unacceptable. *But that is all.* If they do not like what you do, it is not that you are 'wrong', simply that you are choosing to live or act in a way that they find unacceptable.

Where does all this lead us? It means that if someone criticises you, what they are really doing is telling you about their preferences, their choices and their standards. Consider the following example:

> Gerald was seventeen, tall, somewhat gangly and with a teenager's crop of pimples. His mother had sent him in because of his skin problem and the accompanying bad diet, but during the consultation other problems emerged. He had trouble finding and keeping a girlfriend, or at least one that he really liked. He was inclined to blame his skin but eventually a different story emerged. He was still at boarding school and there he mixed with a pretty aggressive group of friends; at home his family were quiet and conservative and so were the friends he had there.
>
> During the previous holiday he had tried to date

the sister of one of his friends, but she had soon managed to avoid him. Later he had learned that she had found him too pushy and aggressive, demanding far more, sexually, than she was willing to give, and that she thought him a boor. Conscious of this, back at school he was a lot more circumspect with his next girlfriend, only to find that she left him because he was a wimp and not sexually exciting.

'What did I do wrong?' was his question to me. 'I tried to do the right thing, I tried to learn, but either way I made a mess of it.'

His problem came from his belief that there was an absolute right and a wrong way to behave in such circumstances. His solution came when he decided how *he* wanted to behave and what was appropriate for him. Once he was clear about this and behaved accordingly, he was impervious to criticism.

A few years later, when he was engaged, I saw him again and his comments were interesting.

'You know what you did with me that day was a real help. I did decide how I wanted things to be and I then started behaving in the way I thought was right for me. I stopped trying to please the girl I was with by imagining what she wanted me to do. At first that meant I missed out on some relationships I would have liked, or at least I thought I would have liked. But I soon realised that if their ideas as to the way the relationship should be were at odds with mine right at the start, then long-term we were probably going to be unsuitable for each other anyway. And the best thing of all is the relationship I now have – which I might have missed out on had I gone on trying to be right for each girl I asked out.'

Not only is he happy now, but he has saved himself a lot of heartache along the way.

Establish your own standards and stick with them. If you do this, you will see other people's criticism simply as their means of telling you about how they would do things and how their way is different to yours. You can then relax knowing that their way is not for you.

Respecting the Beliefs of Others

You can make good use of criticism. No one is an island and few people want to go through their lives unchanged, stuck in a behaviour pattern established in their youth and which may no longer be serving them. If you decide a particular criticism is totally inappropriate you can simply refuse to accept it. On the other hand, you may want to consider the other person's remarks and decide whether or not they have merit.

If you can respect your critic and if you are willing really to hear the other person's point of view as well as feel free to express your own, the whole process of receiving criticism becomes much easier and less painful.

It is much easier if you can get away from the idea of right and wrong. Right and wrong are often only reflections of a particular culture, or even of a particular individual's outlook. You must also avoid the idea that you have to be right or else you have to feel bad about yourself. The most successful people, in any walk of life

or in any role, are the ones who have made the most mistakes, mistakes for which they could have been criticised. Top golfers can be criticised far more often than occasional players for hitting balls into bunkers. Top politicians can be criticised for treading on more toes than club committee members. The person who throws the most dinner parties can be criticised for more flops than the person who never invites people home.

It is not bad to receive criticism. It is not even bad to receive criticism that you endorse and acknowledge. If you do not receive critical comment from others, you will not learn a great deal. If you hear only praise and never criticism, you are probably only receiving half-truths from friends whom you cannot really trust to be honest with you.

If a person is convinced that they are right, it is unlikely you will be able to make them think differently. All you can change is yourself and the way you interpret and use the input you get. Beware of situations where you are both trying to make each other wrong rather than to achieve a positive and mutually satisfactory outcome.

Types of Criticism and How to Deal With Them

Assumed Criticisms

One of the hardest forms of criticism to handle is the type to which you can make no response. This is true whether it be overt, covert or assumed criticism. Let's consider assumed criticism. By this I mean the times when things in your life do not go smoothly and you assume the cause lies in something you have done that other people find unacceptable. Perhaps someone frowns at you instead of smiling. Perhaps you do not get the praise you expected. Perhaps you are not invited to a party or a meeting. Perhaps someone doesn't write to you. There are hundreds of similar situations and I'm sure you can think of a lot of them for yourself.

In any of these situations it is easy to feel criticised and become despondent. Why is this? It is because the assumption you make is that you are at fault. Yet there are always many other potential causes of the situation. When you next see someone frown, make a list of all the possible reasons they have for frowning. They may be worried about a thousand different things that don't concern you. They may be late, they may be focusing on their next meeting, they may be trying to work something out. To understand this fully, you have only to think of the number of times you have frowned for a reason that has nothing to do with an action of the person you are with. You can go further and consider whether or not it is even arrogant of you to assume that their expression was prompted by you.

In any situation where you find yourself feeling criticised, but where nothing specifically critical has been said, write down all the possible reasons there could be for the situation. Let your imagination run riot. Perhaps the other person has a stone in their shoe, perhaps they have just been given a speeding ticket, perhaps someone didn't praise the meal they had cooked. The possibilities are endless. When you have completed your list, you will have your assumption that it is you who is being criticised in a different perspective.

At this point it is worth asking yourself a very important question. Can you know, for certain, if the other person says nothing, whether or not they are really criticising you, frowning at you, even thinking about you, as opposed to having their attention focused on someone or something else? You can always ask, but if you do this too frequently you may be setting up further problems. Few people like to be asked, over and over, 'What is wrong, is it something I have done?' If you cannot know for sure whether or not you are being criticised then it makes sense, as we have said before, to make the assumption that is *the most useful*. It is more useful for you to assume that you are not being criticised than to assume that you are. The only exception to this is if you feel a criticism would have been justified, in which case you can use this prompt to absorb whatever you can learn and make the appropriate commitments to change what you do in the future. In other words, learn, or assume you have not done anything worthy of criticism.

At this point you may also find it valuable to go back to the five-step process discussed in Chapter 8 on Optimists and Pessimists, and review that.

> **Why choose to feel criticised, possibly for no good reason, when you can choose to feel otherwise? If you need some more feedback, ask the other person what is wrong a few times, and compare what you hear with what you had thought or imagined. You will be surprised at how many other reasons people give for doing something that you took to be criticism of yourself.**

Interactive Criticisms

Of course there are times when you get an overt and obvious criticism from someone. These situations can happen many times a day. An American study found that toddlers receive criticism or adverse comments around four hundred and fifty times a day and praise less than forty times. By criticism they meant such things as 'be quiet' (you are too noisy), 'be quick' (you are too slow), 'don't bother me now, I'm busy' (you're a nuisance), and so forth. These may only be minor hurts but they are there and they build up. In adult life you develop a thick skin but similar and greater criticisms occur daily in most people's lives.

By the heading 'Interactive Criticisms' I mean situations where someone has criticised you and it is appropriate for you to respond. This is in contrast to a criticism you may get by letter or second-hand, through the grapevine, or even thrown at you by someone passing, who doesn't wait around to hear what you have to say. In the interactive criticism situation you need something to say, something that will help rather than hinder the communication, and something that will, in the end, leave you feeling good about yourself and, if appropriate, will enable you to learn from the situation.

Typically, there are three things people do in response to interactive criticism:
1. They become defensive and argue back, defending or justifying their position or actions.
2. They crumple and agree that they were stupid, rude, inadequate, wrong, etc.
3. They attack and try to make the other person more 'wrong' than they were themselves.

Following the first option often leads to an argument,

the second leads to pain and the third can mean you lose friends and create enemies.

There are two other options or phrases that you may like to consider using. You should choose whichever is the most appropriate at the time that you are being criticised, which will depend in part on whether or not you agree with the criticism. The phrases are:

1. 'That is an interesting point of view, I will give it some thought.'

2. 'That is an interesting point of view, now would you like to hear mine?'

> *Response One: 'That is an interesting point of view,*
> *I will give it some thought'.*

Consider this response. You would use it if you felt there was some merit in the criticism and were, at least to some extent, in agreement with it. You would also use it if you felt the immediate situation was explosive or that you might be reacting rather than acting – reacting out of anger, pain, guilt or some other emotion, in such a way that saying very much would exacerbate the situation, rather than acting freely and un-emotionally.

By using Response One several things have been accomplished.

a) You have acknowledged the speaker, and that you have have heard what they have said. If, in such a situation, you say nothing, you will only make them cross since people like to know they have been heard. The criticism was made with the intention of creating some effect, whether constructive or destructive.

b) You have also let the critic know that you will think about what they have said, that you are not ignoring them or stonewalling them, nor are you simply walking away and turning your back without considering what they have said.

If the critic is spoiling for a fight and continues to demand your immediate response to their criticism, all you need to say is that you will think about it, that you've already said that you would, and that you want some time to do that. It is difficult for the other person to continue to be critical or aggressive and if they do you can simply repeat the phrase.

Barry told me that on many evenings when he got home his wife verbally attacked him. She would complain that he was late, that he didn't help with the children's bedtime, that he cared more about his work than his family.

'I'm nearly always tired when I get home,' he said, 'and all I want to do is sit down and relax for a while. After that I'm happy to help her. I do understand that she feels trapped in the house all day with just the kids for company.'

'What normally happens?'

'Oh, I usually blow up. I'll tell her I'm tired too, or that I work hard too, and that I pay the bills so she should stop complaining. Later on we usually make up but it's getting so that I hate to go home, knowing all I'll get is criticism.'

I suggested that he use Response One and he agreed to try it. On his next visit, I asked him the result.

'It was very interesting,' was his comment. 'When I got home on Thursday night, she'd obviously had a bad day. The plumber hadn't come and the tap had been dripping. She'd asked me to fix it on Wednesday evening but I'd been too busy with papers which I had to read. Her first words were, "How the hell do you think I am? The bloody tap's been dripping all day and the plumber didn't turn up, though I stayed in all morning. Now I'm behind with the shopping and you'll just have to have a snack meal for dinner. Why can't you be like other husbands and fix things round the house?"'

I waited with interest to hear what he would say next.

'I nearly argued back with her,' he continued, 'then I remembered what you had said, so I simply repeated it, or nearly. What I actually said was, "That's an interesting idea, I'll give it some thought as soon as I've put my things down." Then I walked into the sitting room. It wasn't quite as easy as all that because she was obviously in a very bad mood. She came after me demanding that I answer her right away and so I thought, "Oh well, might as well be killed for a goose as a gander", and I said again, "That too is an interesting demand, I'll think about that too." I expected her to continue, even though one of the children called out at that point, but she went to them.

'Later, over dinner, I brought the matter up. I told her I had been thinking about what she had said when I had got home and I asked her if she would really like me to be like the husband next door. Certainly, he does fix all sorts of things round the house, but he works as a storeman and doesn't have work he brings home in the evenings; nor does he earn nearly as much as I do, so they can't afford some of the things we have. By then she had calmed down of course and we had a good talk. She did agree that I worked harder, that we are better off and that she wouldn't swap, it was just that she was fed up. She said it had made her mad when I hadn't responded to her more fully, on the spot, although she wasn't quite clear as to what she had wanted me to say.

'We also got into a discussion about the arguments we were having. She did see that they were damaging our relationship and she did recognise that it was much better to discuss things when we were both more relaxed. She even added that she had been feeling a bit guilty about the moods she was in when I got home and acknowledged that when I had said I would consider what she had said it had helped her to calm down and wait. So it seems to be working. I guess the real need is for her to find something else to do. At least I no longer feel so criticised, I understand it is her basic frustration that's the problem, not me.'

Many things are obvious in this scenario, including the misunderstandings that are so often a part of relationships. It is all too easy to blame an apparent and immediate cause for a problem that actually has other and deeper causes. Obviously there are times when the criticism is merited, but often it is not, as in this case.

How many times have you said something in anger or on the spur of the moment, in response to a criticism? It is all too easy to do. This method, this phrase, gives you the breathing space to consider what has been said and respond to it in a way that you think is appropriate. **All you need is the presence of mind to use it and not to launch into your usual response, and this comes with time and practice**.

*Response Two: 'That is an interesting point of view,
now would you like to hear mine?'*

You would use this second response if you did not
agree with the speaker and the criticism they had
levelled at you. It accomplishes several things.

You have acknowledged the speaker, as you did in
Response One, and told them that you have heard what
they have said. You have also, subtly and without
aggression, let them know that your point of view is
not the same as theirs. However, you have not insisted
that they are wrong and so put their hackles up. Nor
have you attacked them by immediately throwing your
point of view at them which, in all probability, would
lead to an argument. You have simply let them know,
quietly, that you do have a point of view and that it is
different to theirs. Furthermore, you are offering them
the choice of hearing you or not and are giving the
initiative back to them.

Three results are possible. They will say 'yes'; they
will say 'no'; or they will continue with their comments.

a) If they say 'no' then you MUST walk away. Do not
continue with the conversation. If you do, you have lost
the advantage of this process. It may be frustrating, it
may be maddening, you may be longing to tell them
why they are wrong in their criticism, but resist the
temptation.

If they say 'no' and you either walk away or talk
about something else, they still know that you do not
agree with them and that you have not accepted what
they have said. They also know that you are both aware
that they have refused to listen to your point of view.
All of which leaves them at a disadvantage and enables
you to avoid feeling criticised and found wanting.

b) If they say 'yes', then you can give them your point of view. If they interrupt you, you can ask them to let you talk until you have had your say, since you both know that they agreed to listen to you and gave you permission to tell them what you think. By saying 'yes', they have also acknowledged that there is another possible point of view in addition to their own. By calling it 'my' point of view, you have refrained from trying, even by implication, to insist that it is 'the right' point of view, or that it should be their point of view. In this way you will probably be able to have a reasoned discussion about the situation for which they are criticising you.

c) If they refuse to answer your question at all but continue with their criticism, then you can keep coming back with the same response. In the end, whatever the outcome, you will both know that, in effect, their answer was 'no', with the implications we discussed above.

Jane used Response Two when her teenage son, Bob, complained that he had too little freedom and told her that she was mean and old-fashioned for not letting him go out with his friends in the evening. This normally led to her telling him that she was trying to bring him up on her own and doing the best she could to make ends meet as well, but that all he ever did was criticise her, no matter how hard she tried to give him a normal life, like that of his friends who had both parents.

The next time Bob complained, it was a Tuesday night and he still had homework to do but his friends were going to the cinema. Jane told Bob that he couldn't go, to which his response was:

'That's rotten, how come they can go and I never can. The homework's not that important, it's just that you're too mean, and you don't want me to have any fun.'

To which Jane said, being already prepared in her own mind to do this, 'That's an interesting point of view, now do you want to hear mine?'

'No,' was his immediate and very angry retort, so Jane turned and walked into the kitchen.

She said it was the hardest thing she had ever done. With all her being, she was longing to tell him that his homework was important, that she was working very hard to keep him at school so that he could go to university, that she wasn't mean, that she gave him all the spare money she could afford.

Jane said, 'At first he just stormed off. Then he came back, still angry, and asked again if he could go out and I gave him the same response. Again he stormed off, but I still managed not to say anything more. Then, eventually, he came back and said, 'Oh very well then, what do you want to say?'

After that Jane had been able to put the whole picture to him and, by doing the same thing several times in the ensuing weeks, she gradually sorted things out and felt that Bob understood her situation more and criticised her less. She also came to understand his point of view better and they reallocated some of their funds so that he could get the most enjoyment out of his share.

This way of handling criticism lets you, and the person criticising you, deal with the criticism itself. It often takes away the sting that implies the whole of you is being criticised and allows both people to focus on the specific detail and to see it from more than one point of view. In the end you can and may still agree to differ.

When you are feeling criticised and despondent it is important to separate the specific action or attribute for which you are feeling criticised from the whole of you. Parents often tell their children 'You are bad' when what they really mean is, 'I love you very much and think you are terrific but what you just did is bad.'

Donald used to feel a failure at school when his friends kept saying, 'Oh you're no good, we don't want you on the team'. When he learned to agree that he was no good at sports but that he was great in class and had other things to offer his friends, his life improved. His friends found it was no fun to criticise him for his lack of sporting ability when he agreed with them and they were keen and quick to keep in his good books by acknowledging how much he could and did help explain some of the classwork to them.

Non-Interactive Criticism

It is now time to consider how you handle the criticism that comes at you from a distance or in such a way that you have little or no chance of responding. You may get a telling-off from the boss. You may hear the criticism second-hand. A friend may tell you what someone else said. You may have no way of responding and you may feel hurt. Someone may criticise you and be totally unwilling to hear your point of view. The criticism may not even apply to you: someone might complain that 'nobody' treats them well, or the boss may make a comment about the way 'no one uses their initiative around here except me', and you may take it personally. Your feeling of being criticised may even be self-generated, based on your own self-criticism or on an assumed criticism.

One option is, of course, to ignore the criticism: hide it, bury it and try to keep feeling happy. Do you do this sometimes? Do you do it so effectively that it really does cause no pain? The problem with this method is that even buried pain hurts eventually and you do not learn from it either. In addition, other people are likely to find that communication with you is difficult and unsatisfactory. Think how you feel when somene ignores what you say.

> **The crux of the issue when dealing with criticism in this situation is this: if you take criticism personally, it is easy to get depressed; if you put it at arm's length, it is easy to get the benefits without the pain.**

In the exercise ahead, you will stop taking criticism as a personal attack on you. Instead you will practise putting it at arm's length. You will also put the you that is being criticised at a distance. You will learn to think about what is being said, to explore its implications and to discover whether or not you agree with the criticism. You will learn from the criticism and then, having resolved the issue to your satisfaction, you will be able to relax and let it go. All of this can be done without pain or depression, and will allow you to reap the maximum benefit from the criticism.

To describe the process here, we will use a real life example but I will put a brief description of each step in bold, at the beginning. You can do this process on your own once you have learned it or you can work with a friend and let them read the steps as they go though it with you. You can then swop roles and do the same with your friend. Not only is it helpful to share, it also helps you to learn and remember the process so that you can do it on your own whenever the need arises.

> James had come to see me because he was having problems with his boss. In his view his boss was always criticising him. Sometimes, as he agreed, the criticisms were valid; at other times he felt they weren't. He also complained that his boss never, ever, offered praise, even when James did do a good job. He wanted to know what to say to his boss to sort the situation out and how he could make his boss change. I suggested instead that he work on the way he handled the criticism.

Get into a resourceful and confident state

It is ironic but true that the more self-assurance and confidence you display, the less people criticise you. The more nervous, apprehensive and unsure your posture and your actions, the more likely you are to be criticised. This certainly turned out to be true in James's case.

A useful first step in learning to handle any adverse situation is to put yourself in the most positive and resourceful state you can. You want to start out strong, not weak. Athletes psyche themselves up before an event, not down. You do the same. Think of a time when you felt very successful and confident, possibly a time when you were being praised or receiving applause for something you had done of which you were proud, a time when you felt invincible. Get back to that feeling and keep it with you while you are doing this exercise. If you cannot think of such a time, recall someone who has appeared supremely confident, either in real life, or perhaps in a film. Get inside their skin and take on that feeling. Blend it with a situation of your own where you have felt good. This will help to give you the resources to deal with criticism.

Distance yourself from the situation

I asked James to do this and then to sit back, relax and, if he found it less distracting, to close his eyes. Then I explained the next steps:

'Imagine you are in a large space, watching a scene. First, be aware of a transparent glass screen in front of you. You might even like to put your hands out and feel it. Now, through this glass screen see yourself in the distance and see too the person who is criticising James, also in the distance. Can you do that? How does it feel to see James being criticised?'

'Not so bad. It's not so bad as when I imagine it happening to me, here, and can feel the emotions, but I still don't like it.'

'See what happens when you make him smaller. Does that make it more comfortable?'

'It's better, but I still don't like it.'

'OK, do this next step. See the James in the distance doing what you are doing now, being a watcher. Put a glass screen in front of him and have him watch a third James being criticised. How does that feel?'

'Much better. I can now watch someone watching someone being criticised. That's much easier. In fact it's quite interesting.'

'What's so interesting?'

'Well, somehow it makes a lot more sense now. The watching James can even understand some of the sense behind the criticism that the James in the scene is getting and yet sitting here I don't have to get involved in it at all.'

'Very good.'

When you do this on your own, you do need these three versions of yourself. The reason for doing it step by step is so that you can experience the difference between each remove. If there is only you watching yourself being criticised, you will probably want to jump in in defence of the other you.

At any stage while you are doing this exercise, if you begin to feel negative or unconfident, take time to stop and recreate the positive state you had in the beginning.

Discover the real meaning of the criticism

'James, take a look now at the watching James as he observes James through the second glass screen, being criticised by his boss. As you do this, look at the watching James as he tries to learn the meaning behind the criticism in the scene he is watching. Can you do that now?'

'Yes, I can, and it's funny, it looks quite different.'

'What do you mean?'

'I think it's because I don't feel any emotion, sitting here watching it all. The watching James can see that the boss is really cross with himself, he's cross with his own bosses but he can't complain to them, he wants an office that runs smoothly but he hasn't got enough staff, that's why he's always criticising the ones that he's got . . . But he's cross with James too, he's telling him his work is shoddy.'

At this point James began to look uncomfortable, so I told him to move the whole scene further into the distance and make it smaller again. Sometimes when you get really interested in what is happening you try to get closer to it to see more clearly. Since you can't actually get close to it you bring it closer to you and it gets larger. That does help you to see better but you get more emotionally involved and that is to be avoided. So keep it in the distance, and very small.

'What does he mean by "shoddy"?'

'I don't know.'

'So ask. Get the watching James, as an observer, to ask the boss what he means by shoddy.'

Doing it this way, rather than having the James in the actual scene with the boss ask the question, allows the boss to relate to a third person who is, presumably, unbiased and outside the situation. When James did this, he discovered that the boss didn't like the way his reports looked. This was the fault of the printer which was old, and because the work had to be rushed. When James asked further questions he learned that the boss also liked a different layout and this was something that James could change. The boss then said, in response to further questions from the second James, that he found James's manner disrespectful. So again more questions were in order, and James asked:

'What exactly do you mean by disrespectful?'

The boss, who was still not being challenged by the James in the scene, who was his subordinate, was able to answer the second James without emotion.

'He doesn't acknowledge me properly; he argues, and he doesn't do as I ask immediately.'

At this point it is helpful to acknowledge the boss, not make him feel belittled, so I told James to do this and to explore the matter further.

After James had agreed with the boss that when you had people working for you you had to have their respect, he asked the boss what he would like James to do to demonstrate that he respected him. He found that the boss thought James should jump to his every command, even if previous tasks were not completed, whereas James thought he should complete the tasks in the order he had been given them.

Now obviously here, at least to a certain extent, James is making up what he thinks the boss thinks, but this doesn't really matter. For one thing, the scenario that he makes up for the boss is one of several possible scenarios. It may well have been prompted by some subconscious trigger, such as unconsciously received feedback from the boss or some of James's own unconscious assumptions, which may give real insight into the situation. The thing that matters is that James has gone beyond the point of being the criticised victim to being the explorer, looking for different meanings in the situation. Later, when James is back at work and feeling a lot better about himself, he can actually ask the boss these questions in real life, and find out how the situation can be improved.

Determine your own evaluation of the situation

At this point you have, in effect, two images or films of the situation. You have the real life one of the time when you were criticised. You also have the one you have just made of yourself watching yourself and looking at and assessing the situation and getting feedback. It is time now to compare the two and to assess them. I asked James to do this.

> 'James, I would like you now to have the second you, the observer, look at the film of the real-life event as you recall it. Perhaps you could picture him in a screening room with two projectors and two screens. Have him look at the real-life situation as you recall it. Now have him run the film you have just created with the dialogue with the boss. Compare the two. Which is the more accurate? What do you think of what the boss said? Is it appropriate for the third James, in the film, to feel criticised? Are there changes he might choose to make to improve the relationship? What could he say to the boss that would help? Are there more questions that need to be asked? If so go back to that stage and ask them.'
>
> 'Mmmm . . .' James was thoughtful for a while. Then he said, 'You know, it's interesting. I can see that part of the trouble is that I resent the boss's attitude, and that's silly. I actually could be more helpful. I could explain that I am still busy on the previous task and I could ask him whether or not he wants me to switch. I guess because he is so irritable I actually want to get back at him and that's just making the situation worse. But it's not all my fault. The actual work I do is good, and if I write it

up the way he wants and if I explain about the printer, then maybe he'll grumble less. Anyway, I don't need to feel I'm inadequate, I'm actually quite good at what I do.'

Determine what you will do about the situation

'So what will you do, when you go back to work?'

James thought about this for a while and then decided he would ask to have a talk with the boss, perhaps after work or in a lunch hour. He would then explain the problems he had and ask how the boss would like him to change. After all, as he said, 'I just guessed at what was going on for the boss, maybe he actually thinks differently. But obviously I need to know what he thinks so we can clear the air. At least I can try. If it doesn't work, well, I've done my best.'

I warned James, before he left, about being clear about his goal. It would be no use if he went in feeling belligerent and badly done by, trying to justify himself. Provided his goal was to achieve a positive outcome for both of them he could feel confident of attaining it.

The next time I saw James, I was in for a surprise. He had talked with the boss. He'd agreed with the boss that things weren't going smoothly and he said that he'd like to find out more accurately what was wanted so he could contribute better. That, apparently, had taken the boss somewhat by surprise, but the upshot was that the boss really wanted someone he could talk to, a colleague he could rely on, someone who was articulate, who would offer suggestions, and who would stand up for himself. He had been goading James to try to prompt James to do this, but it had had the opposite effect of pushing James down. After they had talked, they were able to work out a different arrangement, one in which they could both feel happier.

'It was weird,' said James. 'Although the content I had guessed at when working with you was all wrong, the process worked. Because I had learned the process I was able to talk to him better and to ask the questions: that really was the key – finding out what he really thought and wanted.'

It will not always work as it did with James. You may decide you disagree with the criticism. You may decide that the criticism was valid and that you will apologise to the criticiser. You may want to provide more information to the criticiser so that they can better understand your actions. You may need to let them know that you hadn't realised what was happening for them, and that now you know more, you can and will behave differently.

Fred told me that his wife was always criticising him for giving her no respect and for not crediting her with any brains. This was particularly so whenever any new piece of equipment came into the house and he went to great pains to set it up for her. When they talked it through, they found that she felt belittled when he assumed she couldn't do it for herself, whereas he thought he was helping her.

'I told her I hadn't realised that my taking overmade her feel bad. Now I know that, I will leave it to her. In fact I did that last week when we got a new computer game for the children and she got a great kick out of learning it by herself. In the end we had a ball playing with it together – whereas in the old way she would have got cross with me during the time I tried to explain it to her.'

Practise what you are going to do

These changes won't come about automatically. It will be easy for James, or for you, to slip back into the old behaviour pattern. So it is important that you practise. While you are alone practise the way you want to behave in the future. Do this before you go back into the situation so that, when the time comes, it is easier to stick to the new way. Rehearse what you want to say, over and over, in your mind, so you can follow that 'memory' when the situation comes up in real life.

To recap on the process:

(a) Create a state of feeling successful and good about yourself.

(b) Put the situation at a distance: watch yourself watching yourself being criticised.

(c) Still at a distance, watch yourself assessing what the criticism means.

(d) Decide whether you think the criticism is valid or not.

(e) Determine what you are going to do in response to the criticism as you have now assessed it.

(f) Practise this future behaviour so that it becomes easier and more automatic and you avoid falling back into the old pattern.

Offering Constructive and Painless Criticism

Criticism has its uses. Constructive criticism can provide you with lessons that will be to your benefit. You can also offer help to your friends by offering constructive criticism. The important thing is to find a painless way of doing it, and here is one suggestion.

The Sandwich Approach

a) Praise them, tell them something positive about what they did.

b) Offer the positive suggestion as to how they could have done better.

c) Finish with an overall positive comment praising what they did.

As in any sandwich, all three compoments are essential. Sandwich the criticism within two slices of praise. Here are some examples:

Instead of 'I really could have done without your pseudo-cheerful comments when I was upset', try: 'It was really thoughtful of you to try to cheer me up, however I would actually rather you gave me my own space to sort things out. But I know this means you care and I value that, thank you.'

Instead of, 'No, Johnny, that's bad, digging up Mummy's roses', try: 'Johnny, I appreciate your help in the garden, it's terrific. How about digging in your own garden over there, not in Mummy's rose-bed. It's wonderful that you're such a good little gardener.'

If a colleague and you disagree over the way things should be done, instead of criticising them outright you could say: 'You're a great help at what you do and I really like some of your ideas, however in this situation

I think so-and-so. Overall though I think we work well together and I learn a lot from you.'

Practise sandwich criticism with a friend to get the experience of how it feels both to give criticism this way and to receive it. Perhaps you can teach it to people who often criticise you. If nothing else, if they refuse to use it and insist on offering destructive criticism, both you and they will know, at least on some level, that you each recognise what they are doing.

> **When dealing with or giving criticism, be clear about your goal. A lot depends on what you want to achieve. If your goal is to make the other person wrong in your attempt to be right, you won't want to adopt the above strategies. If your goal is to achieve a positive and constructive outcome you are likely to see the value of the exercises in this chapter.**

Chapter Fifteen

Reactive Depression: Keeping It In Its Place

There are time when depression has an identifiable cause; at other times depression is a mood that simply settles over you. In this chapter we are going to be dealing with depression that results from grief over a particular experience or situation.

Whether you commonly feel depressed, or are normally a cheerful person not subject to bouts of depression, you may feel depressed, upset or griefstricken because you have lost someone you love, or something has occurred to cause you pain, or because you have done something you deeply regret. There are ways to deal with this. The processes described in this chapter depend on the fact that there is a specific identifiable event which has led to your present state of mind.

It is important that you understand, from the outset, that when someone you love dies or leaves you, you are grieving for yourself, not for them. You are grieving for *your* loss, for the pain *you* are experiencing, for the void created in *your* life by the absence of the other person. Once you take that step you can recognise that the experience you are going through is your own experience and is of your own creating. Certainly your pain is in response to their absence from your life but it is still your response, your experience, and as such you are creating it. It is not being created by the person you have lost. In turn, this means that you are capable of changing your mood, of creating a new and alternative experience. Let's see what can be done to alleviate the pain, and to do this we will use Barbara's experience.

Barbara came to see me because of her grief over her mother's death. Obviously she and her mother had been very close and the loss of her mother had greatly affected her. Barbara was in her forties, married and with two children in their early teens. Her home life was happy and without undue stress or worry. Once her husband had gone to work and the children had gone to school, it had been Barbara's practice to talk on the phone with her mother. She did this every day, often several times, and on most days she either visited her mother or went out shopping with her.

Two years earlier her mother had died and Barbara had been distraught and depressed ever since.

'My life's over,' she said, 'I haven't been happy since mother's death and I don't see how I can ever be happy again. Without her nothing seems to matter any more.'

'What about your husband, do you get on well, is it a good marriage?'

'Yes it is, and we do get on well enough, but he doesn't understand me like mother did. We don't share so much; he has his own problems.'

'What about your children?'

'Well, I love them of course. But they have their own interests too and they're becoming more and more independent.'

Clearly the relationship with her mother had been the one in which she felt most important, most precious and most protected, and now, without it, she was bereft. Given the other good things in her life, her grief may have seemed disproportionate, but to her it was an enormous loss and that was what we had to work on.

I asked Barbara what she had thought about her mother in the two years since her death. I was interested to find that she didn't mention all the good times they had had, the talks they had shared or the times they'd spent shopping together. Instead she said:

'All I can think about is the pain she went through. I keep seeing her lying in that hospital bed, looking wretched and in such obvious distress, her face grey, her smile gone. Being with her was a misery because she was in such trouble and she was focused on herself all the time, we had none of the sharing we used to. Yet it was almost worse being away from her because I knew we had so little time left.'

Often with people who experience extreme grief and loss it is the bad times they are remembering and the trauma of the ending of the situation or relationship on which they focus, rather than on the good times. In this way they seem to prolong their period of grief. Many people who come to terms with their loss have different memories: either by a conscious decision or by an unconscious process, they choose to remember the good times they had and are often heard to remark, 'It's as if they are still here with me, I feel them all round me.' In other words they still have the experience they used to have when the person was with them. In this way, remembering them brings back happy times and not the pain of the ending.

'What are you seeing now?' I asked, as Barbara gazed over to her left and down towards the floor.

'Can you see her there . . . ?' and I pointed to the place she'd focused on.

'That's right, just where you're pointing. How did you know?'

I avoided the question and said instead, 'Just what are you seeing? Describe it for me in detail. Give me the full details, such as whether you are seeing her in black and white, whether what you are seeing is moving or still, whether or not it has a frame round it or is panoramic. Tell me all about it.'

At first Barbara was vague, not really knowing how to look at what she was seeing as opposed to focusing on the pain she felt when her mind was on her mother. But then she got the hang of it.

'I can see her lying in bed. It's not really still, but it's not moving either, more like a series of snapshots, in black and white. And yes, each one is in an undefined frame, like those old photos you see of great-grandparents, where the edges sort of fade away.'

'Can you reach them, these old-fashioned photos?'

'No, they're too far away. It's like I've lost touch, I can't reach out to her or connect with her any

more. I'm sort of helpless, just as I was at the time
because there was nothing I could do to help, to
make the pain less, and there was nothing I could
do to bring back the closeness, to have her recognise me. I was so afraid of losing her and she
couldn't help me. I know it was selfish, but I
needed her to help me and to tell me that things
would be all right and that she'd get better and still
be there, but she was lost in herself.'

'Is there anything else?'

'Yes, there was, it was the awful smell, part
antiseptics and the usual hospital smell, part the
smell almost of dying, of rotting flesh, ugh, it was
revolting.'

'Can you smell it now?'

'No, but it's funny, it's almost as if I can see the
smell as I look at those grey pictures of her.'

The mind can indeed play strange tricks, I
thought, but I said, 'OK, that's great, you're doing
fine. Now leave that image where it is down there,'
and I pointed to where she was looking.

'The next thing I'd like you to do, if you will, is
to think of someone else whom you have loved,
someone who was close to you, but who you have
now lost.'

Her response was immediate. 'I've never loved
anyone as much as mother, and I don't really think
I've ever lost anyone either, only some friends who
have sort of drifted away as our lives have changed,
but they didn't really cause any pain.'

'What about things you like, what about pets?'

'Oh, that's easy, there was Bimbo.'

'Bimbo?'

'Yes. Bimbo was a poodle, he was glorious, such

a ball of cuddly fun, we all loved him. We got him when the children were small. He'd try to come with us wherever we went and if we had to leave him behind he'd give us this delirious welcome when we got back, leaping all over us and rushing round the house in his excitement. He was great.'

'What happened?'

'He was run over by a delivery van. We took him to the vet and tried to keep him alive. But he was obviously in pain and the vet said his back had been seriously damaged and that we should put him down. We didn't though. We told him to do what he could to save Bimbo. We were just too upset to think of losing him. We decided that even if he was crippled we'd do all we could to keep him alive. But the next morning when we phoned the vet said Bimbo had died in the night. He thought it was internal bleeding.'

'How do you feel when you think about Bimbo?'

I didn't really need to ask for she was smiling as she recalled the fun she'd had with the dog, and this was exactly what I wanted.

'I feel fine,' she said. 'I think we've all got over the loss, but we often talk about him and the things he used to do.'

'How would you like to feel the same way about your mother, when you recall her presence in your life, as you do now about Bimbo?'

Barbara took a while to think about this but finally decided that if she could remember her mother in the same positive and happy way in which she currently remembered Bimbo then she would be a lot happier.

'But what if the change distresses me more? It

might make me feel false, make me feel I'm not being true to her memory.'

'I don't think it will, but you can decide for yourself. If you don't like the change then we can put things back as they were, in fact you'll probably do it automatically for yourself if you don't like the result we get.'

She looked happier at this and nodded for me to go ahead.

'Excellent. So now what I want you to do is this. Think about Bimbo. Where do you see him?'

'Oh, that's easy. It's almost as if I can still feel him, rushing around me, in and out of the rooms, up and down the steps.'

As she said this her eyes were moving, as if following his excited leaping. So I asked her some more questions, just as I had when asking about her mother, such as if she was seeing him in black and white or colour, and to give me other details.

'Oh colour, definitely. And moving of course. It's all around me and . . . no . . . there's no frame to it. Each time I think of him it's as if he's still here, almost as if I can reach out and try to catch him the way we used to when he got so excited.'

It was obvious that although she'd been sad to lose Bimbo, the memory held more pleasure than pain.

Just to be sure that I had her permission to go ahead, I checked again and asked, 'How would it be if you could feel that way whenever you think of your mother? Would that be acceptble?'

Barbara agreed that it would, in fact she said that it would be wonderful. So we proceeded to the next step.

'Now what I want you to do is to think of some of the good times you had with your mother. But think of her as she was when you were together and try to make it just like your memory of Bimbo. Have your mother with you, moving around, doing things with you. Make sure it's in colour, not black and white. Is there a smell?'

She nodded, 'Yes, the perfume she always wore; it brings her presence back so vividly. It lingered on her clothes and I have kept many of them for that reason.'

'Can you smell that smell now?'

'Yes.'

'Have you got her with you? Are you remembering her just the way you remember Bimbo, around you, so she's close?'

'Yes.'

'Good . . . How do you feel, now, about your mother?'

'Wow,' she said. 'That's amazing. For the first time I can think of her without crying.'

'Do you still miss her?'

'Yes I do, but it's also almost as if she is here with me, as if I can still feel the good times we had.'

Often, when you are feeling depressed over something or someone you have lost, the situation is made worse because you are recalling the bad times you had with that person, not the good times. This not only adds to your depression, but it diminishes the experiences you shared together and the relationship you had. This in itself is often depressing and adds to the depression of the loss. It's almost as if you're afraid to remember the good times in case that increases the pain of loss and so increases the grief. This logic rarely works.

> **By focusing on the good times you had, you can keep with you some of the joy you experienced together. This can be true of friends, lovers or relatives; it can also be true of lost opportunities and skills.**

When Barbara thought of Bimbo she smiled and obviously re-experienced some of the joy she had felt with him, even though she still missed him. We had now got her to this point with her mother.

However, it seemed to me that there was more work to do. She did have a loving husband and two children. I wanted to see whether or not we could improve these relationships. Or rather, if we could enable her to get out of these relationships the pleasures she enjoyed in her relationship with her mother.

When I put this to her she insisted it was impossible:

'Mother made me feel good. I felt she approved of me, no matter what I did, and that she would always love me. Whereas I know my husband thinks I'm a bit stupid. He can't understand why I've been depressed over mother's death for so long. He often criticises me.'

I asked her if she would be willing to try anyway, in spite of her present feelings, and she agreed to this. So I took her through the next step, and for this I had her close her eyes, although this isn't always necessary.

'What I want you to do now is to bring to mind the very best times you had with your mother. Good. And now become aware of everything you value about this relationship with your mother. Do you value her approval, the shared jokes, getting advice that agrees with what you want to do, the feeling you can trust her, the feeling that she is on your side? Become clear on these and on all the other details of the things you valued in that relationship. And as you do so you might like to put each valued part of the relationship in a separate container. Can you do that?'

'Yes,' she said, 'I can. They're each in a transparent jar with a lid, like those plastic jars you get bath salts and things in.'

'Good. Now you are ready for the next step. I want you to think about your home, your marriage, your children, your garden, everything to do with your present family. Can you do that now?'

'Yes.'

'Good, excellent. Now I want you to take each of those things you valued in your relationship with your mother and to think about the different ways in which you receive those same things from your own family. And, as you do this, toss the contents of the jars into the images of your home and family. You might like to let the lids come off the jars so the contents can spill into your present life and into the future. Can you see that happening now? Good. As you do this become aware of all the ways in which you have in fact, without noticing it, been receiving those values from your family in the past.'

When Barbara had completed this exercise, and

was ready, she was asked to bring her attention back into the room and to open her eyes. I asked her how she felt.

'You know, it's funny. I suddenly began to see all the ways I do get things I value from my family. I mean, even though Ian does criticise me, I could suddenly see the times when he has approved of me. And I remembered the time I had an argument with the neighbour and he came and stood up for me. And the kids, they often think I'm right, just because I am their mother, and they assume I'm more clever than I really am. I used to believe it was just because they wanted to think they could depend on me, but this time I felt a bit like the way I used to with mother – she always used to think I was bright. I guess when mother was alive I just didn't notice the way my children and Ian are.'

I asked her again how she felt about her mother. The smile on her face was all I needed. It started small and increased in size, accompanied by a look of growing surprise.

'Gosh, that's marvellous,' she said. 'The moment you said that, I started to think of some of the good things we had done together.'

'No black and white pictures in the distance, where you can't reach her?'

'No, it's as if she's right here with me.'

Soon after that she left. Sometimes it really can happen this fast but it can also take longer. I knew that Barbara would still have times of sadness and loneliness, times when she missed her mother. But I was also pretty confident that the deep grieving and depression were largely things of the past.

A couple of weeks later her husband phoned up to express his pleasure at the changes:

'You know, I used to think she was still her mother's girl, as if she was never really part of this family. Now it's suddenly as if we have all of her here, her attention is focused on us. And she seems to have got over that terrible grief.'

This process worked for Barbara. It can also work for you. You can either do it for yourself or have someone help you and guide you through it. Keep in mind that you must find out how you think about the thing over which you are grieving. Then find out how you think about another similar loss that causes you much less or even no pain, and put the original loss into this other context. Then find out what it is you valued in the thing you have lost and scatter those treasures into your present or future situation.

The process applies not only to the death or loss of someone you have loved. It can apply to a variety of other situations as the following example will show.

Kerry was a young man, in his twenties, and a keen soccer player. He practised with his club every Wednesday night, played with them every weekend and spent social time with them on Sundays. They weren't professionals – he had his regular job – but he loved his soccer and it was a major part of his life, particularly his social life.

Then suddenly, and seemingly out of the blue, he got gout. His big toes caused him pain. Medication from the doctor helped a bit, though not totally, and every time he kicked a ball, the pain returned with full force. The club gave him some time off but eventually they decided that they'd have to put another player permanently in his place. This so angered Kerry that he blew up at the coach, abused him and accused him of betrayal, and then he got into a fight. 'That's it,' the coach told him, 'even if your bloody toe does get better, you're not coming back into this team, not so long as I'm coach.'

With a bit of help with his diet and other treatments from us, Kerry's toe did improve but the coach, when approached by one of the players who felt a bit sorry for Kerry, was adamant: no one who had abused and punched him was getting back into his team.

Kerry grieved his loss. He was also angry with himself for his actions and this kept eating into him, he said, and causing nearly as much pain as the loss of his position on the team. He also grieved for the loss of the social life that went with it and the camaraderie of his friends in the club.

'Sure,' he said, 'we still meet up occasionally, but it's not the same if you're not part of the team any longer. And the worst of it is that it's really all my fault. I keep kicking myself for all the things I said to the coach, for calling him a rotten judge of players and a stuffed shirt for not being willing to juggle things till I could get better and so on. I'm particularly sorry I knocked him down in front of half the team. I know he'll never forgive me for that. And somehow that's almost the worst of it – knowing I only have myself to blame.'

I followed the same process with Kerry as I had done with Barbara. Initially he found that when he thought of the team and the position that he'd lost, the images he had of it were situated behind him. Then he thought a bit more and said:

'That's funny, when I think of myself in the team that's behind me, it's in colour and it's full of action. But when I think of the team now, without me, I can see it moving off in front of me and to my right and as I watch it is getting smaller and smaller as it gets further and further away. I have this awful sense of loss as it disappears into the distance without me, leaving me behind.'

My next question almost didn't need to be asked.

'What do you see, then, when you look into the future, your future, and where is that?'

'I'm looking straight ahead, and it's barren, it's like a desert, I can't really see anything there. I just feel alone and abandoned without being part of the team and the club.'

I asked him to think of another, similar situation, when he'd been part of a group and then lost it, but about which he still had good memories. He thought for a while and then said, 'I guess that was when we moved house, when I was a kid. I hated the thought of losing my friends but Dad's business meant we had to move. I lost touch with most of my friends and had to go to a new school, I hated the thought of that.'

'And how do you feel about it now?'

'Oh, it soon wasn't any bother. The new school was great and I made other friends. Mind you, I found I was able to keep in touch with some of my old friends, at least in the holidays, because we hadn't moved all that far away. And it's funny, you know, I actually found some of the old friends weren't really that important, not in themselves; it was being part of a gang that had been important.'

When I asked him to tell me where and how he experienced the memory of his old school group he said, 'They're inside me really, I sort of feel them as being still a part of me. It's like I know other people will like me now and in the future because they did in the past. It's sort of reassuring that I can be a part of a group and get on well with them.'

Clearly his memory of the group he had lost, but was no longer grieving over, was a feeling, an experience, rather than a visual picture which is how he recalled the football club. So I asked him to remember the football club and his friends there in the same way as he did his old school group, as a feeling and as something inside and part of himself.

'Can you do that now?'

'Yes,' he said, 'I can. I just have to go back to a time when I was part of the team and it's the same.'

'OK, now do that strongly, really feel the team as a part of you. Now, while still holding on to that good feeling, look at the pictures you had of the team without you. What is happening?'

'Oh, that's odd, it's changing.'

'What's happening?'

'Well, they're sort of stopping, some of them are turning to wave at me, and they've changed direction. It's as if they are now moving ahead of me parallel to the path I'm taking. I can even see some of them joining up with me from time to time. Perhaps I haven't lost them after all.'

It was tempting to stop there, allowing him to see that, although he might no longer be one of the players, he could still be friends with some of the men. But I wanted more than that for him, so I asked him to determine the benefits he had got from the team.

He said it was the camaraderie, the knowledge that whenever he wanted to he could go down to the club house and be part of a group of friends. Moreover, as a player he was an important part of the group and others looked up to him and recognised that in him.

I then asked Kerry to wrap up each of these benefits he valued – the camaraderie, the belonging and the recognition – and to throw them forward into the future. Not surprisingly, he wrapped them up into balls and then threw them along the route into the future that he could see in front of him. I asked him if he could get a sense of how they could become realities in the months and years to come.

'I can. Goodness, it's as if different men are suddenly appearing from either side, like roads joining a motorway, and heading for the road I'm on. I suddenly get the feeling that I'm going to have lots of other friends in the future and that things are going to start happening. I know I will still see the old friends a bit but I no longer have that sense of being alone and lost.'

After a bit more talk he left. Some years later I ran into him in a local council meeting where, even to me as a guest, it was clear that he was the centre of the group of decision makers and that he was greatly respected. This was confirmed when he broke away a bit later and we had a brief chat. He now had the responsibility for sports venues in the area and agreed that he once again had the sort of social life he enjoyed.

He also added an important rider. He said that not only had the work we had done together helped him through the grief and loss he was feeling at that time but that what we had done had had two further beneficial effects. First, he said, he had realised that it was, and always would be, possible to open new doors. Knowing this, when he had subsequently felt some loss in his life to be irreparable, he had been able to recall that he had overcome a previous loss and that other things had turned up then and would do so again. This knowledge, he felt, had been important. But almost more important to him had been the tool, the method, which we had used to overcome his grief. He had been able to remember the method and to use it on himself at other times to overcome other upsets and losses.

Just as Kerry adopted this method, so too can you. You can use it for loss or grief of any sort. You have just read examples involving death, which is outside the person's control, and a lost opportunity, which was brought about, in part, by the person's own actions. You can employ this same method for many other things. You can make use of it for minor griefs and losses such as the loss of an object, or the loss of a friendship. You can apply it within situations of your own creation or created by other people. You can also use it with things you never had, such as lost opportunities.

  The examples of the beneficial practice of this method are numerous. One woman told me she used it for the sadness she felt at the loss of her youth. Instead of thinking of this as something behind her and out of reach, she was able to bring back many of the feelings of being young. As a result she was able to take on a younger demeanour and a greater sense of a positive future being in front of her again. All of which, not surprisingly, had a positive effect on the future that unfolded. Another woman used it in relation to a miscarriage; another to the loss of her job; and a young boy used it in relation to failed exams and his loss of self-esteem.

One woman married on the rebound and then regretted it when her first love came back into her life. Loyalty made her stay with her husband but she also grieved for the lost opportunity. By employing this method she was able to use the positive experience of the first relationship to enhance her marriage rather than to harm it.

A man had planned to go into business for himself. As the years went by he kept delaying the move until suddenly he found it was too late. After a year spent bitterly berating himself for the lost opportunity, he came in and we went through this process. He was able to apply it to his lost opportunity and even to enhance his last few years, prior to retirement. His wife was most relieved for she had seen him getting more and more bitter and difficult to live with.

You may have had a childhood in which there was abuse, alcoholism, poverty, lack of opportunity. You could adopt this method for the loss of a happy childhood. You could use it if you regret not having children of your own.

The uses of this method are endless. If you feel like being cautious at the start try it on small griefs. Practise it with a friend first, but you will soon be able to do it on your own.

Dealing With Grief Using Your Memory Line

There is another way of dealing with grief and that involves using your memory line (as described in Chapter 12). Think of that line now and float up above it. Turn and float back into the past until you are over the event which grieves you. Then float just a bit further back, until you are over a time shortly before the painful event. Turn and face the future. Then look down and forward to the event and ask yourself, 'Where is the grief now?' You will almost certainly, provided you are truly above and before the event, be unable to feel the emotion associated with it. If there is still some emotion, then float up higher and go a little further back in time.

Once you are able to look forward and down at the event, without experiencing the emotion, float back to the present. You may be surprised to find how good you feel.

Using Questions to Resolve Grief

Another way of helping yourself to resolve grief is to ask yourself questions. Useful questions to ask in grief include:

   (a) 'Why do I feel grief?'
   (b) 'What is the specific loss?'
   (c) 'What does that mean to me?'
   (d) 'What assumptions am I making?'

For instance, one patient complained of being depressed and of experiencing grief but it turned out that the grief was not so much due to the loss of the girlfriend *per se* but resulted from his basic assumption that he would always be alone in the future. His answers to the above questions were (a) 'I'm alone and lonely and so I'm depressed'. (b) 'My girlfriend has left me.' (c) 'It means she doesn't want me.' (d) 'I'm assuming that no one else will want me for long either, so I'm always going to be alone.'

Once you have isolated the underlying cause of your depression you can then deal with this, which is often a lot easier than trying to change the situation over which you are grieving.

Chapter Sixteen

Shame And Guilt: How To Use Them And Then Release Them

Shame and guilt can be devastating emotions and can cause all sorts of problems as well as leading to depression. You may even be feeling guilty over the fact that you are depressed, perhaps thinking that you shouldn't be depressed because there are others so much worse off than you. Sometimes shame and guilt are appropriate, sometimes they are not. Over the years I have been amazed at some of the things over which people can feel shame. Some people's lives are made wretched by the shame they feel over seemingly insignificant events or situations. Other people appear to be able to do the most outrageous things, harmful to others, against all conventions of society, and yet feel no shame at all.

How does shame come about? In general, without attempting to cover every possibility, it occurs in one of four major ways.

a) Direct shame regarding your own self and your actions

'I'm ashamed of having been or done (or not having been or done) . . .'

When you have done something wrong, either by your standards or by those of the society within which you live, shame and regret are appropriate up to a point. Shame and guilt can serve a useful purpose. Ideally you will learn more about your own standards from these emotions and be able to express your regret for whatever it was you did. Ideally too, you will learn from the experience in such a way that you can make moves to prevent the situation arising in the future. If the shame is for yourself you can make changes, if it is due to your association with others of whom you feel ashamed, again you can make the appropriate changes, whatever they may be.

In this way shame and guilt can act as useful barometers, as signposts in learning and development as the individual goes through life. They can be a part of the developing of character and the establishing of values.

The real problem arises if you continue on the path of which you are ashamed or if you continue to feel shame and guilt long after the initial stimulus has passed. For some people feeling shame and guilt is used as a form of self-flagellation. One client was ashamed of where she lived and worked but insisted she should stay there, and that it was all she deserved. Shame and guilt can also be used instead of or in place of correction, as in the case of the drunken husband who goes on beating his wife and expecting her understanding because he expresses his shame when he is sober.

It is important here to distinguish between guilt that is appropriate and that which is not. However, even appropriate guilt is a pretty useless and destructive emotion unless you channel it into something beneficial. It is all very well to feel guilty if you have cheated someone, but it does your victim little good and creates problems for you that you then pass on to others in a variety of ways. If you truly have cause to feel guilty then pay your dues, make amends, learn the lessons you can, resolve to put them into practice in future and then put the situation behind you. If you don't you will feel depressed, which will do you no good and will also have a negative rather than a beneficial effect on other people's lives.

Having said that, it is still true to say that much of the guilt that leads to depression is inappropriate guilt. Let's find out what I mean by that.

> Robert said that he had been feeling depressed for months, even years. He and Wendy had been married for three years before they had finally agreed the whole thing had been a mistake. Wendy had been miserable out on the farm, although before the marriage she had been certain she would enjoy it. She blamed the divorce on the farm's isolation and on Robert's unwillingness to leave it whenever social events occurred. Since the divorce Robert had felt depressed and lonely, missing Wendy, sure also that the whole thing had been his fault. He knew she wasn't happy either and he was guilt-ridden, blaming himself and insisting there must have been things he could have done to make the marriage work. This form of guilt at best is inappropriate and at worst destructive.
>
> Just as some people seem to choose to be victims to get sympathy, so do others seem to create guilt as a way of demanding other people's attention and exoneration. I asked Robert what he had done about the way he felt.

'I've discussed it with lots of people,' was his response. 'They all say I'm not to blame. I did my best, Wendy just wasn't suited to country life, the isolation and the lack of company.'

I wondered where he'd been to have all these people to talk to, but it soon became obvious that he'd spent a lot of time phoning his friends and discussing his situation at length. This may have helped reduce his feeling of loneliness, though he said it hadn't, but it did nothing to resolve the depression.

When Robert and I had finished working together he was able to leave behind his guilt and his hankering after Wendy. He was still unhappy for a while but was able to feel more positive when he understood his situation and Wendy's role in it and started to look for a partner who did enjoy country life.

When people feel ashamed they also, often, feel ashamed of feeling ashamed. Not only have they done something bad, but they have done it in spite of recognising that it is bad and so the pain goes deeper. For some people shame covers something specific, for others it is more total, they are simply ashamed of being themselves. This latter problem often starts in very early childhood. Many mistakes in childhood are made unwittingly. You do something, such as taking a toy from a sibling or friend, hitting the cat, smearing tomato paste on the chair, or refusing to come when called, simply as part of your exploration of this new world you are in. A harassed mother is apt to say, 'No, don't do that, you're a bad boy/girl.' Unfortunately distinction is rarely made between the person and the specific act.

'You are bad' is the usual paraphrase and your sense of shame may move without break from the deed to the whole of you. To reduce your sense of shame you may need to build up your sense of self-worth and practise separating the deed from your self.

b) Direct shame regarding someone else's action

'I'm ashamed that my friend/relative/colleague did (or didn't) do . . .'

It is hardly appropriate to take responsibility for someone else's actions. That would mean you were taking away their sovereignty, their individuality, depriving them of self-responsibility and authority and making or endeavouring to make them dependent on you. If you don't want to be associated with someone then move away. Otherwise admit that they are responsible for themselves.

c) Indirect shame based on assumption of another person's assessment of you

'I'm ashamed that other people think I'm . . . poor/ uneducated/stupid/mean . . .'

Much shame comes from what you assume people think. That is mind reading, and mind reading is rarely successful. Furthermore, since you could have assumed they were thinking any one of a variety of thoughts, what you actually assumed they were thinking is more a reflection of your thoughts than of theirs.

d) Indirect shame based on your assumption of another person's assessment of your friend/relative/ colleague

'I'm ashamed of what other people think of my friend/ relative/colleague . . .'

Again, shame arises here from second guessing other people's thoughts. Remember: if you cannot know *for sure* what someone else is thinking, it is wise and beneficial to accept the *most useful* belief.

If you frequently feel ashamed of what you have done, it probably means you have continued to act against either your own standards or the standards of others. You might then want to look at your mission statement and your values. (Both of these are topics covered in Part Three.) It is possible that either you are not living up to them or that you have outgrown them and should consider changing them. For instance, an aim as a child may have been to 'be obedient'. If you are still trying to follow this as an adult and feel ashameed when you act independently, it may well be time to change this value to one more appropriate to an adult.

You may find that you have two or more beliefs in conflict and want to be more specific about the value of each. Let's say your values included 'always tell the truth' and 'don't hurt people'. You would be in conflict with yourself if telling the truth meant hurting someone. Whichever course of action you adopted you would feel shame since you would have violated one of your beliefs. Once you recognise this conflict and prioritise the values you can follow whichever is the more important to you and avoid the assumption of shame in violating the lesser one.

Are your values your own? Perhaps you are trying to live by someone else's standards rather than by your own. If so, and if you act instinctively and naturally, you may find yourself constantly acting out of line with the values you are trying to adopt. Set your own standards and live by them, only then can you be true to yourself. The other person's standards may be fine for them but you definitely need your own.

Or perhaps your values are your own but you are spending time with people whose standards are totally different and feel ashamed, either on their behalf or of yourself, when with them. If you feel honesty is important and you are working in an office where winning is more important than honesty, you may want to think about moving. If your friends swear and you think that is wrong, you may experience shame and embarrassment when your family meets them. Perhaps it is time to change your friends or reassess your values.

In other words shame can be the result of self-assessment or assessment from other people and it can reflect on or relate to you directly, or on those with whom you feel associated in some way.

Methods For Dealing With Shame and Guilt In Unresolved Situations

If you feel you have done something wrong and this is depressing you, then do all you can to put the matter right, to resolve the situation. If you regret something you have said or done then make the appropriate apology, but be careful, make sure that you are making the apology for the right reasons.

For instance, if you have been rude or unkind and the other person knows it, then go ahead and express your regret. If you have said something unkind about them to a third person, then do what you can to correct that with the third person. If you think your remarks will get back to the first person and you feel sorry for what you have said and want to reduce their pain, then apologise. But if you are apologising only to save your own hide, just in case they find out, then you have some deeper thinking to do. Similarly, if you have done something of which they are unaware and you are about to confess all only to ease your own guilt, causing them pain in the process, you might want to rethink that course of action. Unfaithful wives or husbands may soothe their own guilty consciences by making a full confession to an unsuspecting spouse, yet cause additional pain if they do so. If you are about to let a friend down, telling them so in advance and asking for their forgiveness is probably motivated by a desire for your own peace of mind rather than a wish to correct a situation of which you may feel ashamed.

If you can make reparations for whatever is causing you to feel shame, then do so. Notice that by recognising that something you have done is in some way shame-worthy, you have at least demonstrated your awareness of what you believe to be right and wrong in this situation. Do all that you can to correct the situation. Learn all you can from it. Resolve to use this knowledge in the future to avoid a repetition. Then be willing to let the matter rest.

Often, when you feel you have done something wrong, either by commission or omission, you will be able to put the matter right relatively easily, at least logistically if not emotionally. You may even be surprised at some of the outcomes. Communication should be simple, a mere matter of expressing yourself to the other person or people. So often, however, it is an area fraught with pitfalls and pain as poor communication is followed by misinterpretation and false assumptions.

You may have said something you regret. In which case consider what you can say to put things to rights. You may not be able to take back your words or deeds but you can apologise. You can do whatever you can, or whatever is appropriate, to explain the situation and try to correct it.

Betina told me she had been out with a girlfriend, Marianne, one evening and had had several drinks in the pub when two men had come over to their table and started talking to them. The men had then suggested the four of them go off to a strip joint and 'have a good time' together. Marianne had said a definite 'No' and looked critical when Betina elected to go with them on her own anyway. Betina had said yes because she wanted company, male company, and because there was no man in her life at the time, but afterwards she had felt ashamed, knowing that this was not something she would normally have done.

Ever since that evening she had felt uncomfortable around Marianne, as if she had cheapened herself. I suggested she speak to Marianne about the situation, and explain to her that the real trigger for her behaviour had been the loss of her boyfriend, and that she was feeling particularly down and 'what the hell' at the time, but Betina said no, that was too uncomfortable. Emotionally it would be difficult, but the alternative, the loss of Marianne's company and friendship, was also painful.

Eventually, after further discussion, Betina decided to write Marianne a note. In this she explained the situation and asked if they could still be friends. To her surprise Betina found that her friend had had an altogether different experience.

'After she got my note,' said Betina, 'she came round to see me and I could hardly believe it. *She* was feeling ashamed of the way she had let me down. She said that she had known I was feeling low because Bob had left, and that she had felt that she should have come with me when I needed her support. In the end, the good talk we had about the way we both felt has brought us even closer together. Now that I know she doesn't think the less of me for the situation I can feel comfortable and we are good friends again.'

In this case Betina's feeling of shame was self-induced, then transferred, in her mind, to another person and reflected back to her. It was also induced by her mind reading, by the assumption that her friend thought the less of her. Once full communication was established the whole situation could be defused to the benefit of both of them. Both of them had been feeling ashamed, and both were depressed. So often feelings of shame are brought about by what you think other people think, yet other people rarely think what you think they think.

If you do not feel you can talk to the person most concerned with the situation about which you feel shame, then consider writing them a letter. Write and explain the frame of mind you were in at the time, why you did what you did, how you felt about it then and how you feel about it now. When you do this be very clear about your intentions: be sure you do not use it as a chance to blame the other person and to justify your own actions, thus compounding the problem.

When it is not appropriate, or possible, to communicate with the other person or people concerned, it may be a help to write the letter anyway, and then either post it into the fireplace or put it away somewhere. This can help you to sort out your ideas or to get things off your chest. The other person may be dead, they may not be interested in, or aware of, whatever it is that is causing you shame. There may be too many people involved.

When you have done all you can to achieve what you feel is the best possible outcome under the present circumstances, then be willing to accept that. Be willing to accept yourself as a worthwhile human being. Be willing to acknowledge yourself for doing your best and to pat yourself on the back for what you have achieved, and are continuing to achieve, rather than continuing to pull yourself down for what you are not. Recognise that you did the very best you could at that particular point in your history.

No one goes out to do harm to themselves intentionally. Even if this may seem to be the case there is nearly always some underlying perceived gain, no matter how convoluted. In general, however much people succeed or fail they usually do the best they can do at that particular moment in time. If, having done something, you feel shame, then your values have changed, you have learned something.

Do you feel shame now for not having known how to spell 'necessarily' in a school test when you were ten years old? Of course not. You did your very best and since then you have learned. Shame for that spelling mistake would be inappropriate and pointless. Many other shames may be similarly inappropriate if you can see them in that light.

Are you setting yourself up for a fall? Are you insisting that you should be right and correct all the time? To err is human. The most successful people have made the most mistakes. Be willing to accept that you will do things that, later on, you will learn to do better.

Reframing, or showing the situation in a different light and with a different meaning, can be useful. One patient was jolted out of her shame when I said, 'How arrogant of you to assume that you should always be right and never have done any wrong. At least this shows you are human.' Of course this doesn't always work, and you want to careful when you use such a method, but in this case it did the trick.

Do your best and then be willing to accept yourself as you are. Refusing to do this is wilfully to cause yourself pain.

Methods For Dealing With Shame And Guilt In Resolved Situations

Much shame and guilt is experienced even when you have done all you can to resolve a situation and learned all you can from it. Under these circumstances is shame a useful emotion? No. Much of the time it simply eats into you, makes you feel depressed and provides very little benefit for anyone else. Some people might say that if you have done something wrong you should continue to feel shame and you should continue to suffer and be depressed, but let's work towards a more positive assumption.

Let's assume you have done all you can to resolve the situation and you still feel guilty. What now? One method of changing the situation can be to follow the exercise described in the chapter dealing with criticism (Chapter 14). It is amazing how much less dreadful a deed can seem when you watch an observing you watching a distant you experiencing the emotion. It is sad but true that we are often more tolerant of other people's foibles and mistakes than we are of our own.

One client felt totally incapable of being seen in a swimsuit because of the cellulite on her thighs, so she turned down all invitations where this might be expected of her. This depressed her but was less painful to her than letting other people see her cellulite. With other people she was far more tolerant, feeling it hardly mattered. When she watched herself watching someone else refusing to go to the beach she laughed and felt far less shame.

The following case history shows how, by changing your perspective, you can control shame and guilt and get out of a painful and depressing situation.

> Gerald had come to see me because of his embarrassment over the way he handled social situations. He said he kept saying the wrong things and then feeling ashamed of the way he had behaved. No matter how hard he tried, he said, he somehow always seemed to commit a *faux pas*.
>
> In this case Gerald was obviously doing the best he could in the situation, given his character and temperament. What was needed was a way to reduce his shame and so make him more comfortable and at ease and, quite possibly, thus increase his chance of saying the right thing.
>
> I asked Gerald to think about a situation of which he felt ashamed and of the people he felt were criticising him and then describe how they looked to him. He said it was like being in the middle of a goldfish bowl. He imagined himself at the social event once again with everyone standing around him in a circle. Further questioning elicited the fact

that they all seemed to be taller than him and leaning over him, touching each other in a complete circle so he couldn't get out. Because of their height they cut out the light and so he was in the dark. He felt criticised, ashamed and without escape.

When I asked him about other times when he had made a mistake but had felt no shame and had only focused on how to correct the situation, he relaxed visibly and smiled as he recognised that in that situation other people, if they were involved, were smaller than him and further away. If they were looking at him they had an expression of curiosity on their faces as they wondered how he was going to correct the situation, and the scene was bathed in light.

I then asked him to go back to the first situation, make the people smaller, move them further away, change the expressions on their faces and turn up the lighting. Again he relaxed and was able to say that he felt much less shame now for his lack of social graces. Later still, Gerald reported that as a result of carrying out this process he had been able to relax the next time he was with a group of people and had behaved more appropriately.

Shame and guilt can be destructive and depressing if you let them, but if you examine the underlying causes, resolve to change them and make use of the processes described in this chapter, you will be able to control their effect on your life and lift the depression they may be causing.

Chapter Seventeen

Don't Fight Yourself –
Resolve The Conflict

Whenever you feel depressed or have chosen to make yourself feel depressed, at least a part of you is still wanting you to be happy, otherwise you would be enjoying the situation – in which case you wouldn't be totally depressed! In other words, while a part of you is creating the depression, another part of you is recognising the undesirability of this and is striving in the opposite direction.

It is possible to work with these two parts and find out the ultimate goals for each part. In almost every instance each part is striving for a valuable and common goal. Perhaps the part that wants you to be happy is striving for peace and security. The part that is creating the depression may be aiming for the same goal by a different road. For instance, one patient discovered a part of herself that made her depressed so that she would be aware of how bad things were. In this way she would not live in false optimism and not be disappointed when things went wrong, and she could be secure and at peace.

When the unconscious becomes aware of this

common purpose, it is possible to let the two parts come together, either now or at an appropriate time in the future, and the unconscious mind can then use the preferred, often the happier, way of achieving that outcome.

Inner Conflict

In Chapter 6 we touched on the concept of parts. Here we will be making specific use of this concept and focusing on the presence of two parts at any one time.

Have you ever heard your internal voice saying 'Part of me wants to do this, but part of me wants to do that'? Part of you may want to go out and another part of you may want to stay home. You may want to be with your partner one Sunday because that would make you happiest, yet feel you should spend some time with your mother because she is unwell. You may want to have a career but feel this would be unfair to the children. You may want to spend time with your colleagues after work, yet feel you'd also like to go home to the family. You may want to exercise to keep fit and at the same time spend a lazy day lounging in front of the television. An obvious conflict, for more than half the population is experienced daily when their desire to be slim is in conflict with their desire to eat. You may want to spend more time in the garden, yet also want to go down to the shops.

There are thousands of different ways in which you can be pulled in opposite directions, one part of you wanting to do one thing, another wanting to do something totally different. In fact, while it may seem that the two aims are totally different, often, as we shall see, they do have something in common.

If you allow yourself to be pulled in different directions without resolving the situation you can get awfully depressed. You may feel that you are never able to do what you want, simply because, whatever you do, you always think of the other things that you aren't doing. Resolving this inner conflict can be a major step forward in eliminating depression, and the process is surprisingly simple.

The first thing you need to do is to isolate the two parts that are in conflict. If there are more than two parts you can work them off in pairs, as we will do in the following example, until they are all reconciled, rather like a knock-out tennis tournament which works its way towards one finalist. Alternatively, you can deal with them all at once, in a parts' party. We will discuss that later too.

> Annette wanted to be slim. She was only a few pounds overweight and when she was at home she had no problem avoiding overeating and could even lose a pound or two. The difficulties started when she was away from home. Her work as a flight attendant meant that she was often away and, worst of all, eating out. Boredom on the flights regularly led to her nibbling at whatever was available. This was commonly nuts, cheese, biscuits or something equally fattening. On stop-overs she would go out with some of the crew and this was where the problem worsened. Often they were people she did not know particularly well, and she felt shy. Inevitably she would then drink more than she had meant to, feeling that only that way could she loosen up, be fun and have other people like her. Then she would eat more than she had meant to, searching for the

good feeling she felt she ought to be having in a fun crowd, yet getting more and more depressed, particularly the next morning when she could just feel that another pound or two had crept on.

I asked Annette to sit in front of me, with no desk between us, and to hold each of her hands, palm up, a few inches above her lap. There were no arms on the chair so her hands and arms were floating freely. I then asked her to become aware of the two parts of her and describe them to me as she put one part in each hand.

As she looked at her left hand I asked, 'Which part is in that hand?'

'That's the part that eats and drinks too much.'

'Can you see it clearly now?'

She looked a bit confused, so I explained that I wanted her to have a very clear picture of herself when she was overeating and overdrinking.

'Where are you?'

'I'm in an Indian restaurant.'

'OK, describe what you have been doing and then tell me, in detail, what is happening. As you do that make a very clear picture of everything, as if you were watching a replay in miniature taking place on your left hand.'

'I'm sitting next to one of the officers and there are some flight attendants on my left. I'm being offered a drink and I'm accepting it, even though I don't really want it. I'm a bit scared of the officer. His name is Bill. He's a junior officer but he's still a lot senior to me. The others seem at ease with him, so it must be my fault. So I say yes, I'll have another drink while we order. Then when everyone orders a meat dish I do the same, even though I would rather have vegetables, but I don't want to seem different to the others.'

'What happens next?'

'I feel full, I know I've eaten too much, and drunk too much, not enough to be drunk but more than I wanted. And the worst of it is that I still don't feel good, and I know I'll feel fat and miserable in the morning.'

She continued to gaze down at her left hand as she spoke.

'OK, well done. Now leave the scene there in that hand.'

'You know, it's funny,' she interrupted me, 'it's heavy, almost as if I can actually feel the weight of the scene on my hand. It's warm too.'

This is a common experience. Many people find that the image they have created is so real that the hand actually feels as if it is carrying it.

I next asked Annette to do the same thing with the other hand, her right hand, only this time she was to imagine the part of her that wanted to be slim. She didn't find this quite as easy as the content was less obvious, but it too soon came into form and she was able to describe it.

'I can see me slim. I look good, I've lost all the weight I want and I can fit into clothes easily. In fact I have a whole new wardrobe of clothes I love.'

'What about eating?'

'That seems to be easy. I can see her saying no to food when she doesn't absolutely want it, and no to glasses of wine too.'

'And what's happening as a result?'

'Well, obviously I don't feel depressed any more. I look happy and confident.'

'Good, very good.'

If you are doing this process on your own, keep giving yourself compliments and acknowledgement for how well you are doing.

'Now, which situation, which hand, would you like to deal with first?'

'The right one.'

'OK, I wonder if you can help me to understand things a bit more?'

'Mmm.'

It was clear that she enjoyed focusing on this desirable image of herself.

'Can you explain to me the purpose of this part, the purpose behind her saying no to food and wanting to be slim?'

'To look good.'

'And the purpose of looking good, what is it?'

'Well, to be liked I suppose.'

'Good, and what's the purpose of being liked?'

This took a bit longer, but eventually she said, 'To feel good about myself.'

'And what's the purpose of feeling good about yourself?'

'Well, to feel good, to feel happy . . .'

Clearly that was it. When I asked her the purpose of feeling happy, she said it was to feel good, and the purpose of feeling good about herself was to be happy. So I thanked her and asked her to focus on the other hand, the left hand. After a few minutes, to give her the time to get back in touch with that part, I asked her the same questions.

'Could you explain to me the purpose of choosing to eat and drink more than she really wants?'

'To be popular and to be fun. If she doesn't, they may not like her, she won't be part of the crowd.'

'And what is the purpose of being liked?'

'So she can feel accepted, be part of the crowd that does things.'

'And the purpose of that is?'

'To be liked, to know I'm popular.'

'And the purpose of that is?'

'To feel good about myself, to be happy.'

There we were. Ultimately the two, totally different types of behaviour, leading ostensibly in opposite directions – to being slim on the one hand and being overweight on the other – had, as their ultimate objective, the same goal: that she should feel good about herself and be happy.

I commented on this and then watched for a few minutes as Annette digested the idea. At the same time her hands, still held flat and floating above her knees, began to drift a bit closer together. Eventually I commented on this too.

'Notice that, as you become increasingly aware of the common goal of these two parts of you, that your hands are beginning to come together. As the desire for this to happen increases let them drift . . . that's right . . . until they touch. Very good. And as they come together you may feel a desire to bring them in towards your body . . . good . . . to any part of your body . . . your chest . . . good, that's right. Bring these two parts, now joined, in to you, making them an integral part of yourself, and knowing that, in future, you will be able to achieve this goal in the best way possible, the way that best suits your long-term goal of being slim and looking good as well as being liked, feeling good about yourself and being happy.'

As I said all this, her hands were sometimes leading and, just occasionally, following what I was saying. At the end she sat there quietly looking somewhat stunned.

'That's amazing, I really feel as if something has shifted inside me.'

'It has,' I told her. 'You will feel very different in future, and next time you are in a social situation where you would previously have had more to drink and eat than you really wanted, I want you to notice how you feel. Be aware of the differences in the way you feel and what you think and do.'

She came in to see me three weeks later full of stories. She had been on a long flight across Asia and had been out with the crew several times. She said it had been surprisingly easy to stick to her plan except for a couple of times when the pressure had been heavy.

To help her further I suggested that the next time, just before she set out, she should rehearse in her mind how she wanted to behave. She was to create a very clear picture of the way she wanted to conduct herself and to see herself doing this. Then, when the time came, all she would have to do was enact what she had already rehearsed. She told me later that this had done the trick and as a result she was able to lose weight when she was at home or eating alone, and to maintain it, instead of gaining weight, when she was in a group.

This may not sound a very profound exercise when you first read it and that was my thought initially, but I have been impressed by the impact it has. It is an NLP technique and, almost without exception, I find it produces both a significant effect at the time and, which is the real aim, a definite change in the person's long-term behaviour.

Sometimes the two hands may not want to come together. If this happens to you, don't force them, find out when would be an appropriate time for them to do this.

Ronald was the head of a small advertising agency and his inner conflict concerned the way he related to his staff. On the one hand, he wanted to be friends with them, to join in some of the fun and chatter that went on in the office, particularly towards the end of the day. On the other hand, he felt that, as the boss, he had to be somewhat aloof and in control as they had deadlines to meet and the work had to be good.

He found that the common purpose of both his behaviour patterns – remaining aloof and being the efficient boss, versus being one of the crowd and friends with all his staff – was to run a good company and be a success. When he realised this, and when both parts had been fully acknowledged and complimented for the great job they were doing, he still found that his two hands would only come partway together, so I asked him to consider when would be the appropriate time for them to join up. He told me that would be six weeks away. So I told him that was fine, and that he could rest easy and feel at peace within himself knowing that in six weeks' time these two, seemingly contradictory parts of himself would be able to come together in harmony.

When he had finished the exercise I asked him what was happening in six weeks' time. At first he wasn't sure what I meant but then when he thought six weeks ahead he realised that that was when their current project, the largest they had ever handled, would be finished. He had been working on this for some months and was looking forward to its completion.

Obviously for Ronald this was the time when he could relax. This was the time when he could feel free to be both one of the gang and the efficient boss. Simply the facts of knowing that there was an end to the present situation was enough to stop him worrying at night and getting despondent over the fact that he felt he was not as popular with his staff as he could be.

Once he understood the situation and his unconscious fears had surfaced, he was even able to articulate them to his staff and promise that both he and the office would be able to relax once this all-important deadline had passed.

Multiple Conflicts

There is a possibility that several parts of you might be in conflict and as a result you might experience great difficulty resolving the situation which is depressing you. This happened for Sara.

Sara had many hobbies. She was a keen sportswoman, enjoying many sports but especially racket sports such as tennis, squash and badminton. She was also enthusiastic about her career as a freelance writer and reporter. Since this didn't pay particularly well, she added to her income by running her own marketing company. At one time she had played tennis several times a week, before work, in the evenings and also during the weekend. Then her other activities had taken over, she had been asked to write a couple of books and her life was very full. She reduced her tennis playing to one night a week but that depressed her. Gardening was important and energetic but she felt she was becoming less fit than she had been. Her social life was also vital to her and she tried to maintain time for that too.

I refrained from trying to find out what each part was trying to achieve as this would have been time consuming. Instead, I decided to institute a parts' party.

Notice here that there is an inbuilt assumption in this work. It is always assumed that each part is trying to achieve something positive for you. After all, each part is a part of you. Each part depends on your existence and well-being for its own existence. It is reasonable to assume that it has your well-being at heart. It is important to take pains to acknowledge each part for the valuable role that it plays in the individual's life. Only in this way will you get the full co-operation of each part as you endeavour to resolve these situations.

Sara was asked to close her eyes and to call up each of the parts involved. She brought up the gardening part in her gardening clothes, the tennis-player part in tennis clothes and carrying her racket. She brought up the career woman, the

writer, the social part and any others that needed
to be there, all dressed appropriately for their roles.

I asked her to seat all the parts round a table and
then let the tennis-playing part state her case. After
that, each of the other parts was to explain what
more time devoted to tennis would mean for it in
particular.

I asked Sara if I could talk to her tennis-playing
part and, on receiving her agreement, asked her
what she, as that part, really wanted.

'What I really want,' said Sara as the tennis-
playing part, 'is to be able to play tennis on the
weekends the way I used to and possibly on
another night during the week or else for an hour
on a couple of mornings before work.'

I thanked the part and then asked Sara, in her
role as each of the other parts, what that would
mean.

'Well,' said the gardening part, 'that would mean
I couldn't keep up with the garden and much of it
would be taken over by weeds. Either I would have
to stop growing flowers and the place would not
look so attractive, or I would have to stop growing
vegetables and then she (Sara) would have to buy
commercially grown ones.'

'And I,' said the career part, 'would have less
time to concentrate on commercial situations,
which often flow on into the evenings.'

The writing part added, 'Of course I would write
less, much of my best writing time is in the early
morning, before the day starts.'

The social part was horrified. 'Hopeless! I have
enough trouble getting her to listen to me as it is. If

she plays more tennis we can kiss her social life good-bye.'

The tennis part listened to this thoughtfully and then made its own decision. 'Given all the other things Sara's different parts would miss out on I realise I am selfish in wanting more time for tennis. One night a week and the occasional social game at the weekend is enough and I will stop giving Sara a hard time.'

Two weeks later Sara was able to report in happily.

'It's interesting,' she said, 'I used to get depressed at how little time I had for playing tennis. Now I realise how much else I do with my time, and what I'd have to give up to play more tennis. I'm happy now with the amount of time I have for tennis and a lot less depressed. After all I'd hate to give up all the other things I do.'

There are many ways to resolve inner tensions between parts when you feel you are at odds with yourself and this is causing your depression. Here you have a couple of ways. Try them out and use them to your advantage.

Chapter Eighteen

Making Decisions More Easily

Does decision making make you miserable? Some people make decisions simply and easily. It's almost as if they know what they want to do before they even think about it. Other people agonise over decision making, causing themselves pain and stress in the process and then, since they are often unhappy with the decisions they do make, more pain and distress afterwards as they wonder about the wisdom of the decisions they have made.

There are many reasons why you may find decision making difficult. Some specific examples will help to show you a few of them.

> Ann was always thrown into a quandary when asked what she would like to do, whether it was her husband asking what she would like to do at the weekend, a friend asking her if she would be able to help with baby-sitting or another friend wanting her to go shopping. She even had trouble when shopping, finding it difficult to come to a decision not only on major purchases such as big household items or clothes, but on the daily shopping for food. Which brand should she buy, what

should she give the family for dinner? These were all questions that caused her enormous distress. When we talked, she found that the problem stemmed from the fact that she was always wondering what other people would think of her choice and what decision they would make, and since the decision would vary from person to person and she couldn't please everyone, she could never make a satisfactory decision.

Barry was always looking for the 'right' decision, feeling that if he could find that then he could stop worrying. He spent so long agonising over how he could discover this right decision, who he could ask, what he could read, how he could learn, that he rarely got round to making decisions until it was too late and circumstances had changed and made them for him.

Colette would make decisions quickly and then feel sure it couldn't be that simple and that she must have missed some vital information and made a mistake.

David made decisions quickly and then felt he had to stick to them, no matter what, even if he did think, after considering his choice, that perhaps an alternative decision would have been a better one. He was too afraid of looking weak and indecisive.

Edwina would wait patiently until she saw what someone else chose or decided and then would copy that decision, feeling that the other person must surely know something she didn't and so should be followed.

Frank made decisions easily but the moment he had made them he felt trapped, and so had to cancel the decision and make another and so on *ad infinitum*.

Georgia would panic and then plunge. When in a restaurant, for instance, she would gaze at the menu in panic, not knowing what to choose until, in desperation and faced by a waitress whose patience was running out, she would make a blind stab at the menu and choose whatever item her finger landed on.

Harry was incapable of making a decision without asking for advice. Not only did he want advice but he wanted someone else to make the decision for him, knowing then, that if things worked out well, he could bask in his success, and if it was a poor decision he would have someone else to blame.

Isobel spent all her energy on information gathering and would be exhausted and depressed long before she was ready to analyse it and come to her conclusion.

John would make a decision and then spend hours wondering how to find out if it was the right one.

Kathleen simply knew she made bad decisions, so whatever decision she made she knew it would be wrong and she began to get depressed the moment she even thought about making a decision.

Leonard could only make decisions if there was something in his past that would help. If he was deciding what book to read, what food to eat, where to go for a holiday or what to plant in his garden, he could only do it if he had previously read a similar book or eaten a similar food, or if he had been to those places or planted those plants in his garden before. Thus he found it difficult to create anything new in his life and this depressed him.

Marjorie made decisions quickly and easily and then lapsed into depression as she worried that other people would think her too strong and aggressive and feel she had trampled on them.

Nigel had led a sheltered childhood where first his parents and then his teachers had made his decisions for him. His wife had then taken over this role. Whenever he had to make a decision for himself he felt lonely, feeling that this meant there was no one there who cared.

Odelle was a strong woman married to a man who was content to let her run their lives. After the divorce she suddenly found herself terrified of making decisions because that, she now felt, led to loss.

Patrick was the eternal peacemaker. Unfortunately this also meant that he could see the good in each possible choice in a decision-making situation. Whatever he decided on, he then felt depressed about all the other options that he had abandoned.

Queenie made decisions based entirely on instinct and the way she felt. She would, for instance, buy clothes because they felt good. After she had made her choice she would walk out of the shop and then assess everything else in other shop windows on the basis of looks and wish she had bought something smarter, giving no thought now to how the other clothes would feel.

Roger felt that, as a man, he was supposed to be the head of the household. As such he had to make all the decisions. If his wife made decisions, he could either agree, in which case he felt diminished and emasculated, or disagree, in which case he felt rotten since he knew that in the 1990s couples were supposed to act as equal partners.

Susan knew that if she had to make decisions it meant that there was no one around to make them for her and that this meant no one would take care of her, so she was alone. Thus whenever she had to make a decision, she felt lonely and depressed.

Thomas knew that if he made decisions, other people would expect him to act on them. Since he doubted his ability to do this he postponed decision making for as long as possible. He was often told that he was hopeless, indecisive or lacking in direction, but all of these seemed to him to be less terrible than suddenly to find other people demanding that he perform in situations in which he doubted his ability.

Ursula had had to make decisions for the first time when her mother had died and she had hated it. The eldest of three children, she had suddenly found the weight of adulthood pressing on her thirteen years. Decision making for her, as an adult, meant loss: loss of the mother she'd had, and loss of the freedom that would have been hers had she not had the responsibility of her younger brother and sister.

Vincent knew that decisions meant that you had to close doors. Every time he made a decision he felt an enormous sense of loss for all the other opportunities to which he had, by his decision, said no, and for the things he felt were now gone from his life for ever as a result. In this way each decision made him more conscious of life and time running out.

Wendy wanted to make easy decisions but every time she was faced with one she found there were several different voices running around inside her head. One would say, 'No, don't do this, stay on the safe and narrow that you know'; another would say, 'Go for it. You only have one life and you deserve some fun'; another would focus on the loss, the diminished bank account, the things she wouldn't be able to do as a result of the decision. When she went shopping she knew she should buy the cheapest and be economical, she also knew she should buy well and feel good. Whatever she did she was unhappy with her decisions.

Xerxes felt that decision making was beneath him. If he had to make decisions then his staff weren't doing their job properly. If this happened it meant they weren't paying him proper respect and he would fly into a tantrum. Being forced to make decisions made him both very angry and very distressed.

Yvonne was afraid of decisions. She knew that if anything went wrong, she would be blamed, yet if she didn't make a decision she would also be blamed, this time for procrastinating. She dreaded going to work and woke up depressed every morning, except on Sundays when she could hide in bed – unless the phone rang and a friend asked her to decide what she would do that day.

Zanadu hated making decisions. He hated to hurt people and he knew that every time he made a decision there was someone who would be hurt.

You will doubtless think of a multitude of variations on these themes and you will probably recognise yourself in some of the examples above. In all of them, the problem lies not so much in the decision making itself but in underlying factors. Certainly there are times when you may feel that a decision between two or more options is so finely poised that it is difficult to make, but more often than not, if decision making is regularly difficult and depressing for you, it is the underlying emotions and fears with which you have to work.

Make Decisions For Yourself

It is important to recognise that you have to make decisions for yourself. Ultimately, no one else can make them for you, for even if you let them, it is still you who is making the decision, only you are doing it by default instead of by positive action. Moreover, you must be aware that it is you who has to suffer the consequences of these decisions. Although letting others decide for you gives you someone to blame if things go wrong, it is, nonetheless, rarely a comfortable way to approach decision making. You can cause yourself more emotional stress by the blame and resentment you heap on the person who has made a bad decision for you, and the victim status you create for yourself, than by accepting responsibility for your own decisions in the first place.

You will nearly always find that, whatever decision you make, you cannot please everyone around you. They are all individuals and they will all have their own opinions both as to what decision they would have made in a similar situation and what decision they think you ought to have made. If you make your decisions and choices on the basis of 'what will other people think' or on the basis of a desire to please others or to look good in their eyes, you will always be able to find someone who thinks you made the wrong decision. Inevitably this way of running your life leads to stress and depression.

It may take courage to make decisions for yourself but ultimately it will be an important part of your way out of depression. To be able to make your own decisions is part and parcel of self-development and of acknowledging yourself and taking control of your life. This in the end usually leads to greater peace and happiness for everyone concerned, than spending time trying to please others and wondering what they will think. Once you have recognised clearly, just what sort of person you want to be and what you stand for (see Part Three), making decisions becomes easier.

There Is No 'Right' Decision

Recognise that there is no 'correct' or 'right' decision, that there is only what you want to do at the time. In any given situation, different people will make different decisions and whatever the decision it may work out well for one person and badly for another.

Patrick and Michael, successful businessmen, who travelled a lot, were both faced with the decision of whether or not to purchase the sports car of their dreams. In the end they made different decisions. The cars were vintage and luxurious but they would cost more than the sensible choice of a new and modern car. On the face of it, the vintage car would be cheaper in the long-term as it would not depreciate in value, but what about the running costs and repairs, and what would friends think, was it being bought for show, was it too much of an indulgence, what about the responsibility, security, the limitations of not being able to subject it to rough wear and tear? These had to be balanced against the pleasure of it and the chance to fulfil a dream.

Was there a 'right' decision? Of course not. Patrick bought it and loved every minute of it. Every time he got in he revelled in the look, the feel and the nostalgia of it. He spent time looking after it, was willing to make adjustments such as using taxis to avoid leaving it for extended periods at airports and kept in mind, each time there was a repair bill, the fact that there was no depreciation. Michael chose the modern car. Whenever he felt like it at the weekends he took off with no thought for the miles he added, he left it at the airport knowing it was insured and replaceable and congratulated himself on his trouble-free motoring pleasure.

Had they reversed their decisions, Patrick would have for ever regretted the lost opportunity to live a dream and Michael would have chafed at the restrictions and limitations of having to look after a vintage car.

Since there are no 'right' decisions in large or small situations, you might as well stop looking for them now. It is impossible for you to know the full consequences of any decision you make. You may make what you think is a bad decision and then find that some wonderful benefits and results appear in the future. You may make a decision you come to regret and focus on how much better your life would have been had you made it differently, but you cannot know how the other choice would have turned out.

What you can do is decide (a) to make decisions on the basis of what you think is right for you, at that moment in time; (b) use your values and mission statement and your memory line to assist you in making such decisions (see later in this chapter and in Parts One and Three); (c) recognise that you are doing the best that you can at that particular moment; and (d) trust yourself to have done what is best for you and believe that good will come from the decision in either obvious or roundabout ways.

Positive Decision Making – Discover And Prioritise Your Values

One aspect of easy decision making depends on knowing what you want. To achieve this you will want some of the tools from the chapters in Part Three. Once you know what your values are and once you can define your mission statement you will find it a lot easier to make decisions.

I have worked with many people who have agonised over major decisions in their lives, such as changing jobs, where to live or which house to buy, whether or not to marry and so forth. In many instances, the decision making has been complicated even when they have tried to be analytical and list the points in favour of each option. In this case, another tool is often necessary, as we shall see.

Mary was a successful career woman. She was getting married and moving to another city in two months' time and she could not continue in her present job for logistical reasons. She had to decide whether she would apply for a new job near her new home, or stay at home and adapt her life around her new husband. She could think of five good reasons for getting a job: she liked to be independent, the money would be useful, she'd have her experience to fall back on if the marriage didn't work out, she liked what she was doing and she thought she'd be bored at home all day. On the other hand there were three good reasons not to get a job: she would be able to furnish and create their home the way they wanted it, they would have time together for fun in the weekends, instead of doing chores then, and finally, she rather thought her husband would prefer her not to work, although he kept telling her that she was free to choose.

The problem, as she explained to me, was that there were more reasons to work than not, yet when she made the decision to go job hunting she got depressed. Equally, she felt her decision to stay out of the workforce after the move was emotional rather than logical, which was not like her; she felt she wouldn't be pulling her weight, that she would be a wimp by opting for the choice with the least number of benefits.

I asked Mary to list her values (as described in Part Three) and the decision became simple. Her values, in order of priority, were a successful marriage, creating a family life and building a family, career, consideration for others, personal growth, etc. When she did the weighted scores (see Part Three) it quickly became obvious that her best decision was for her not to continue with her career but to build the home and adapt to her husband's lifestyle since these were her *highest* priorities.

Listing and prioritising values is an excellent tool for making decisions, particularly big ones where you have time to sit down and carry out the process in full. It is less suitable for making minor or quick, on-the-spot decisions, although even then it can be useful. One woman always battled with her conscience in the supermarket when deciding whether to buy a cheaper food, one that would cook quickly, one that was popular with the family or one that was healthy. After she had run her values she recognised that nutritional quality and ease of cooking were more important than economy and popularity and she kept this thought in mind every time she went shopping from then on.

Decision Making Strategies and Processes

There are several other processes which can help you to make decisions more easily and successfully than you do at present. You can develop these strategies quickly and easily with just a small amount of practice and use them for the myriad small decisions you have to make every day, as well as in larger decision-making situations.

Remember How A Good Decision Feels

Just as there is no 'right' decision, so too there is no 'right' decision-making process. One way to find out what works for you is to think of a time when you made a good decision simply and easily. Do this at a time when you can relax and concentrate and go back to that time in your mind. How did you make the decision? Did you make a picture? Did you go on your feelings? Did you go through a multiple step process and if so what was it? At this point you are quite possibly saying you 'just knew', but even 'just knowing' has to involve a way of knowing. How did you just know? Almost certainly you had a picture, made a comparison, or referred to a reference point. One of my clients discussed each option with herself. When the voices in her head were the loudest she knew that was the best choice. Another client pictured all the possibilities and the one in the brightest colour was, he knew from experience, the best choice for him. Another found he would argue with himself, then make the comparison with different situations in the past, create a picture of the one that sounded best, and if that felt good he had his decision.

There are many other ways of 'experiencing' a good decision. Often they are highly individual but work for the person concerned. The best thing is for you to discover how you made a good decision in the past and then to practise using it consciously. If you cannot decide what your method is, try one outlined here and find out whether or not it works well for you.

See, Hear and Feel Your Decision

When you make a decision you are, in some way or another, checking out each option and then coming to a conclusion. Let's say you are deciding what to wear. You may consider the way the outfit would look, you may focus on how it feels, you may listen to a voice inside your head analysing the choices, you may make comparisons with events in the past or with mental pictures of the future, you may make a quick choice or you may evaluate your choice repeatedly against different criteria.

> Barbara hated to get up. She knew that once she was out of bed she had only a limited time in which to decide what to wear. She would make half a dozen choices, find fault with each of them, reject the lot, and then in desperation close her eyes and grab a hanger, wearing whatever outfit came to hand. She had just been offered a new job in which her looks and grooming would be important as well as her warm personality and her ability to get along well with people. She was on the verge of turning it down, terrified about how she would know what to wear each morning.
>
> I suggested the following steps, which she learned, practised and then put into action. First she was to pick an outfit, create a picture of herself dressed in it, imagine the way it would feel, physically, when she wore it, listen to any voices chattering inside her head, and so discover the way she felt, emotionally, about this outfit. After that she was to do the same thing with another outfit and another. Finally she was to make her choice on the

overall feeling for each. Since she was a warm and emotional person her feelings always played a major role in the decision making but this way the feelings would be based on a wider input than just instinctive feelings.

As human beings we process information in three main ways, visually, auditively and emotionally or with our feelings. We can abbreviate this to Visual, Auditory, Emotion or V, A, E. If you want to follow up this concept further there are many books on Neurolinguistic Programming (NLP) which you can read and from which you will undoubtedly learn fascinating things about the way the human mind works. For now it is enough to focus on the basics of this.

Barbara had, in effect, been guided to assess each outfit using all three of these (V, A, E) and then to make her final decision based on E, her overall feeling. This is commonly an effective strategy for decision making. Once she practised this Barbara could either continue to use it or adapt it slightly to suit herself. Whatever she did would be better than her present method.

When deciding what to do for the day you can do the same thing. For each option picture the day (V), listen to what you are saying to yourself about it (A), and then find out how that feels (E). Repeat this for each option and then evaluate your responses.

Some people have a tough time using their imagination to discover what the future will be like as a result of their decision. Faced with an empty room or one with which I am dissatisfied I have a hard time figuring out how to change it for the better. My strategy used to be to look through magazines until I saw something I liked and then copy that. Since the magazine picture was often not exactly what I wanted this was rarely entirely satisfactory. Some people, it seemed to me, simply saw an empty space and could instantly imagine a finished result that they would like. I used to envy them.

Now I use the above procedure and visualise the options and examine my feelings about them. I create a possible new look, any look, just so long as it is different and a step in the right direction. I might change the colour, alter one piece of furniture or whatever. Then I ask myself what I think of it and find out how the change feels. I don't aim for perfection the first time, I simply mentally make a change, and then find out how I feel about it. When I have created half a dozen possibilities I evaluate them and pick the best. Then I do it again. Eventually I have several possibilities that have made it to the final evaluation and I am able to choose the one that appeals the most.

Physical movements may help you to see, hear or feel the outcome of your decisions more clearly. As a child, when asked a difficult question at school my eyes would go straight up. An irritated teacher would often demand that I look at her, saying, 'Look at me, the answer is not written on the ceiling'. But it was. If I looked up I could, in my mind, visualise the page on which the information was written. My best friend, on the other hand, always looked down at her feet when faced with a similar situation and the irritated teacher would say, 'Look at me, not at the floor, when I'm speaking to you, that's rude'. This made things difficult for her as she operated largely in her feelings and by looking down she could access them and find the answer to the question. A third friend was dominantly auditory. We were all impressed by the fact that she took very few notes in class but seemed to remember everything the teachers said. On the other hand she had trouble remembering things she had read. When she was asked questions her eye used to move off sideways, in a line with her ears, and our irritated teacher considered her sly. A wiser woman would have been able to help all three of us make optimum use of the way our brains worked.

When you are trying to decide something on the basis of how it will look, turn your eyes up and to the right. (Keep in mind that, for most people, their future is on their right rather than on their left. If yours is to your left, change the direction you look towards accordingly.) When you are listening to the words you are saying to yourself, slide your eyes in the direction of your ears; and when you are finding out how the result will feel then look down.

You can use these procedures to help you make better decisions, and to feel more confident in them. However, be willing to be flexible. There will be times when it is appropriate to change the basis on which you make decisions. There is little point in deciding on what to wear based on the sound of the material even if you are dominantly auditory, or on which concert to go to by what the performers look like, even if you are dominantly visual.

If you are already familiar with NLP you will realise that this is a very simplified version of the concept and that there are exceptions to these rules that we have ignored. Nonetheless, this brief description will provide excellent results. Again, if you would like to explore these ideas further please refer to the many books written on Neurolinguistic Programming.

Making Decisions With the Aid of Your Memory Line

Just as seeing, hearing and feeling the effect of a decision can help you make up your mind, so can envisaging its consequences on your memory line.

Sometimes people make decisions with little thought to the long-term consequences. Dieters are a classic case: their thoughts are on immediate gratification rather than the weight they will gain. Too much drinking, or inappropriate or casual sex with regrets the next day are other examples. You may be choosing to leave school for the immediate reward of a job and an income rather than assessing the long-term benefits of higher education. You may be spending unwisely for immediate pleasure rather than considering long-term security. Your temper may lead you to decide to 'have it out' with the person concerned for the immediate goal of letting off steam when a better long-term option would be to wait until things have calmed down. Using your memory line can help you evaluate a decision and estimate its future consequences.

Remember how in Chapter 12, you discovered the way your memory line is constructed and where to look to find your future and your past. You can use this knowledge to help you make a decision. When you are trying to determine the outcome of your decisions, turn to your future. When you are trying to make comparisons with something in your past experience, look along your memory line to your past. Do the following for each option that is open to you and that you wish to include. Make the first decision. Create the future the way you think it will be as a result. Then move up and out along your memory line to this point in the future. Find out how this future feels. Look ahead to the futures that evolve from this point. Then turn and look backwards to now and find out about the steps that have brought you to this point. Is this a future that you want? Do the same thing with each possible decision. Find out which outcome you prefer. Practise doing this. Making decisions will not be so difficult once you can envisage the consequences.

Lack of Choices – Widening Your Options

Sometimes it is not your decision making that is at fault: you may actually be working with insufficient choices.

The dieter who goes home from work to a lonely flat and heads straight for the fridge may be doing the only thing she can think of that will cheer her up. She needs more choices. The alcoholic who heads for the nearest pub after work may be doing the only thing he can think of to avoid his unhappy marriage at home. He needs more choices. The compulsive shopper may be doing the only thing she can think of to fill an aimless day. The person who keeps choosing the wrong job may not believe he deserves the better ones.

If what you are doing is not working for you and you are telling yourself you keep making rotten decisions, it may help you to list the options you felt you had at the time and then, if appropriate, you can create more options.

If you eat compulsively in the evenings, then list other ways you could have a good time. Don't try to force yourself to do this on the way to the fridge. Do it in a quiet time when the loneliness and the desire to eat are not on top of you. Once you have decided on alternatives, such as making social arrangements, giving yourself a facial or taking up a hobby, you will find it easier to opt for those choices rather than the fridge to satisfy your need. Once you have decided on positive ways to improve your marriage you will find it easier to go home instead of into the pub. Once you have created a list of alternative ways to fill your day, shopping won't be your only option; and once you have developed your self-esteem you will be able to imagine not only being offered a better job but being successful in it and thus have the courage to decide to take it.

Decision making is with us every moment of the day. For people who are sure of themselves, who make decisions quickly and easily, this may be an unconscious process. If you are one of these people, you may even be unaware of all the decisions you make and of how you make them. But from the moment you wake up until the moment you fall asleep you are making decisions. Even if you remain motionless you have to make a decision: a decision not to move. You decide to move, to stay still, to speak or not and what to say. You are constantly deciding what to do. At some point, for everybody, decisions stop being easy and automatic and demand your conscious attention. Getting up and cleaning your teeth may be automatic, what to wear may demand your attention. Driving to work may be automatic, parking the car may demand a conscious decision. You may go through your normal routine, week after week, but have trouble making bigger decisions and so remain stuck in a rut.

If, or when, decision making is difficult, it can cause you distress. If this is the case or if you make bad decisions and feel depressed with the results, then put some thought and energy into what we have discussed here and you will almost certainly find that you can make better decisions and make them more easily than in the past. As a result you will have less reason to be depressed.

Chapter Nineteen

Do You Simply Have To Do It? – Getting Rid Of Compulsive Behaviour

'I always do it,' wailed Teressa. 'Every time something goes wrong, I eat.'

'Every time?'

'Oh, you know what I mean, not every single time maybe, but it seems to be the way I deal with things. When I'm bored, I eat; when someone criticises me, I eat; when I'm depressed, I eat. And the dreadful thing is, I do it when I'm not even hungry. I just find myself heading for the kitchen and I eat whatever I can lay my hands on. It might be biscuits or a chocolate bar; if I can't find something sweet I may eat some cheese, nuts, crisps, whatever I can find.'

'Does it help?'

'No. Of course not, and that's why I'm here. All that happens is I get fat, and that makes me more depressed.'

Does this sound familiar? Do you have some behaviour you resort to when you feel depressed? Eating is a common one. Think back to what happened when you were a child. Were you promised a treat when you behaved, or a treat if you would just cheer up and stop crying immediately? You probably were; most children are. And was the treat usually food? Almost certainly it was. Think about what you hear all around you. 'Stop crying and I'll buy you an ice-cream later.' 'Be quiet now, I have to think about what I'm doing. If you're good you can have a sweet later.' 'Do your homework and you can have a hamburger and a coke later.' It's all bribery of course, but worse still, it instils a message into the brain at an early age that tells it that the solution to many of life's problems is to seek a reward or compensation by eating or perhaps drinking. My experience with clients tells me that heading for the fridge or the larder is also a common compulsion when they are already depressed.

It is very easy to set up a vicious cycle here. You may start out by being depressed, turn to food as a solace and then get more depressed as you gain weight but go back to eating even more as an attempt to cheer yourself up and build up the cycle this way. Alternatively, you may start out eating compulsively, gain weight or feel disgusted with yourself as a result, become depressed and then turn again to food for solace, and so again find yourself in the cycle.

In other words, the depression can lead to the compulsive behaviour, whatever it is, or the compulsive behaviour can lead to the depression. Either way you can begin to feel there is no way out. The solution, at least in part, is to learn how to eliminate the compulsion.

*

Notice that at the beginning of the chapter I asked Teressa if eating compulsively helped her mood. It's always worthwhile asking that question. Sometimes the compulsive behaviour provides no benefit. At other times it does, at least for a little while. Graham's behaviour was as compulsive as Teressa's, but it did seem to help, at the time at least.

> Every time Graham was criticised he argued back. He told the other person exactly why he had done what he had and why his own action had been better than the criticiser's course of action. This made him feel good, at least for a while. The problem was that it was losing him friends.
>
> 'I can't help myself,' he said, 'even when I know the other person is right I argue back, I can't stop myself, the words are coming out even before I think about them. It really is something I must change. I know I hurt people and drive them away and as a result I'm often lonely and that makes me feel miserable. I guess I'm just a horrid person, I'd rather fight other people, at least verbally and emotionally, than let them hurt me, yet in the end, of course, I get hurt anyway. If only there was a way to stop this.'

As we have seen, the compulsive behaviour can come about as a result of your depression, it may also be the cause of your depression, or at least a contributing factor. Other forms of compulsive behaviour may be less harmful or destructive than those of Teressa or Graham, yet just as closely linked with their depression.

Susan had an absolute compulsion to check all the locks, doors, and windows, each time she left home. She said it could take her ages to leave the house. She'd check all the windows and doors, go out, get into the car, and then worry that she had missed one, or had left a power point switched on. Back she'd go and check them all over again. It was no use her husband doing it for her, or assuring her that he'd checked everything as well. She trusted him even less than she trusted herself in this.

There is nothing wrong with checking all the windows and doors when you leave home. The problem comes if you have to do it five times before you can go out. Other people feel a compulsive need to straighten pictures, plump up cushions, wash their hands, fidget with an object, pick at their cuticles or spin a ring on their finger. These and many other compulsive behaviours can be very distressing, both to the person doing them and to the people who have to watch them or live with them, and can even put marriages at risk.

Mandy came in with her husband. He explained that she had this absolute fixation about washing her hands when around food. She washed her hands before going into the kitchen, before touching food and, while cooking, after every single time she touched a utensil or surface. It had reached the stage when she now insisted that he and the children do the same thing. Now, he said, she was starting to make the same rules in the dining room and it was become a serious problem for the whole family.

Whenever a compulsive behaviour pattern starts you begin to lose personal freedom. When the behaviour interferes with your life and your relationships, when it interferes with your goals or objectives and when it worries you and makes you feel depressed, it is high time to deal with it.

Few people with compulsions are happy, many are depressed. Even if the compulsion is to do something good or helpful, it may also be a problem. A colleague, whose elderly and recently widowed mother lived alone, felt compelled to phone her mother every morning to see how she was, even though she knew her mother was irritated by the implication that she couldn't look after herself. It is possible to rationalise such compulsions, yet they may still be compulsions rather than choices made in freedom. Obviously, checking up on other people can be an expression of care and concern, but it can also be a compulsion, something you simply have to do, no matter what. Expressions of appropriate care and concern are fine, but compulsions can frustrate others and yourself and can make or keep you depressed. You may even find you are depressed if you don't do them and then depressed all over again when you have done them, recognising their hold over you.

There is usually a reason why you do something compulsively. It will not be immediately obvious, but an underlying cause for your behaviour no doubt exists. Somewhere in your past *not* doing the compulsive behaviour has probably been linked to pain or discomfort in some way, or alternatively doing it has been linked with pleasure or reward. Not washing your hands can be linked to being called dirty, leaving home without locking up leaves you and your home open to violation. These are relatively obvious underlying reasons, but there can be other still deeper ones as well. Finding the reason is the first step to getting rid of the compulsion.

Discovering The Reason Behind Your Compulsion

One client went to the pub compulsively on the way home from work each evening, even when he knew it would cause problems at home and he was already depressed at the state of his marriage. He was able to change this pattern when he understood that he did it so his colleagues, with whom he drank, wouldn't think badly of him. His fear of their censure stemmed from his assumption that he was unpopular because he was a foreigner.

The technique of 'Running a phrase', described in Chapter Three, was used to elicit this information:

Russell was asked to run the phrase 'A benefit I get from going to the pub is . . .' and produced the following completions '. . . I can relax after work', '. . . I can be part of the crowd', '. . . I can be like the other guys.'

This seemed relatively straightforward and he got stuck at this point so I changed tack and asked him to run the phrase 'Something I would lose if I didn't go to the pub with them is . . .' and he completed with '. . . their friendship'. This one appeared to cause him some distress so I asked him to run 'A reason they might not want me for a friend is . . .' and got '. . . because I'm a foreigner'.

As so often happens on these occasions, he looked startled and said, 'Goodness, I didn't know I felt like that, but when I think about it I guess I do. I'm conscious of being a foreigner and not knowing how to fit in. They all go to the pub so I guess I've sort of assumed that I have to go too. I don't know how important this is in their social life. I suppose I think that if I don't go I'll have shown my foreignness and the fact that I don't know how to fit in socially. It would show that I'm not one of them. I suppose too,' he continued after a pause, 'that I do feel that I have to try to make up for being a foreigner. After all, in my country we really didn't much like the foreigners that came in, they were always the oppressors. But I love this country and I want to stay here and make friends and be accepted.'

We discussed other ways in which he could be friendly, possibly have a drink after work occasionally, but on most days still go straight home to his wife, who was also feeling lost and at sea in a new country. There is little point in removing a compulsion that serves a positive purpose without replacing it with some other more constructive means of achieving this same goal. At first Russell couldn't see how to do this so I used the same technique of running a phrase to solve this problem. The great thing about this method is that it bypasses the conscious mind and lets the creative subconscious have a say.

'Another way I could make friendships is . . .' prompted 'join in conversations more, even though my English is not good', and '. . . share my ideas

with them more', and '. . . go to football matches
with them on Saturdays'.

Once Russell could go to the pub some nights
and on others go home comfortably, straight after
work and without feeling cut off from his work
mates, he had a new freedom.

This brings us back to the concept of choices that has
been discussed many times previously in this book. It
is not so much whether or not you perform a particular
action that is important. It is important that you have
the choice as to whether or not you do so. When you
have no choices you have no freedom. When you have
choices, even if your behaviour doesn't change notice-
ably, you have freedom.

Finding What Attracts You To Your Compulsion

Another way of elminating compulsions depends on
isolating what it is, inside your brain, that makes that
action so compulsive, and what the triggers are that set
the action in process.

To see how this works we will use a simple example
of a compulsion that is easy to identify and work with.
You will then be able to expand this and apply it to
whatever compulsion you have that you would like to
change or 'demote'. By this I mean that a useful goal is
to 'demote' the compulsion into an optional behaviour,
one that you can perform when you choose to, in
freedom. There is little point, for instance, in eliminating all desire to make sure the doors and windows are
locked and closed when you leave the house, but there
is great benefit in giving you back your freedom of
choice in this regard.

A very common compulsion is to eat chocolate, so we will use this as an example. Martin had originally come in to see me about his skin. At thirty-four he still had the acne which had first appeared in his early teens and he was thoroughly depressed about it. Everything he had tried had been unsuccessful. However he was also addicted to chocolates and, since they can cause pimples, we decided to work on this addiction.

Whenever Martin saw a box or a bar of chocolate he felt he simply had to eat some. It was impossible to keep chocolate out of the house because both his wife and children liked it too and continued to buy it and once Martin knew it was there it was only a matter of time, usually a very short time, before he started eating it. Initially he would tell himself he would only have one piece but inevitably the first led to the next and the next.

I asked Martin to think of something else, similar, that he did not have the compulsion to eat and about which he felt neutral. I suggested other sweets or biscuits but he said he rather liked those too. He suggested olives because he disliked them but that was not a good idea; it had to be something about which he felt neutral, with no strong feelings either way. Eventually he settled on corn chips. These, he said, he could leave alone unless he was really hungry. For this method of handling compulsions you need two similar situations, one in which you experience the compulsion, the other in which there is no compulsion but also no negative feeling. Here is what happened with Martin.

'Martin, I would like you to focus on what you

experience when you see or think of chocolate. Describe that experience to me.'

'I feel it. I can feel that warm smooth feeling and the taste of it in my mouth.'

'That's fine, but something has to happen before that, perhaps you picture the chocolates first? How do they look?'

'They're brown of course.'

'What else? What in particular do you notice? Check on the details of the way they look.'

'They look mellow, that's the best way I can put it. Then I immediately get that warm smooth feeling in my mouth.'

'Great. Now think about crisps. What do you experience when you think about corn chips?'

'I feel them as sharp and scratchy. And yes, that's funny, if I picture them they have a sort of stark light to them, sort of angular and sharp.'

'Excellent. Now imagine the two of them side by side. Which seems closer?'

'Oh the chocolates. They seem to grow in size and fill the space, crowding out the corn chips. The chips are definitely further away, sort of in the background.'

'Good, now we have several factors to work with. The look, the lighting, the distance and the feeling.'

The next step with Martin was to discover which of these factors was the strongest in motivating him to eat the chocolates, the look, the light, the position or the feeling. I asked him to consider the chocolates and make them even larger and closer. When this happened he felt he wanted them more than before; the same was true when he looked at their smooth round shape as compared to the shape of the chips. The real change occurred when he changed the lighting. When he softened the lighting and made it more subdued and intimate his response was immediate.

'Oh now I *really* want to eat them. That light is so comforting and it makes the feel of them in my mouth even more real and compelling.'

'What happens when you sharpen the light? Imagine bright floodlights or strong sunlight on them, so you can see shadows and details. You may even want to have them glitter as the corn chips did. What happens now?'

'That's funny, they don't seem so appealing. In fact there's little comfort in the thought of eating them, just as there isn't in the thought of eating the chips.'

'Excellent.'

So in Martin's case we might simply have stopped at this point, telling him that every time he thought of chocolates he was to shine a very bright light on them in his mind and make them seem as undesirable as corn chips did, unless he was hungry.

This can work but the trouble is that you have to remember to do the process each time and if you are determined to eat the chocolates it is all too easy to give in to the compulsion before you can think about the process. If you can 'blow out' the experience, you can remove the compulsion all together.

The next instruction to Martin was that he was to think of a box of chocolates and rapidly fade the light down, dimmer and dimmer and continue making it even dimmer and then tell me what happened.

He paused for a moment and then gathered his thoughts. 'Gosh,' he said. 'It was like going down into the centre of the earth. First I imagined the light getting dimmer and initially the thought of the chocolate was really appealing. Then as the light faded even further I suddenly felt as if I was being drawn into a deep vortex, sort of down into these muddy depths. It even got a bit scary. I felt as if I was losing touch with reality, drowning. It certainly didn't have the comfort of eating chocolates.'

We chatted for a bit while I let him have time for his emotions to settle and the experience to take effect. Then I got out some chocolates I had brought in for the purpose and passed the box to him. The expression on his face was all I needed; clearly the experience was different this time and he was able to say no to them without any struggle.

Linda had a compulsion to do crossword puzzles and we had to work a bit harder to eliminate this one. She said that doing the puzzles was wasting a lot of her time. If she saw a puzzle, she had to do it; if she couldn't finish it she got depressed with herself and told herself she was stupid.

'I read the paper after my husband and children have left in the morning and there they are, right in front of me, the crossword puzzles – two of them. I *have* to do them and I *have* to finish them, otherwise the day's hopeless. It's the same with the ones in magazines or the days the television guide arrives – they're bad days, when they come.

'Everyone else has an interesting time,' she continued, 'they're off to work, school or college, they're all doing something worthwhile with their lives. Whereas here I am, stuck at home, doing the rotten housework, too stupid even to complete the crossword puzzles. But I have to keep trying. I can't seem to leave them alone.'

In fighting Linda's compulsion we chose something else that she saw in the newspaper just as regularly but about which she felt totally neutral, namely, bridge games. Linda said that the print on crosswords drew her and that she felt that there were lines of light going from her eyes to each of the squares and that the entire crossword rose above the level of the page and then got larger in size and the print got darker. When she did notice a bridge game it was just a passing blur, along with all the other writing, of the same colour and intensity and lying flat within the page.

When Linda focused the lines of light onto the crossword, brought it up off the level of the page and let it become larger she had an increasing compulsion to work on it. Encouraging her to leave it on the plane of the paper, as she saw the bridge game, was of little help.

'I can't control that, it simply leaps off the paper and comes towards me, with the beams to each square getting shorter and shorter.'

'What happens if you push it further away, further than the newspaper?'

'I can't do that, it just comes up towards me.'

So we moved on to the next step, the overdose or 'blow out'. Have you ever thought that if you worked in a sweet shop, or could eat yourself stupid on sweets or chocolates, you could fix your chocolate compulsion? Working in a chocolate factory is a dream for many people but I have rarely known it to eliminate the compulsion, not, at least, in the long term. It's amazing how resilient some compulsions can be. Now, however, as I told Linda, we were going to break her compulsion by doing just that, by overdosing her with crosswords. We were going to do this in a specifically structured way.

I told her to focus on the crossword and repeat the process that occurred when she was driven to work on it. She was to strengthen the lines of light to it, lift it further off the page and have it spread out wider in every direction. She was also to do this *as fast as she possibly could* and to take the process to the extreme.

'Wow,' was her initial reaction as she pulled her head back and out of the way. 'That really exploded in my face. It's a bit overwhelming though, I mean I feel I *really* want to do the crossword.'

I asked her to repeat the process several times. Each time her reaction was similar and she looked quite uncomfortable. Then suddenly she simply looked slightly puzzled.

'What's happening now?'

'It was funny. In the end, that last time, I could see only one square and then it became a blur. It was almost as if my face was in the puzzle and I could only see behind it, I couldn't see the puzzle any more.'

As an enthusiastic puzzle-solver myself I had one handy, so after talking for a bit and allowing the process to settle I reached for it and offered her the paper open at the puzzle. Linda gazed at it for a moment and frowned.

'You know, I don't feel like I need to do it any more.'

'Make it bigger, lift it off the page, can you do that?'

'No, I can't. How strange.'

We have eliminated Linda's compulsion to do the crossword puzzles each day. It is important to recognise, however, that we had also found an underlying cause of her compulsive behaviour – belief that she was stupid since she didn't go out to work but stayed at home, did the housework and vegetated. While that no longer led her to need to do the puzzles, it was still an issue to resolve. But that's another story.

You can use this process for any compulsive behaviour whether it be locking windows, clicking your fingers, rocking your chair or whatever. Find out how you respond to it in comparision to how you respond to something that is equivalent but about which you feel neutral. Find the major factor or factors that drive you to it as a compulsion and then exaggerate the main one to the extent that it becomes so much larger than life that it collapses and you are left with nothing. You may be able to do this just once as in Martin's case or you may have to do it repeatedly as Linda did. Make sure you do this part very fast as doing it slowly can have the effect of increasing the desirability or the compulsion.

You can also use this procedure with emotions such as impatience, fear, anger, guilt and even depression itself. However, my suggestion here would be that you find a practitioner to help you. This is a Neurolinguistic Programming procedure, so find yourself an NLP practitioner. The reason for this lies in the fact that in the process of overdosing on the experience or allowing it to enlarge to such an extent that it dissipates or explodes, you have for a brief while an intensification of the experience. If this gets a bit overwhelming and there is no one there to keep you at it, you might stop at this point and in this way you could dig yourself into a deeper depression. It is much better to deal with emotional compulsions under the guidance of someone who is competent in this field. However, you can certainly use this procedure on other compulsive behaviours which cause your depression.

Chapter Twenty

So You're Alone – Join The Rest Of Us

Many people tell me that they are depressed because they're lonely, because they're alone. Everyone is alone. Everyone is an island. The middle of a large city can be the loneliest place in the world. A desert island with three people on it can feel crowded. Loneliness is a state of mind, and we have already seen that you create your own state of mind.

I used to know a woman whose constant complaint was that she was alone. She was divorced and had two children in their early teens. She frequently insisted that being alone, as she was, was a terrible thing. Her two children loved her and would have been thrilled to have her happy and interested in their activities, but the implication of her constant complaint of loneliness made them feel rejected. She avoided parents' functions and turned down overtures from other mothers. What she wanted, of course, was a new husband. Any invitations to social occasions, which arrived progressively less frequently, were met by the question, 'Who will I meet, what's in this for me?' When she arrived and found that there was no one interesting there – i.e.

no slim, handsome and wealthy single man, who was immediately bowled over by her, dropped to his knees and begged for a date – she got depressed. The few single men she did meet were all 'too something' – too stuffy, too old, too limited financially, too dull or, worst of all, too interested in other things and unable to focus their attention completely on her. She remained unhappy.

If you cannot give, you cannot receive. If you cannot give warmth and friendship to everyone, at least until you make clear distinctions in your own mind as to your preferences, if you cannot be interested in other people for themselves without prejudging them, above all if you assess people and situations only in relation to their value to yourself personally, to what you want, then you will almost certainly be lonely. After all, everyone else is like you: they want people to take an interest in them.

If you are going to be unhappy until people are taking a passionate interest in you and your affairs, you had better learn to take an equally passionate interest in them and theirs first. If you are not interested in them, you can hardly expect them to be interested in you.

No one is going to suddenly whip you out of your depression. You have to pull yourself out, to fight your apathy and take the decision to find ways out of your loneliness. It can be done and *you* have to do it. Waiting for the proverbial fairy to wave the magic wand could leave you at eighty, grey-haired, alone and still depressed.

In any large city there are millions of things to do, and they need not cost money. I know that for a fact. I have lived in London on a shoe-string, not only as an undergraduate but later as a mature student with little money but more adult tastes, and found a million things to do. You can too. Above all, *talk to people*. They are only people, after all, just like you. Would you bite a stranger who passed a pleasant comment? Probably not. Nor will they bite you. The comment might come to nothing but silence will certainly not break down any barriers. And you never know where the conversation may lead. At worst you might lend a little excitement and interest to someone else's life – after all, they could be lonely, just like you. A lot of people are.

Go to art galleries: many of them are free, particularly those whose aim is to sell paintings. You might even make the first night and score a glass of champagne. Talk to people. You and the person standing beside you are there presumably because of a common interest in the paintings, so talk about them. You never know who you might meet and what it might lead to. Even if the person you meet is not exciting, he or she may have some interesting friends. You could also learn more about the paintings in particular and art in general.

Go to museums. Visit stately homes or historic houses. Join classes. Learn a new skill. There are hundreds of interesting classes on a myriad of different subjects. Some of them are free, others are available for a very small cost. They may be run by schools, colleges or universities, by the local council or privately. They may be run by local businesses, such as classes on antiques or wines, or they may be run by people who, just like you, felt alone and decided to meet people by teaching.

Join clubs. If you have an interesting car, join the club for that type of car. You may not be interested in how the cylinders work but it is a way of meeting people. Join country-dancing clubs. Get involved in local politics or other action groups – organisations always need new people. Repertory theatres often have need of volunteers. Offer to help. There are always charities wanting free help and you will meet a lot of people that way. Offer to visit people in hospitals, help with meals-on-wheels.

That's all very well, I can hear you saying, but that's all lonely and dull. They're a bunch of miserable people too. I want people who will cheer me up. So do they. And when you can learn the joy of giving you can be open to receiving. Besides you can make friends with the other givers who are, almost by definition, people who like to give and to share with others.

Once you have joined the class, club or whatever, keep your goals in mind. If you are lonely, you have probably joined with the aim of finding people who will help you out of your loneliness. It may be that you are looking for a partner, at any rate you are probably looking for friends. However, when you are desperate to meet someone you can distort relationships even before they start, so make finding friends your secondary aim and make your primary aim the obvious one: learning the subject, helping the council, or whatever. At the same time make the effort to get to know the people, talk to them before and after the classes and so forth.

Put yourself in their shoes. If you were running a craft class and someone arrived and said, 'I don't really have an interest in this craft. I'm actually here to find a bosom friend,' how would you feel? If you were organising the local fête or a recruiting drive for your political party, and someone joined in and then asked to be introduced to the best-looking eligible person of the opposite sex, would you feel you had a reliable and valuable addition to your group? Of course not.

Start with the end in mind, the true end, not the apparent or intermediate goal. What do I mean by that? You may have started out looking for a friend, someone who will care for you and lead you out of depression, be it someone of the same or the opposite sex. You may have joined this particular activity hoping to find such a person. Yet your true goal, the true end to keep in mind, is to rise out of depression. This could come about by finding friends or a partner, but it could also come about by learning to contribute, by discovering a hobby that absorbs your attention, by making a larger group of general friends or by some other means. Be open to any outcome in your quest for leaving loneliness and lifting depression.

> **Take a true interest in the activities you undertake: the efforts you make to get out of your rut could surprise you, you never know what might happen.**

One of the main aims in life for most people is to find a mate. In Western cultures we have it in our minds that to be single is to be alone and miserable, to be part of a couple is to find happiness. We still, by and large, hold on to the romantic notion that being one of a couple is the road to eternal bliss. What nonsense. It can be, of course, but being on your own, with the freedom to create your life as you want it, can be equally wonderful.

We hold on to this belief in the joy of being part of a couple in spite of the many miserable marriages and the large number of divorces we see around us. We held on to it in the last century when a large number of marriages were arranged and you felt yourself to be pretty lucky if you even liked your husband or wife. We also hold on to it in the face of the many single and happy people we can see.

There is no question that to find a partner with whom you can share your soul, your hopes and dreams, your life, and in whom you find joy is a wonderful experience. It does happen. It can even happen more than once in a lifetime. But for many people it does not happen even once. If you base your criteria for happiness versus depression on whether or not you are with someone who loves you exclusively and whom you love totally, then you might be setting yourself on course for long-term unhappiness.

For one thing, you create your own experience. If you are constantly checking to find if someone loves you and can make you happy, without thinking of how much you can love them and give them happiness, any relationship has a limited future. To pull yourself out of depression you first have to learn to give and then you will be able to receive. You have to be happy and express happiness for others to want to be with you and share in your pleasure. You have to be loving and be able to express it before others will want to share their love with you. You have to be interested in others for them to become interested in you.

If you are not happy with yourself, how can you expect someone else to be happy with you? You know yourself better than anyone else does. If you find yourself poor company, if you don't like yourself, if you tell the world how inadequate you are, how dull and uninteresting, they will probably take your word for it and leave you alone.

Think of a party you have been to recently. Who did people flock around and listen to? Was it the outgoing person who smiled and laughed a lot, willing to share their warmth with others, the person who was interested in other people in general and you in particular? Or was it the quiet, lonely person who waited for someone to come and rescue them? Who would you rather be with – a warm and friendly person who is interested in you or someone who is depressed and interested only in themselves? Now, ask yourself which category a stranger would put you in.

'Fake it till you make it.' This does not mean being false. It does not mean pretending to be something you are not. It does mean finding the best bits of yourself and sharing these with other people, and the world in general.

Remember, you are what you think. There are some things you do well, others you do less well. How do you measure those criteria anyway, compared to what or compared to whom? Do you think a top tennis player who failed to make the Wimbledon finals hasn't called themselves a failure? Yet I'm sure there are others who made the first round of the qualifying tournament and lost, but who thought they had achieved success beyond their wildest dreams. Focus on your successes, no matter what their size.

You may not be the most beautiful, the wealthiest or the wittiest. But you can be the warmest, the friendliest and the most interested. You may not be brilliant at maths but you can speak another language. You may be hopeless at sports but good at creating a home. You may not be the latest entrepreneur but you may be an equally essential, reliable assistant.

You are neither happy nor sad. There are times when

you are happy and times when you are sad. Leave the sad person at home and take the happy one out to meet other people.

You are neither intelligent nor stupid. There are times when you are one and times when you are the other. Focus on the times when you have felt intelligent and interesting and take that emotion out with you.

Faking it until you make it is focusing on the best of you, however big or small a part of you you feel that to be, and sharing that with others. The results can be amazing.

No matter what the situation, you will find some people who can be happy and others who are depressed. It is up to the individual, it is up to you. Which would you rather be?

Renee was miserable. She came to see me because she was forty-seven, lonely, bored with her work and unhappy at home in the evenings. None of my suggestions got her going until I suggested she get a pet. The next thing I knew, she had two tiny kittens who, it seemed, occupied all her waking thoughts. She could hardly wait to get home to them and play in the evenings. The result? She became happier, she talked about them, she shared her enthusiasm and she started to smile at work. Another woman invited her round to her house to see her own cat. This in turn led to an invitation to a Scottish country-dancing group and Renee's social life improved from there on.

Elaine Benson also found it difficult to overcome her apathy. Eventually, however, she joined a local church group, visiting people who couldn't get out and go shopping. She liked shopping anyway and now she had a purpose in doing it and somewhere to go each morning. Initially she found it all rather depressing, but then she made friends with some of the others and eventually went so far as to comment on how lucky she was to be able to get out and about. The next thing I heard, she was learning to play bridge with one of the other helpers. 'A bunch of old people wasting their time round a card table and no one talking to anyone except to criticise and argue' was how she had first described bridge when I had suggested that as an option. That had obviously all changed when she had found a younger woman to lead her in.

Do you live in the country? Is your social circle limited to a few people in a village? Then you are lucky in that you belong to a small community and can get to know people more easily. Make the overtures. Invite people home. Start a bridge group, a craft group, a help group. Initiate a theatre group to go by coach to the city once a month. Are there no classes, clubs or socials in your neighbourhood? Then start one. Have open house one evening a week. Organise a film evening and take home a video.

I love opera but, like many people, find a year can go by without making the effort to book. So I started an opera night at home that has been going, at the time of writing, once a month for twelve years. Starting from the first operas of the 1590s we have worked our way, using tapes and videos, up to the twentieth century. People bring a plate of food, a bottle of wine and we have an amazing, if often unbalanced, meal, served during the first interval, and a fun evening learning about a new opera, and all at almost no cost. You too can do the same. You may not like opera, but you can build this social gathering round ballet, music, films, anything.

I made this suggestion to a client, a shy bachelor, who immediately replied that no one would bother to go to his house for a movie when they could just as easily go to the cinema. He was surprised when, in time, he tried it and found that his friends admired his enterprise and were delighted to come out to a low-cost dinner and film, and particularly commented on the fact that it was nice to do this with friends as opposed to going to an anonymous cinema, and that they enjoyed the chat afterwards.

It is not only single people who can feel alone and depressed. One couple were finding they were so busy with the new business they had bought that they were losing touch with their friends as they could spare only the occasional night for social activities. We evolved the idea of a restaurant night. They chose a street where nearly every second building was a restaurant and they and four other couples all met up once a week and dined at the next restaurant down the street. They then evolved a plan whereby each week one couple could bring a guest couple and in this way many new friendships were made.

Another couple came to see me and both were depressed and feeling the fun had gone out of their lives. We eventually evolved a different scenario for them. One evening a week and one weekend a month became their special times. They chose a Tuesday. On the first Tuesday she had to devise a surprise night out for him, incorporating the things she knew he liked to do. The next Tuesday it was his turn and he thought of what he would suggest were they single and he trying to woo her and give her pleasure. In this way they each had the pleasure of receiving a night out doing what they loved and then the pleasure of creating for and giving to the other person a night they would enjoy. However dull the week, they knew they had Tuesdays to look forward to. Each month they also had a weekend to anticipate. Sometimes they went away, often they stayed at home but one partner had the weekend planned full of fun things to do and the next month they reversed roles. Since then I have used this idea for many clients and it's even saved a marriage.

Notice that in the above I say 'we evolved'. There is little point in my telling them, or you, what to do. With input from me and from other sources you will evolve your own solution to the problem. Maybe all you need is a little push or a few ideas.

Notice, too, that all the solutions involve some effort on your part. There is no one 'out there' to whom you are the most important person in the world, although you might keep hoping to find such a person. Everyone, without fail, is more interested in themselves than in you. And this is how it should be. Even the most giving person is giving because it pleases them to do so, but to follow this idea is to lead us off track.

The one person to whom you are supremely important is you and it is you who must make the effort to fashion your life the way you would like it to be. If your life is not the way you want it to be then you only have yourself to blame. No one can let you down unless you are leaning on them. Lean on yourself: you are far more reliable. It may be harder to do this when you are depressed than when you are happy, but the rewards are definitely worth the effort.

Chapter Twenty-one

Eradicate the Destructive Power of Jealousy and Other Unwanted Emotions

In Part Two we have covered a number of emotions that are either created by depression or can cause depression. For example, you may feel depressed because you feel other people are criticising you; alternatively your depression may be leading to criticism, either from yourself or from other people. Either way, if you can learn how to handle criticism, you can lift your depression. Similarly, shame, indecision and compulsive behaviour can either lead to depression or be a consequence of depression. The problem with writing this section has been knowing where to stop. Jealousy, anger, hate, fear, regrets, all these and more are emotions that can cause depression or result from it.

Ask yourself which emotions are the result of or trigger your depression and then explore ways to deal with them. Most of the time you will find that these emotions serve no useful purpose and that often they are counter-productive. This is the case with jealousy:

Jealousy

Jealousy is a particularly useless and harmful emotion. It eats into the person involved, sours relationships, and never serves a useful purpose.

> Tony came to see me because he was depressed. He went on to explain that his big fear was that his girlfriend would leave him.
>
> 'We've lived together for a couple of years now, and I'm pretty sure she's faithful. But she works erratic hours as a flight attendant and I know she meets lots of interesting people while she's working. She has to stay away at nights too, when she is on a long-haul, and I'm afraid she'll meet someone else.'
>
> 'What do you do about it?' I asked.
>
> 'Well, I ask her of course, but she always laughs at me and tells me not to be stupid, it's me she loves. But I don't know . . .' and his voice trailed off. Then he continued, 'Recently I've taken to phoning her wherever she's staying and once I thought I heard the sound of a man's voice in her room. When I asked her about it afterwards, she just got impatient with me. And now it seems as if she's doing more away-shifts than ever.'
>
> We talked some more and it seemed to me that his girlfriend was getting fed up with the suspicion. I suggested that this could be the case and discussed possibilities with him regarding trust and self-esteem, but he looked unimpressed. Finally I asked, 'Is what you are doing now working?'
>
> 'What do you mean?'
>
> 'Is the way you are presently handling the situ-

ation – phoning her late at night, checking up on her schedules, asking her if she's faithful – is that improving the situation?'

'No, in fact it's probably making it worse. If things go on like this I can see us separating. We fight so much more than we used to and she gets impatient with me and then retreats into herself.'

'So, would you be willing to change what you are presently doing?'

Tony thought about this for a while and then agreed to try.

Addictions and Preferences

It was time to talk to Tony about 'Addictions and Preferences'.* The things, people and situations you want in your life are either such that you have a strong preference for them or you are addicted to them. A preference is something you want but you can live without. The wanting may be mild, like having a preference for one film over another, for going out to dinner rather than staying home, for not having to do the school run or for having time to yourself to write letters or be with friends. Or the wanting may be strong, such as the desire to stay married, to have no harm come to your children or to others whom you love, or to achieve a particular goal that is very important to you. Although preference may seem a mild word, you can feel very strongly indeed about a preference. It can be one of the most important things in your life, but it is not your life, it is not all-consuming.

Addictions, on the other hand, are things, people or situations that you simply have to have. You just know that without them your world will fall apart, you will be miserable and you won't be able to cope. You can be addicted to big things such as your lover not leaving you, as in Tony's case, or to small things, such as a friend phoning you, getting things done your way, getting even with someone, keeping an object that is precious to you. If you are addicted to smaller things, like your husband being home from work on time, the boss smiling at you or a friend phoning, when these don't happen your day, your mood, the occasion are spoilt by the way you feel. If these things were a preference you would be able to say, 'What a pity! I would like that to have happened, but it hasn't, and it's no big deal.'

Addictions and preferences can be equally strong. The difference is that with a preference, although you recognise that it is extremely important to you, you know your life, happiness, peace of mind and self-esteem do not depend on your having it. With an addiction you are seriously afraid of the result if you don't manage to have or keep it.

Addictions can jerk you around emotionally, like a puppet on strings. You are at the mercy of the addiction: your mood depends on it. You will be saying things like, 'It made me angry', or 'It's not my fault, so and so came late and spoilt things', or, 'I have a right to be mad, she treated me badly', or 'It's their fault, they didn't show proper respect'. Preferences leave you in control of your mood and your actions, free to do and be as you wish or decide. You do not blame outside factors but take full responsibility for yourself.

Sadly, feeling addicted to something is more likely to cause you pain than pleasure. You are miserable if you don't have it, but you are also unhappy when you do, fearing the devastation that would occur if you lost it. Having a preference, on the other hand, allows you to enjoy all the pleasures without anticipating pain. If you do lose the preference, you know you will cope. You may be sad, you may be unhappy for a while, but you do know that you will cope, that you will be OK and that you can move on to the next stage of your life.

People with addictions can be manipulated. If you are addicted to having someone like you, you will jump when they frown and do whatever you think it will take to please them. If you are addicted to something, 'fear of loss' can be a powerful motivating factor. The threat of losing something to which you are addicted can really pull your strings. People who have only preferences cannot be manipulated; they may willingly enter into a negotiation or bargain, but the resulting decision they make will have been made in freedom and within their own set of values.

People who have an inner self-assurance, who are content with themselves and are comfortable being self-reliant, tend to have preferences rather than addictions. People who do not have that inner peace and security tend to have addictions, especially in regard to the major things in their lives.

> Tony was clearly addicted to his girlfriend. He felt his world would fall apart if she left him: it would mean that he was no good, a failure, and had been made a fool of. He didn't know how he would cope on his own; he doubted that he would find someone else. It was time to convert his girlfriend into a preference. He could see this for himself after we had discussed the difference between addictions and preferences in some detail.
>
> I then suggested that he act 'as if', and explained what I meant:

'Act as if you totally trust her. Act as if you are absolutely positive she won't leave you. Act as if, and this is a hard one, it is fine with you whether she goes or stays, but at the same time let her know that you would much, very much, rather she stayed.'

Clearly, Tony was going to have a hard time doing this, but he conceded that he had nothing to lose and said he was willing to try. In the meantime we agreed to work on his own self-esteem.

The outcome was favourable. He did it in his own way. He didn't tell her what I had suggested, but he stopped phoning her to check up on her. Instead, when she was away on a long trip, he pre-arranged a time when it would be possible to phone for a chat. He stopped asking if she had gone out with anyone. He also started to create a more active social life of his own for when she was away and started to enjoy himself. Even more importantly, he kept working on making her and his relationship with her a preference rather than an addiction. None of this came easily, but it worked. When I saw him some weeks later, he told me that she was doing fewer long-distance trips, that she had even said he was such fun to be with these days that she hated to be away, and they were getting closer together again as a result.

It is difficult to be jealous over a preference and easy to be jealous over something or someone when you are addicted to it or them. Since jealousy is so painful to the person experiencing it, so unpleasant for the other people affected by it and destructive to the very thing you are trying to protect, you would do well to work on your own addictions and convert them into preferences.

Other Unwanted Emotions

Fear and worry can lead to depression. Anger can get you depressed, or, if not the anger itself, then the results and consequences of anger. Hopes that are not fulfilled can lead to depression. So many other emotions can be contributing to your depression or resulting from it. As part of the process of lifting your own depression, you will find it valuable to identify, isolate and work on these emotions.

> **Keep in mind, at all times, that you are the architect of your own life. If you are depressed and if you don't want to be depressed, then there are things that you can do to change the situation.**

Severe Depression

For most people, depression is a mild or moderate emotion. It is a grey cloud hanging over your life; it is unpleasant but manageable. It is something you can work on and change, if not easily then with a little determination and will-power.

For some people, however, the depression can be extreme. It can be so strong, so overwhelming that it may seem to be bigger than you, something that takes control and leaves you powerless. *It is if you think it is.* No matter how severe the depression, I have found that if the person is really willing to work on it, really willing to do whatever it takes to make positive changes, results can be achieved. It may not be possible to convert deep, endogenous depression into happy optimism, but it is certainly possible to make significant changes.

Notice, however, that you have really to want to make the changes. It is an active rather than a passive process. There is no point in waiting for the black cloud to go away, waiting for the morning when you wake up happy. You do have to come to terms with it, grapple with it, and welcome each small advance that you make. However, if you do this, you will find it worth the effort.

No matter how deep the depression, if you believe it is an insoluble problem, if you believe you are powerless to do anything about it, it will get worse. If you are willing to assume, as is simply demonstrated in many ways, that you do have and can have as much control over your moods as you are willing to take, you can lighten the depression.

What is the alternative? Remain heavily depressed? Rely on chemical drugs that alter your mind and your moods but have other adverse effects? Give up, and endure life in this state?

It is far better to take the positive step of turning round and grappling with the problem than running away. You may not be able to do this on your own if the problem is severe, but there are many professionals who will be able to work with you. Find an NLP practitioner. Find someone who does positive psychotherapy using some of the ideas and concepts covered here. Find, read and work with this and other books at the same time.

It's bootstrap stuff, but you can do it.

*For further analysis of this see *Stress – Recognise and Resolve* by Xandria K. Williams, Charles Letts (Holdings) Ltd (UK) 1993.

PART III

Creating Your Future

In Part One of this book we considered the past and the present and your responsibility for it and power over it. We included the concept that blame is not implied or appropriate and that you are not at fault for anything in your life that you have created. Whatever you have done, at some subconscious level you have had your reasons for doing what you did. We assumed that you had done the very best you could at that time and that whatever you created served some useful benefit. The great value of this philosophy is that it gives you the ability and the power to create the future any way you want it. Since you have created your past life and emotions and currently have an input into your present state and emotions, you can continue to do this and so fashion your own future.

In Part Two we covered a variety of ways of dealing with many different emotions and types of behaviour. Obviously we could not include all emotions and behaviours but we covered many of those which often either lead to depression or result from depression. This was a very practical section, and if you have put all the ideas into practice, you will already be experiencing many differences in your life.

In this third section we are going to look to the future. You will learn how to decide what type of person you want to be, how to motivate yourself, what goals you have, and how to attain them. Just as you cannot know how to reach your destination if you don't know where you are at the start, so you cannot reach your goal if you do not know where or what it is.

If you do not change the direction in which you are heading, you will end up where you are going.

or

If you always do what you've always done, you will always get what you've always got.

If you like where you are and where you are going, then keep doing what you are doing. If you would like to improve the future, you will want to start by designing it, and this is what we will be doing in Part III.

It is time now both to design the future and to define the way to reach it.

Enjoy the journey.

Chapter Twenty-Two

What Are Your Values? – Knowing What You Want Is The First Step In Creating Your Future

Clearly you are not happy with the way things are at present. If you were, both for yourself and for other people, you would hardly be reading this book. If the present is not perfect, then you have to decide whether or not you want to make changes for the future. If you choose to continue with the imperfect present, then you have some soul searching to do. Why would you choose to stay unhappy? You may be deriving some benefit from the present state of things; you may be too afraid to change; you may be enjoying the sympathy; you may believe you don't deserve anything better; or you may have some other reason.

The chances are, however, that you want the future to be better than the present. Even if now is a relatively happy time, there will almost certainly be improvements that you dream of or could consider creating for yourself.

The first step in creating the future you desire is to remember that the future starts now. The next second is the future.

Values

You are about to start planning the rest of your life, and there are some important questions to answer, some important assessments to make. A good way to start, and one that allows you to lay a really firm foundation for what you want in the future, is by determining your values, determining what factors you choose to live by and what general characteristics you want in your life. Find out what you really want in your life and what is less important to you. Discover what things you believe to be worthwhile and desirable. Some people want freedom, others look for security. Some want love, others want independence. You may value honesty or cleverness, peace or excitement, success or comfort, variety or routine. You may like to have people depend on you, you may want possessions, children, money, opportunity, skills. It is necessary to discover your values, then to rank them and to decide which of these values are the most important to you. After that you can begin to shape your future.

Start by taking pen and paper – now, not at some time in the future – and making a list of what you value most in your life. Don't worry about which values are the most important, just write down anything that comes into your head that you would like to have in life. It can be a quality, an emotion, a situation, an object: anything that you value should be written down.

> Gerald was a quiet bachelor in his early thirties, working in a government job and restlessly uneasy about his life. He felt depressed because most of his friends were married with children and he felt he was missing out. When he was asked to list his

values, he produced the following list: security, wealth, wife, children, nice home, being the boss, good job, freedom to be with my own friends, time alone.

Ranking your values

The next step is to rank these values in order of their importance, a task that is not always as easy as it sounds.

> When Gerald first considered his list and I asked him which was the most important, he was uncertain.
>
> 'Well, I want to be wealthy, but I think I want security more, yet security sometimes stops me being free and freedom is more important than wealth, yet I need money to be free, I think. Then there's a family . . . I would like a good home life . . . they give you security but take away freedom and reduce your wealth . . .' and his voice trailed away in some confusion.

There's a simple way of doing it. First, write the values down in a list. In Gerald's case the list looked like this, in the order he'd thought of them and written them down:

Security
Wealth
Wife
Children
Nice home
Being the boss

Peace
Good job
Being with friends
Time alone

I started off by putting a dot beside 'security', the value at the top of the list, and asked him, 'Is security more important than wealth? (The value below it).

Gerald answered, 'No.'

So I put a dot beside 'wealth' which was now the most important value we'd covered and asked, 'Is wealth more important than a wife?' He answered. 'Yes.' So I stayed with wealth and asked, 'Is wealth more important than children?' 'Yes.' Again I moved on, 'Is wealth more important than a nice home?' 'Yes.' 'Is wealth more important than being the boss?' 'Yes.' When we got down to 'Is wealth more important than being with friends?' Gerald said 'No.' So I put a dot beside 'being with friends' which was now his most important value to this point, and asked, 'Is being with friends more important than time alone?' 'Yes.'

Thus we established that 'being with friends' was his most important value and I wrote the number one beside it. By then the list looked like this:

- Security
- Wealth
  Wife
  Children
  Nice home
  Being the boss
  Peace
  Good job

1 ● Being with friends
    Time alone

The next step is to go back to the previous dot, which at this stage is the next most important value, and find out how far down the list you can go with it. So I asked, 'Is wealth more important than time alone?' (We'd already checked it out against all the others.) 'Yes.' So I put '2' beside wealth and went back to 'Security', comparing it to each entry on the list by asking, 'Is security more important than . . .' Gerald had trouble when we got to 'Is security more important than being the boss', but eventually decided it was and carried on down to the bottom so that security became his third value.

The next value, working down the list, was 'wife' so I put a dot beside that and asked, 'Is a wife more important than children?' 'No.' A dot went beside 'children' and I asked, 'Are children more important than a nice home?' 'No.' Another dot and I asked, 'Is a nice home more important than being the boss?' 'Yes.' This meant I could continue so I asked, 'Is a nice home more important than peace?' 'No.' A dot beside 'peace' and I asked, 'Is peace more important than a good job?' 'No.' A dot beside 'good job'. 'Is a good job more important than time alone?' 'Yes.' A good job was his fourth value and the list looked like this:

3 ● Security
2 ● Wealth
  ● Wife
  ● Children
  ● Nice home
    Being the boss

- Peace
4	● Good job
1	● Being with friends
	Time alone

I went back up to the lowest unnumbered dot, 'peace', and asked, 'Is peace more important than time alone?' 'Yes.' So peace was marked as number 5. Up again to the next highest unnumbered dot which was 'nice home'. I'd already discovered that this was more important than 'being the boss', so I asked, 'Is a nice home more important than time alone?' 'Yes.' So that was number six. We moved up to children, the next dot up without a number. 'Are children more important than being the boss?' 'No.' We marked a dot by 'being the boss'. 'Is being the boss more important than time alone?' 'Yes.' So 'being the boss' is number seven. The list had changed again. It now looked like this:

3	● Security
2	● Wealth
	● Wife
	● Children
6	● Nice home
7	● Being the boss
5	● Peace
4	● Good job
1	● Being with friends
	Time alone

By continuing in this vein we got the following list, ranked in sequence:

1 Being with friends
2 Wealth
3 Security
4 A good job
5 Peace
6 A nice home
7 Being the boss
8 Time alone
9 Children
10 Wife

Once Gerald took a good look at that list he relaxed visibly.

'You know that does make sense. My friends are very important to me. I guess I've been feeling depressed because they've been marrying and so have less time to spare for me as a bachelor. I don't really want to marry, I just thought I ought to, to be part of the crowd. And while I want to be wealthy, I also want security. I'd rather be wealthy by not spending it on a wife and family than by getting a riskier and more stressful job. Even being the boss would reduce the peace and security, yet if I remain single I will be my own boss in my private life and have time alone.'

This may not be everyone's idea of the good life, but it suited Gerald. More importantly, by recognising consciously what he had been feeling at the unconscious level, he was able to rationalise his emotions and start creating the life he wanted, without doubts and without being pulled in different directions. This is the benefit of sorting out your values.

Away-From Values

Some people find that there is a measure of conflict within their values. For instance, Gerald wanted both a secure job and to be his own boss. He was able to rationalise this by being his own boss in private whilst at work having the peace and security of working for someone else who would tell him what to do.

Sometimes there are greater conflicts between values, and, more importantly, sometimes these conflicts are hidden and go unrecognised. They can still cause a lot of inner conflict and problems, as the following example will show:

> Wendy was in her early twenties. She had a good job as a research assistant, had been married for a year and was looking forward to having a family in the near future, yet she felt depressed. She had even started wondering if she had been wise to get married in the first place, if she should stay married and, if she did, if she should reconsider the whole question of having children. Yet when she thought about getting a divorce or not having children, she also got depressed. Like squirrels in a cage, these thoughts had been scurrying around her brain for several weeks by the time she came to see me.
>
> When asked, Wendy listed her values as: husband, children, happy home, financial security, travel, friends, love, happiness, trust. When she ranked them they changed sequence slightly to: love, happiness, husband, children, travel, friends, financial security, happy home, trust.
>
> I then asked her to list her 'away-from values' – the things she did not want to have in her life.

Among these she listed: being trapped, meanness, housework, infidelity, having too many demands on her time, and gossip. She was then asked to rank them, just as she had ranked her 'toward values'. Her number one 'away-from' value, the thing she most wanted to avoid, was being trapped, and her two lists looked like this:

Love	Being trapped
Happiness	Having too many demands on her time
Husband	Housework
Children	Infidelity
Travel	Meanness
Friends	Gossip
Financial Security	
Happy home	
Trust	

When she saw these two lists side by side, she realised why she was feeling depressed. On the face of it her 'wants' were clear enough: a happy home and family. But what she was feeling subconsciously and what was depressing her was what this would mean for her in terms of personal freedom. She was beginning to feel trapped, her number one 'away-from' value, and to sense the enormous demands that would be made on her by having children to rear and a home to look after. Even her desire for travel, she realised, was more a desire for the freedom it implied. Her challenge was to find a way to have the home and family she wanted without feeling trapped and without losing her personal freedom to an unacceptable extent.

The last time we talked, Wendy was considering how she could have children, keep her job to ensure financial freedom and have sufficient income to pay for a nanny so that she and her husband could still travel together and she could keep some of her independence. Obviously it was going to be a challenging juggling act, but at least she had identified the problem and could set about solving it.

Determine Your Own Values

Exercise:

List both your 'toward values' and your 'away-from values'. Go on, do it now. You might think you know what they are but when you actually list them you might get a surprise. Then rank them, this might give you even more surprises. Then look for any possible conflicts and determine how you can resolve these.

You can use different time frames. Assess what is of value to you for the next year and then for the next ten years. You may realise that you want to do certain things for a short while and then change them later to fit in with your ten-year plan.

Working On Values in Specific Contexts

You can work on the values that relate to the whole of your life, as Wendy and Gerald did, or you can work on your values within a specific context. If you are unhappy about your social life, then ask yourself what it is that you value in your social life and what are the things you want to avoid in your social life. You can then make the necessary changes. Perhaps you are buying a car and can't decide between a sporty model that makes you feel good and a sensible family car which will meet all your practical needs. List your values in relation to a car, rank them and then find out which model comes off best.

You can also use this method to help you make decisions. You may be wondering whether to move house or stay put, whether to stay with your family or leave home and live on your own. You may be wondering whether or not to marry a particular person or what career you want. You can use this method of determining your values to help sort out your real wants.

Jeffrey had a good job in a merchant bank but had been getting somewhat restless and fed up recently. As a result he had put out feelers and been offered two jobs in two other banks. All three jobs had advantages and disadvantages and for the past three weeks his mind had been going round and round in circles. One day he thought he would stay where he was, the next that he would move to one bank, the next that he'd change and move to the other one. The whole thing was getting him down and he was feeling progressively more anxious and depressed as time went on, for he knew that the jobs would not remain open for ever and that, if something wasn't decided soon, his present employers would learn that he was restless, which might compromise his future if he did decide not to move.

I suggested that he sort out his values and then see which bank most satisfied them.

'Oh that's no use, I've already done that,' was his response. I suppose I should not have been surprised, bankers might well be expected to measure and weigh their decisions. I asked him how he had done it.

'Simple. I listed all the things I wanted in a job and then ticked them off against each bank.'

'And did it help?'

'No, they could each supply about half to two-thirds of my needs and no one bank stood out clearly ahead of all the others. Even when I thought of going to the one that scored best, I didn't feel all that happy. And that didn't make sense to me so I got more depressed, thinking how stupid I was for not being able to work out what I wanted.'

When I saw Jeffrey's lists it was clear that he hadn't ranked them, he'd merely made a list and scored a point for each bank that could satisfy a particular want. I suggested that he first rank his values, of which he had seventeen, so it was a fairly lengthy process. Then I had him draw up a table with the ranked values, listed from the top down, on the left hand side and then three columns, one for each bank, to the right. Each bank that could satisfy the first of the seventeen wants he was to give a score of seventeen points. Each bank that could satisfy the next want was to get sixteen points and so on down the list, the lowest want only scoring the bank that could provide it with one point. It was then a simple matter to add up the points for each bank.

The results were interesting. One bank satisfied

only eight of his needs but these eight needs were in the top ten of his values. The other two banks could satisfy ten and eleven of his wants respectively but they were mostly lower-ranked values, not the most important ones. The aggregate of the values of the first bank was 102 and of the other two 71 and 80. Clearly the first bank – which on the basis of the number of criteria satisfied seemed the least likely one to please Jeffrey – was the one which was most able to offer him what he really valued.

Since decision making is a not a simple mechanistic process, I then asked Jeffrey to examine the result. I asked him to tell himself that he had made his decision and to close his eyes and visualise himself in the new bank that had scored best and find out how he felt. The smile on his face was answer enough. He said that all along he'd wanted, at the emotional and gut level, to pick this bank but that since it had satisfied only eight of his needs he'd felt that he should be a sensible banker and accept one of the other two jobs which met more of his criteria.

There are many ways you can use this process to help you in your life. Have fun with it. Work with a friend or several friends. By realising how different your values are to other people's, you come to know yourself better and to respect your needs rather than trying to fit into a mould made by others.

The next step for you is to go on to the next chapter and determine your 'statement of purpose' or your 'mission statement'. This is a statement about the sort of person you are, what you value, what you want to achieve and what you stand for. Now that you have a clearer understanding of your values, this next step will be a lot easier.

Chapter Twenty-three

Who Are You and What Do You Stand For?

Now that you have established your values, you are ready to define who you are and what you stand for – in other words to write your mission statement or your statement of purpose. First, let me ask a question. Did you receive any surprises when you ranked your values? Many people do. Something that you felt was important, perhaps overwhelmingly important, may have appeared near the bottom of the list. You can learn a lot about yourself by exploring and ranking your values.

So, on to the mission statement. What is it? It is a clear and precise statement of who you are, what your standards are and what you want to be. Most people drift through life with no clear idea of where they are going, what they stand for or what they want to achieve. Doing this may work satisfactorily, but if it does it will be more by luck and instinct than by good judgement. Many people reach the end of their life and look back on it with no particular satisfaction: they may wonder what they did with it, where the time went and what they accomplished. They may ask themselves whether or not it was all really worthwhile, or if they could have done more or better. Too many people say 'I didn't achieve . . . but never mind, my children will', as if their children can make up for their failures and omissions for them. This doesn't work.

When you think back on your own life to this point you may wonder what you have done with it. You may wish you could have your time over again to live it differently. You may feel that you have done a lot of things you didn't particularly want to do and have omitted many things you did want to do. At least from this point on you can take a firm, conscious and well-thought-out hold on the future.

It is very easy to drift through life. As a child your parents told you what to do. You may have had to make certain choices at school as to which subjects you studied and which you dropped. You certainly had the final say in how hard you studied, what you achieved, and who your friends were. However these decisions were all made within a limited environment and largely dictated by your parents, the teachers and the other children around you.

You then chose a career or a job. This may have been chosen by you on the basis of some strong desire and a clear undertanding of the full implications of your particular path, but this is rarely the case. It is more likely that you chose on the basis of wanting to continue to study your favourite subject, or to fit in with what other people were doing, or to do what your parents suggested or expected, or acted on some other somewhat random stimulus.

You follow the tramlines dictated by your chosen career. You join in the social life of your friends and suddenly you are on the tramlines that lead to marriage, then to a house and a mortgage, then to children, then to the need for more money to make ends meet, to cope with the children's schooling, to see them through college, to provide for your retirement – and there it is. Suddenly you are retiring and you look back and wonder at what you have done and not done.

Along the way you may have made a number of decisions that worked for you and a number that didn't. It is possible that you had trouble making decisions, not knowing what was going to be for the best, or what you really wanted to do. We have already covered this topic to some extent but this chapter will help you further.

All these problems or missed opportunities can be avoided and life can be far richer if you have a clear idea of exactly who you are, what you stand for and what you want to do or achieve in life. A lack of answers to these questions can lead to problems and depression as you seem to drift aimlessly through a pointless life. A mission statement makes things a lot easier.

If you get depressed when you have to stay in at nights studying, it helps to know that this is leading you to your goal of having the appropriate qualifications so that you can fulfil your mission of, for example, being able to help people. If people criticise you for being aggressive and too ambitious, it helps if you recognise that this is helping you to your goal of building a business empire. Conversely, if you are not sure how to decide whether or not to go on putting up with your boss, to skip a holiday, or to spend time on the local committee you can use your mission statement as a test. If what you are doing is in line with your ultimate purpose, then continue. If it is not, then consider what changes you can make that would be appropriate.

Having a clear mission statement can act as a light at the end of the tunnel for many people experiencing depression.

Creating a Mission Statement

Start thinking about what you want your statement to say. Some people have suggested that a good way to do this is to picture your own funeral. Imagine the scene, perhaps put yourself up on the ceiling and look down on it. Someone stands up to tell the others who you were, what you were like and what you meant in their life. Then the next person does the same. What would you like them to say? How would you like to be remembered?

If a funeral is too depressing, then think of your one hundredth birthday. All your friends are there. The occasion is being written up in the local paper. How would you like them to describe you and what you have done and achieved in life?

Both of these can be good ways of getting some ideas for your mission statement, but I do have one problem with them. You are relying heavily on what other people think of you. We have already talked about taking full responsibility for your own life, making your own decisions and doing what seems right to you, no matter what other people think. If you try to live your life so that, at the end, other people will think well of you, you could fall into the normal traps that trip people up. You can never please everyone all the time, so you will always find someone who is criticising you.

If you think of your funeral or your hundredth

birthday, you may find that many of the onlookers think well of you and you feel proud of yourself. However, you may also find that some of them think you were too ambitious and career-oriented, others that you were too timid and could have achieved more. Some may be thinking you were too social, others that you were too aloof. Some may think you spent too much time having fun, others that you were too serious. Some may not understand your drive to explore, to risk danger, to travel. Others may think that you let people make use of you, not understanding your need to give, or think you too critical and not understand your desire for perfection.

If these assessments reflect what you know people currently in your life think of you, you may end up trying to make a mission statement for yourself that is acceptable to them and this is a mistake. This is not what we are seeking here. Mind you, if you are sure you want your mission statement to include such statements as '. . . do or be whatever I have to do or be to get approval from so-and-so . . .' and you are comfortable with that, then maybe this is right for you.

In fact, when you aim to become what you think will please other people it is often your own subconscious that you are assessing. In other words, if you think other people think you should do your duty and so you have this as a part of your mission statement, it may be that, subconsciously, *you* think you should do your duty. The expectations that you assume other people have of you may well be, in reality, simply reflections of your subconscious attitudes.

There are times when it is useful to ask someone how they would like to be remembered, particularly when they have no idea what they want to do or to achieve.

Even if you do not know what you want to do, you probably know how you would like other people to think and feel about you.

However, I would suggest that you do your own assessing. Mentally go forward to the far end of this life, a life of which you are proud and of which you can say 'I did it my way', content in the knowledge that you are pleased with what you have created and secure in your self-assessment rather than dependent on the assessment of others.

Think back to your values. What is important to you? How can you build these values into a life with which you will be pleased?

Create your own mission statement. Make it positive. Avoid phrases like 'I want to avoid conflict' or 'I don't want to be poor'. State what you *do* want, not what you don't.

Your mission statement should be a description of yourself and of what you value and think is important. It should cover the things you want to be, do and achieve. Include everything in it. 'What the mind can conceive of you can bring into reality.' The first steps are to conceive the ideas and formulate them.

Your mission statement is likely to be a dynamic and changing statement, not something that is static and carved in stone. Initially you may be only half pleased with it. Give yourself time. Spend some time thinking about it, making changes as they occur to you. Gradually it will come to feel right, to feel like an exact description of what you want to be and do. My first attempts were only fair but I worked at it, sometimes expanding what I had already written, sometimes starting all over again, until suddenly I felt like exclaiming, 'Eureka! That's it, that's exactly right, that is who I am now, at this stage in my life, and what I want to do and what I think is important for me in the foreseeable future.'

When I had reached this point I realised that all my earlier attempts had been somewhat self-conscious. I had written them with the thought that someone else might read them. I had written them with a view to 'looking good'.

When you write your mission statement, write it for yourself. No one else is going to read it. Have in mind a safe place where no one will find it and think only about yourself as you write it. If you imagine someone leaning over your shoulder, you may write it for them rather than for yourself and it will not be an honest and true statement.

Once you have written it and done all the alterations you want, find a quiet place and time and read it over to yourself. Ask yourself if you are totally comfortable with it, *by your standards*.

Do not worry what other people think. To live your life in happiness and peace, you have to live by your own standards. Having said that, of course, your standards may be that you fit in with other people and you may feel, as a conscious and positive decision, that this is important. In which case, say so and do it. This is much better than fitting in with others automatically and then wondering, years later, why you never made a decision of your own. It is important to be sure that you have chosen the path you are on.

By the time you have finished with your mission statement, you should have a sense of peace, security and pride. Although I said write it in private, by the time it is complete, and provided it is truly in line with the way you see yourself, you will probably be perfectly happy to have other people read it. But that is up to you.

> Nellie came to see me feeling vaguely depressed and frustrated with her life. She'd been all right, she said, quite content really, until her elder sister, who lived in Europe, came to stay on one of her frequent visits. This sister was a successful career woman, married with a child who was taken care of after school by a friend. She would look at the quiet, suburban life that Nellie led and tell her how dull she was, that she had achieved nothing, that she should stand up for herself and make a life for herself, instead of being a doormat to everyone around her. At the end of each visit Nellie became depressed, promised herself she would do something – but then let things drift on as they were, often feeling more inadequate as a result. The sister had left two days before Nellie came into my office and she was feeling very low.
>
> Nellie listed her values in the following order: love, husband, children, home and extended family, caring for others, having lots of friends, security, honesty, peace, routine. I then asked her to write a mission statement. She had trouble with this at first but when she returned and showed it to me it read:
>
> 'I am a warm and caring person who is the centre of the family. My husband, children and home come first. Once that is secure I contribute as much as I can to our extended families and the local community. I like caring for others and providing security and comfort. I do this by being there for them, providing a warm and hospitable house into

which they are welcome at any time. I support the school by being on the parents' committee, I support my church by contributing time to fund-raising and being on the list of women who are available for people in distress. I value honesty, do not like conflict and am willing to give in rather than fight unless by so doing I hurt my family or friends. If there is conflict between the demands of my family and of the community, the family comes first. I am quiet in social gatherings and do not mind if no one notices me – I enjoy listening to others. I do not mind not being well-off, but love, friendship and a chance to help others are essential in my life.'

Once Nellie had sorted out these ideas, she was able to see that the life her sister had chosen would not suit her at all. She may seem dull to others, she told me, but she realised now that she was doing exactly what she wanted. She saw clearly the benefits she provided, felt comfortable with what her sister saw as her limitations and was content to continue as she was.

The next time her sister visited her, Nellie was able to say this. Her dislike of conflict had, in the past, led her to agree with her sister and say that yes, she should get out and achieve something for herself. Now that she had a clear idea of her own mission statement she was able to say quietly but firmly that she was leading the life she wanted to lead, that she had made a conscious choice to be the person she was, she wasn't stuck there by default, and that she didn't want to change. What's more, she reported, much to her surprise, her sister didn't argue. Obviously, her quiet certainty had been apparent. The final benefit was in the lifting of her depression. She was able to enjoy the visits without feeling criticised or inadequate or getting depressed.

Tony had a different story. He was going through his second divorce and felt depressed and concerned about this. He was feeling guilty and torn between the latest failed marriage and the demands of his job. When he came into the office he asked:

'How come other men manage to have a wife and family and a successful career. Is there something wrong with me which makes me mess up relationships? After all, two failed marriages and I'm only thirty-four. I'll marry again presumably, but what if that fails too? All my friends are saying it's my fault and that I'm a selfish bastard. Yet I work hard, I provided well for her and the two children, and I'll go on doing so. I don't see where I went wrong.'

When Tony listed his values and ranked them, his list gave the first clues to the answer to his questions. His most important values were: success, achievement, job satisfaction, money, being a leader, making a name for myself and freedom. Home and family came next and finally leisure activities. He was then asked to write his mission statement. It read:

'Achievement is important. I aim to be a successful businessman, to build my companies into a strong empire, to be successful on the international scene and make a name for myself. I am a leader to whom others look for advice, information and guidance in that they see and copy what I do. I wish to be known for my honesty and integrity but above all for what I have achieved, coming from a poor background and with limited education. I will show the world who I really am. A home and family are important as a place to go to at the end of the day. I'm proud of the lifestyle I can provide for my family and I need the nourishment and nurture they provide me. When I have free time, I want to spend it with my sons who will grow up to inherit what I have created.'

As we looked at this together, the reasons for his divorces became obvious to both of us. I asked him what he felt he had contributed to the marriages.

'Not much, obviously. I guess I almost used it as a luxury motel, one that I paid for handsomely and expected to fulfil my needs. I suppose, if I'm honest, I thought of it as being there when I needed it and pushed it out of my mind when I was busy. I travel a lot and work long hours. I guess I did take them all for granted. I felt that I worked hard and provided well, and that they should have tried to understand me. But neither wife did, and they were somewhat the same really, when I think of it. But how can I change?'

'Do you want to change?'

'Yes, of course, no, well, no, not really. But a man must have a home and family.'

There were several options open to Tony. He could change nothing, marry for a third time and probably face a third divorce. His first two wives had indeed been similar: unless Tony made some conscious decisions, the third would probably follow suit. He could refuse to marry again, saying it was bound to fail, and live a bachelor existence that he clearly did not relish. Or he could take a long, hard look at his mission statement and decide what type of woman would fit in with it. He could then share it with her, preferably before they got married, and they could create a lifestyle that suited both of their individual natures and would be mutually satisfying.

Nellie's problem came from trying to fit in with what other people, including her sister, expected of her and then feeling depressed when she didn't achieve this. Tony's problem came from trying to run his domestic life along conventional lines when that didn't really suit him since he was a particularly ambitious and creative person, and then getting depressed when he experienced failure. When each of them had a clear idea of their own purpose and the way they wanted to live their lives they were able to make decisions and create a lifestyle that led to their own inner satisfaction.

Remember, like your values in the last chapter, or your goals and scripts in the next two, your mission statement is not written in concrete. If a time comes when you feel that you wish to change it, then do so. People evolve as they grow. Their goals and ambitions change, their values alter. You are free to change your self-assessment and your statement at any time you wish. Your statement should not be seen as a straitjacket but rather as a tool to enable you to live your life to the fullest with a minimum of depression, uncertainty, doubt or guilt. However, for many people their mission statement remains essentially the same throughout life. You may add to it, you may get new insights into it, the concepts may deepen as you explore their full meaning but this process can only enrich your life.

What if you find your statement or purpose is at odds with those around you? What if, to live it fully, you have to make changes, possibly serious changes, in your life as it is at present? Then you have some choices to make:

You can choose to adapt to fit in with other people and the present situation and accept the consequences. You may decide that you are in a marriage, job, relationship, country or some other situation that is not really what you want, not in line with your mission statement. You may feel trapped, yet at the same time you may feel that you cannot now make the break. Then that is your decision. Accept it as such. Do not, afterwards, blame other people or circumstances for your dissatisfactions. Instead, say to yourself something like, 'In some ways I do want to change. I would rather be somewhere else but I have decided that the problems associated with making the change are not acceptable. The benefit of the change is not sufficient to warrant the disruption or pain it would cause. This is my decision and I will not blame those around me for it.' If this is what you feel then you will probably want to change your mission statement accordingly. You might add something like, 'I value my freedom and would like to leave home but I put an even higher value on not hurting people to whom I have already made a commitment.'

There is nothing more poisonous than making a sacrifice for someone else and then secretly, or even overtly, blaming them for your dissatisfactions for ever afterwards. I have a friend whose childhood reverberated with her mother's instruction to 'Look what I have given up for you, look what I put up with.' The implication being that she would have divorced and married again if there had not been a child involved. By definition, if you have remained bound by rather than changed your situation, then you have shown your own set of values and you must recognise them as yours. My friend's mother valued a continuing marriage and home for her daughter above freedom for herself. Had she accepted this as her own decision and not blamed her daughter, she could have created a happier life for the three of them and built a better relationship with her daughter.

The other choice open to you if you are not fulfilling your mission statement is to make the changes that are important to you. Again there will be consequences which you must accept. If your job is not in line with what you want to do in life and you decide to leave, then do not blame others if you land up unemployed. Take another good look at your mission statement and get on with it.

You can often cause more pain to others as well as to yourself by trying to pretend you are someone you are not, rather than being yourself and accepting full responsibility for the outcome. If your mission statement puts you at odds with society, society will soon let you know and again you will have to accept the consequences. If, for instance, you think wealth is more important than respect for other people's property and you get caught stealing, you must accept the penalties. However, most people are willing to live within the written laws of society and find it difficult only when they try to live within laws they feel are imposed by 'what other people think' and 'doing the right thing', or try to live up to someone else's expectations. These problems can be avoided when you have a very clear idea of your own mission statement.

Your options may not always be perfect, but it is up to you to assess those available and to choose the best of them. One way to do this is to be very clear on who you are and the guidelines by which you choose to live.

Create your life the way you want it to be. Be proud of yourself and take responsibility for yourself.

Chapter Twenty-four

Knowing What You Want – The Importance of Goals and Goal Setting

If you are depressed, miserable, unhappy, dissatisfied, if you are in a bad mood, down in the dumps, fed up, bored, restless or in any other way discontented then clearly the present is not the way you want it to be. One way out of the situation is to stop focusing on what is wrong with your life and what you want to get rid of and focus instead on what you do want in your life. Once you know what you do want, you can start to work towards this and away from what is wrong with the present situation.

Many people drift through their lives with no particular goals and no real idea of where they want to go or even where they are going. Sometimes that works. I have a friend who left school not knowing what she wanted to do but it hardly mattered since she fell in love and married soon after that. She has three children, a happy home life, a good marriage and is content to fit in with her husband's career. I talked to her once about setting goals and she said, 'What's the point? If I set a goal I would have to take control and that would surely disrupt our family life. My goal might not fit in with what my husband wanted to do, it might mean I wasn't here when one of the children needed me. I have never planned, I have simply been blessed. My life is good. I guess if I do have a goal it is for things to stay as good as they are now, even perhaps with a few more of the ups and fewer of the downs. But everyone has ups and downs and really our downs are small and fundamentally we are a strong team and we work things out.' She was fortunate.

For you, since you are reading this book and so are probably not happy with your life at present, it is definitely time to work on your goals. For many people a way out of depression is to know where they are heading, not only in the greater context of their whole life, but on a daily, weekly, monthly or yearly basis. Setting goals for the short-term, medium-term, and long-term, is one way to achieve this. It is less easy to feel depressed about being poor when you are on course for your goal of being wealthy in five years' time than when you don't know where you are headed and assume you will be poor for ever.

There are many excellent books on goal setting and so we will not go into the subject in great detail. The purpose here is to show how it can help you deal with depression and to give you some general ideas.

Setting Goals

So, it is time to set goals. If you do not know where you want to be, then no map in the world will help you get there. Worse still, if you do not know where you want to go, you cannot tell whether or not you are heading in the right direction, there are no signs along the way to acknowledge and confirm that you are aiming for your goal, and there is no light at the end of the tunnel that could bring some cheer or purpose into your life.

If you have followed the suggestions made so far in this book, you have already taken two major steps towards setting your goals. First, you have established your values. Second, you have written your mission statement. At the time, formulating your mission statement may have seemed somewhat like a repetition of writing your values: for some people it is, for others the two are sufficiently different to throw new light onto what they really want. In this chapter you will find out how to use both your acknowledged values and your mission statement to help you to set your goals.

Goals must be specific. There is no point in having a goal of 'getting wealthier'. Your unconscious mind is a funny thing. It has no sense of humour and will take you literally. If you commit to 'being wealthier' your unconscious mind will help you to achieve that goal until it deems you to be wealthier. This could be when you have earned, won or made enough to lead the wealthy jet-set life, it could be when you have doubled your current assets or it could be when you have acquired as little as a few more coins in your pocket. Even having a few more coins means that you are wealthier than you were before, even if it is not what you think you had in mind, and certainly not enough to lift your depression.

If you want to be wealthier, specify exactly by how much. Specify what form you want the wealth to take. Do you want money, do you want assets, do you want an increased income? Do you want to achieve this yourself or have someone around to provide for you? Or do you mean a richer life emotionally?

A common goal, especially if you are depressed, is 'I want to be happy'. Clearly that is not specific, nor does it satisfy the next criterion of being measurable. If you want to be happy, then you will have to define exactly what being happy will feel like, what it will take to make you happy and how you will know when you are happy.

If a goal is not measurable, how will you know when you have achieved it? How will you know you are wealthy unless you have defined for yourself the exact amount of money which, in your mind, constitutes wealthy. If you want to be successful you must include in that goal a yardstick as to exactly what success will mean. Will it mean writing a better report, keeping the house tidier, having fewer rows, winning an award or a promotion? If you want to lose weight, you must specify exactly how much you want to lose. If you don't, the minute you have lost a pound or a kilo your subconscious may decide that that is enough. Conversely, no matter how much you lose, you may still feel depressed, wanting to lose more.

Failing to make goals measurable is a great way to remain depressed. Let's say your goal is to have financial security. If you make it measurable you will have to put a number on this and define exactly what you mean by financial security. It may be an amount in the bank, an annual income, or an amount that you save each month. When you have achieved this you can then say to yourself, 'This was what I defined as financial security. I now have it and it is appropriate for me to relax and stop worrying'. What happens if, on the other hand, you do not put the numbers in place but you do achieve these assets or incomes? You can say to yourself, 'This is all very well, but what if it isn't enough? I really need more, other people have more, it could be taken away from me'. And you can continue to feel depressed.

If you would like to have more friends and think that this would make you feel less depressed, define what you mean by 'more friends'. Specify how many friends you want and how close the relationship should be.

Goals must be achievable but not insignificant. There is no point in having goals that are so small that they make hardly any difference in your life. If your goals are to have one more shirt or blouse to wear, or enough money to go to one movie, or to get to work five minutes earlier, or to deliver one more meals-on-wheels, or to do, have or be anything that is not considerably more than what you are doing, having or being right now, the difference will probably not be enough to stop you feeling depressed. Obviously, there are exceptions to this. If you have absolutely no money for a movie and there is just one film that you passionately want to see, achieving this could lift your depression. But, in general, for goals to be of value and for their fulfilment to pull you out of depression, they must be big and demanding enough so that their achievement makes a significant and powerful difference in your life.

Many clients, when I have suggested this process of goal setting to them, have said something like, 'That won't make any difference, I already know what I want, I just don't have it or can't get it.' If you have a little voice saying this, ignore it. Other clients say that they already know what they want and writing it down will make no difference. But they are wrong.

> **Consider and then *write down* your goals,
> even if you think you know exactly what you
> want and that you don't need to make the effort,
> and even if you are sure there is no way of
> achieving them.**

There are four stages to goal setting:

The first step is to list your values. This should be easy for you, provided you have worked chronologically through this third section of the book and have discovered and ranked your values as described in Chapter 22.

Now, carry out step two: draw four columns down a page and head them 'Values', 'Long-term Goals', 'Short-term Goals' and 'Daily Tasks'. Put the first value at the top of the left-hand column. Then consider the long-term goals you will need to achieve to gain this value. Each time you think of one put it down below and to the right of the value and immediately consider what short-term goals would help you to achieve this result. As you think of each short-term goal write it in the appropriate column on a line lower than the corresponding long-term goal. Then move on one step further and list, also below and to the right, all the daily tasks you would need to perform to achieve the short-term goal. When you have listed all the daily tasks for the first short-term goal, work on the next short-term goal. Do this until the first long-term goal is complete, then move on to the next long-term goal. When you have completed all the long-term goals for the first value then move on to the next value. At any stage, if you wish to add additional long- or short-term goals do so and complete them.

Let's take an example. Perhaps you are single and

your value is 'A loving family life'. A long-term goal would then be to be married. A short-term goal would be to meet possible partners, and appropriate daily tasks would be to accept invitations, invite friends round, join a club, enrol in a class. Another long-term goal to enable you to achieve this value might be to have a better relationship with a parent; a short-term goal might then be to have a good talk with them and the appropriate daily tasks might including phoning them up, writing or visiting. You might also have a short-term goal of trying to understand them better and a daily task might be to learn more about people and relationships.

Your second value might be 'Happiness' and you note long- and short-term goals and daily tasks which might help achieve that. The results might then look something like the table on pages 348–9.

It is almost inevitable that there will be some repetition of the daily tasks and you will find that there are things that you can do which will help you to achieve a number of goals, such as learning French in the example.

When you have completed this table for every value in your life, take a look at the result and consider all the things you can do to get out of depression. But do not stop here. It is important not only to set the goals but to chart the course and to establish a routine for achieving and monitoring them. It is also important to commit to doing this on an ongoing, daily basis.

The final two steps are, of course, all important. First, transfer these daily tasks into your diary on every day that is appropriate. As in the table, you might decide to phone your father each weekend: write it down. You might put 'learn ten French words' on every day. You might decide to enter 'see a travel agent' a few times, until you have all the maps and information you need. Second, do the tasks you have allotted and do them *every time* you have indicated that they should be done.

Even if you do nothing more than set your goals you will achieve a small step out of depression. At least you will clarify your thinking and show yourself that there are many things you could be doing to change your present situation. But what you achieve in this way is only minor when compared to what you can achieve by actually following through and carrying out your daily tasks and thus attaining your goals.

> **Keep the daily tasks positive. Rather than saying 'don't get cross with the children' you might want to put 'try to see the world from the children's point of view'. Instead of 'don't be late for work' you might want to put 'get out of bed when the alarm rings'.**

Discovering Goals

You may say you do not have any goals, that you do not know what you want, that you don't know what would make you happy. Many clients who have come into my practice have said just that. They have been able to tell me everything that is wrong with their lives but have been totally incapable of telling me what they want to do.

> Eileen was in her mid-thirties, single, living alone and working as a secretary in a job that bored her. She had a few girlfriends but no social life that

Values	Long-term Goals
A loving family life	Get married
	Get closer to Dad
Be happy	Spend more time on fun things
	Travel

Short-term Goals	**Daily Tasks**
Meet my partner	Accept invitations Throw a party Join a club Learn French
Find the courage to talk to him	Visit him more often Get some advice

Understand him better	Read books about
	   relationships
	Take time to
	   consider his point
	   of view

Find a job I enjoy more	Read job advertisements Talk to people
Have the money	Save each week
Plan a trip	See a travel agent Learn French

satisfied, no boyfriend, no hobbies and no interests. She didn't like living alone but she hadn't found anyone she wanted to live with and didn't think that would be a lot of fun anyway. Although she was bored at work she was unable to think of what else she would rather do and was depressed that she had no qualifications.

'What would you like to qualify in?'

'I don't know, but if I had something perhaps I could get a better job.'

Not much help there.

'Would you like to travel?'

'Yes, but I have no money.'

'Where would you like to go if you did have the money?'

'That's the trouble, I don't know. There's so much unrest in lots of countries, and besides, travelling by yourself is no fun.'

I asked her a succession of questions but she had no positive answers to give. Try as she might, she could come up with nothing she would like to do, nowhere she particularly wanted to be and no hobby or interest that could attract her attention. She had tried doing one or two classes but was not sufficiently interested to stick to them and, as she said, there was no one particularly interesting doing them. By this I understood she meant no interesting man. As I explained in Chapter 18, on being alone, there is no point in pursuing a hobby or activity unless you can open yourself up to the possibility of enjoying it for itself, as well as using it to achieve other goals.

Eileen was not being difficult, she genuinely couldn't think of anything she wanted to do.

'I'd love to have interests and hobbies,' she said. 'I'd love to feel happy just lying on the beach with friends even. I just find it boring though.'

Eileen could not think of anything she wanted to do, so a proactive list of goals was out of the question. But she did respond when I asked her how she would like to be remembered.

'I'd like to be thought of as someone who was kind, someone who didn't like to see other people hurt. I'd like to think people liked me and understood me. I know I'm quiet and not very sociable but I'd like to think they thought well of me and knew I wouldn't hurt anyone. I'd want them to think I hadn't done anything bad and to understand that I had done the best I could. I'd want them to feel concern for me, even, perhaps, to wish they'd done more to help me.' Here she looked a bit sheepish. 'I mean, no one really cares at the moment. Perhaps they would recognise the difficult time I've had and how lonely I've been.'

It was clear from this that Eileen's dominant temperament was Melancholic (see Chapter 7). She was also in immature melancholic, with her attention focused almost entirely on herself. From her statement on how she would like to be remembered it was obvious her goals were not things she wanted to do, but things she didn't want to do, such as hurting people. So I set her the task of creating a life for herself which would allow her to reach these goals. I suggested that she make it a goal to create a life for which she would at least be remembered in the way she wanted, for the hurt she *hadn't* caused and the sacrifices she *had* made.

Eileen was comfortable with this. It seemed to

her to be a much more achievable and manageable goal than the goal of trying to be happy. She was able to get a job as a secretary/receptionist in a hospice. The hours were long and irregular so she had little time to miss the social life she didn't have. She sympathised with the terminally ill and had sufficient reasons for grieving and being despondent when one of the patients died. Her friends started to comment on the wonderful work she was doing which gave her a quiet satisfaction. It also gave her a little more confidence in social situations since people commented favourably on what she did when she was introduced.

Her sense of self no longer revolved around her depression but centred on the fact that she was someone who cared, someone who made sacrifices, someone who gave to others in such a way that other people thought well of her and accepted her for what she was.

Nicholas was another person who was depressed and dissatisfied with his life yet who didn't know what he wanted and had no success when I asked him to write down his goals.

'There's nothing really that I want to do,' was his response. 'I dunno. We should go away on holiday I suppose, like a couple we know. But I can't decide what to do and besides, you never know just what the places will be like, do you? You might get there and find they're a disappointment and you've wasted your money. An upheaval for nothing.'

He felt he was stuck in a routine job in a factory storeroom but could think of no other job he particularly wanted to do. He had a quiet marriage that ran to a predictable routine but lacked any excitement. His wife even cooked the same meal once every seven days, so he always knew what he would have to eat when he got home. Saturday mornings they went shopping, later on he went down to the pub and on Sundays he did odd jobs round the place or helped friends with theirs and in the evening they visited friends or friends came round. Either way they had a few beers and watched television. He and his wife rarely talked.

I asked him what was wrong with his life.

'Nothing really, I suppose. It's just that it's always the same and my friends tell me I should do something about it. They are always going off on holidays or doing interesting things. They have good jobs, and people look up to them. A couple have moved house recently and said I should do the same. I feel they are all getting somewhere and my life stays the same.'

'Do you mind it staying the same?'

'Not really. It's just their comments I guess. After all, we have a nice house . . .'

'Do you need a new job? What about the pay?'

'No, that's fine. I got a rise recently and I'm pretty well paid. It's just that I've been in this job for nearly twenty years and the others keep telling me I'm a stick-in-the-mud.'

Since asking him to write his goals had proved unsuccessful, I asked Nicholas to write a mission statement, having explained what that was. Again I had little success. He clearly didn't feel there was anything particular he wanted to achieve in his life. So finally I asked him how he would like to be remembered, what he would like his friends to say about him if he were no longer around. This he found much easier.

'They'd say I was reliable. They know they can always count on me. So can the boss – in fact he's said so. He told me the other day it was a great benefit to him that he knew I kept a close watch on the stores and that the records were always straight. My books are always up to date. My wife says much the same: that I'm reliable and that she can always be sure a pay packet will come in and that we are saving a bit each week. She also knows exactly when I'll be home so she can cook a meal on time.

'They'd say I was tidy and organised and that I didn't mind doing the boring jobs. I usually keep the records at the local football club, have done for years. I have asked them to find someone else but they say other people soon get bored at that sort of job and they'd rather I continued. And I don't mind really – it's something I know.'

As he spoke Nicholas was obviously getting a clearer picture of himself and was learning to value himself for what he was and for what he had to offer. He still said he didn't have goals and that he didn't have anything new he particularly wanted to achieve in life. What he did want, and did eventually decide was his goal, was to continue his life as it was with no upheavals, changes or disasters. He realised he liked to be the reliable one, the constant anchor in his circle of friends. He learned to value these features and to stop trying to be like the others.

Nicholas set about recognising and enhancing his own particular qualities. He had felt stressed at the thought that he was in some way inadequate and at the prospect of having to make changes. Now, every time someone asked him why he didn't do something different he learned to state that he valued what he had and what he did. In this way his discontent fell away and so did his stress, and he found that the depression gradually lifted and that he could settle down contentedly and enjoy his routines and the quiet sharing he experienced with his wife.

If you are depressed and dissatisfied with your life as it is now, change it. To do this in a positive way, work with your values, your mission statement and your goals to help you to learn where you want to go and what you want to achieve.

If you have difficulty with these, ask yourself how you would like to be remembered or how you want people to think of you and what you would like them to be saying about you. Either way make sure that, ultimately, you make your values, your mission statement and your goals yours and take full responsibility for them. Do this in such a way that it pleases you. Negative emotions will then drop away, you will have more inner peace and contentment yourself and as a result you will have more resources to share with others.

Find out what is positive and beneficial for you in any of these methods and then build on this.

Chapter Twenty-five

_____

Getting Motivated

Throughout this book you have been given a number of
ideas and concepts to consider. You have been presented with a host of practical things to do that can help
you stop feeling depressed. Yet, sadly, the time when
you are feeling depressed is probably the time when
you feel least motivated to do anything. It's a sad irony
that when you are happy and don't particularly want
things to change in your life, you have the most energy
and resources to do things. When you are depressed
you have the least energy and resources available, and
may feel that making the necessary changes is too
difficult a task and one with which you cannot cope at
this time. Even though you may not like your present
frame of mind, you may lack the motivation to do
anything about it. So it is appropriate here, before we
move on to the final step into the future, to have a
chapter aimed at helping you motivate yourself to bring
about the changes you want.

One important step in this direction involves learning
how you currently motivate yourself to do things. In
general there are five main ways in which people
motivate themselves. The first three are, I find, generally less helpful than the last two, although each can be

turned round and put to good use in the right situation, as you will see:

1. Drive Yourself To Get Started

Some people try to motive themselves by listing all the things they ought to do and then saying to themselves 'You *should* do so and so.' As soon as they hear this, and particularly words such as 'should', 'ought', 'must', 'have to', they rebel. Another voice inside their heads will say such things as 'Why?' and 'Who are you to tell me what to do', or 'I'll do it when I feel like it'. The result is procrastination as they wage this internal battle with themselves. 'I ought to' and 'I must' fight with 'why should I?' and 'I don't want to', 'I haven't the energy' and 'it probably won't work anyway'. A stalemate then ensues while the person does nothing and continues to feel depressed. He or she may eventually get on and do whatever it is they feel they have to do, but only after they have spent a lot of time in continued depression and after a considerable struggle.

You can change this very simply. Just alter the words you use. Choose to do something; don't feel obliged to do it. Choosing to act, whilst acknowledging your own freedom in making the choice, is usually a lot easier than doing something because you feel you are being forced to, even if it is you doing the forcing.

Typically you will have grown up with a number of adults telling you what to do. 'Ought', 'must', 'should', 'have to', 'you'll be sorry if you don't', you'll be punished if you don't', 'you have to whether you like it to not', 'you must because I say so', 'don't ask questions, just do as you're told': these and many other instructions probably formed part of your childhood, first from parents and then from teachers, group leaders, other children's parents, older children and even your peers. You finally leave school, reach adulthood and, quite possibly, tell yourself you will no longer let other people boss you around and tell you what to do. No wonder you rebel the moment your inner voice starts telling you to do things.

So defuse the situation. Change the words. Instead of 'I ought to do so and so' say 'I choose to do so and so'. Instead of 'I must' or 'I have to', you could use 'I want to' or 'I would like to'.

Simply by changing the wording you can bypass the rebellious spirit in you that has you resisting as an automatic knee-jerk reaction. This simple change can alter your attitude towards the task from one of disgruntled duty into one of pleasant anticipation.

> Jamie was nineteen and had come in with his mother. He had left school at seventeen and was, according to her, throwing his life away.
>
> 'All he does is sit round the house saying he's fed up. I know it's hard for kids these days to get a job, but he won't even try. He doesn't see his friends any more either, even though I tell him to go out and get out of my way. His dad's tried to help with getting a job, told him all sorts of things he could do. We've done the best we can but he just sits around, watches television and feels miserable. We don't know what to do, that's why I've brought him in.'
>
> I suggested that she sit in the waiting-room while Jamie and I had a chat.
>
> 'What would you like to do?' was my first question.

Clearly it took him by surprise.

'I don't know? I haven't thought about it much. They just keep telling me what I ought to be doing. I thought that would stop when I left school. I hate being ordered around.'

'That's fine, I can understand that. So what about discovering what you would like to do and then we'll figure out ways in which you would like to achieve it?'

As we worked together I asked Jamie to focus on using positive and desirable words of self-choice and self-motivation ('I choose to', 'I would like to' etc) rather than instructions or phrases containing implied duties. It was as if a heavy blanket of grey clouds lifted from him. In the end what he decided he wanted to do was pretty much the same as his parents had been telling him to do, but we didn't comment on that.

Jamie did want to get a job, he did want to go out with his friends. At the same time he also wanted to rebel by doing the opposite to what his parents had been telling him to do, regardless of what that was.

I was able to talk to his parents, explain what was happening and counsel them to stop giving him instructions and instead to leave him free to choose what he himself wanted. You can do the same for your subconscious. Change the words you use and your subconscious will get the message.

2. Increase The Pain of Not Making the Effort

The only way that some people can motivate themselves to do whatever it is that is required, is to make the thought of *not* doing it so bad and uncomfortable that they would rather get on with the effort of doing it than procrastinate further and reap the consequences.

Perhaps friends have been sympathising with you and are now getting impatient at your own lack of effort in dealing with the situation. Perhaps you are getting so depressed that you would rather make the effort to change than remain in your present mood. Perhaps your depression is risking your marriage, your job, your welcome at the club or something else which is import-ant to you. Or perhaps you have overheard someone who has been sympathetic to your face saying that really, though they are trying to help you, they do feel you are being a wimp. Whatever the final stimulus, at some point the pain of not making the effort to do what has to be done becomes greater than the pain and effort of doing it, and you make a start.

There are times when this strategy of doing things to avoid pain is effective. If your job depends on your being absolutely sure everything is as it should be, it is appropriate to use this pain strategy. A doctor might use this strategy to make sure he or she has done everything possible for a patient. Lawyers, accountants and agents might be motivated to take extra care by the thought of the litigation, loss or dismissal that could occur if they were negligent. Pilots and engineers might use this motivation to ensure that planes are in perfect condition before take-off.

This 'pain motivation' works well when moving away from disasters, but if it is your only method of motiv-ation there is likely to be a lot of stress and depression in your life. For moving towards a more positive and happy future it is not usually the best method of getting yourself motivated to make the necessary changes in your life.

There are other problems with this method of motivation. One is that by focusing on what you are leaving rather than where you are going you may reach a destination you do not like. If, for instance, you have recently divorced but feel depressed and lonely at being single again, this method of motivation might have you rushing into another marriage simply to stop being lonely, without proper thought as to whether or not this second marriage is really what you want.

Another problem with this method is that when you create a better set of circumstances and your depression begins to lift and the pain lessens, you may stop in your efforts and have to go through the cycle again, waiting until the pain is once more unbearable before further improvement is possible.

Angela was in her mid-forties when she came to see me. A few years earlier she had been through a difficult divorce. There had been little money left at the end of it. She had rented a small flat, planning to buy later when she had assessed the market carefully. She had a safe if not very interesting job as a secretary in an import-export house in the city which meant a lot of travelling each day.

'It's as if my life ended with the divorce,' she said. 'We lived well, we used to entertain a lot, I enjoyed cooking and creating dinner parties. We went to theatres and did things with friends, we dined out and so forth. What I didn't know was that he had this other woman too, and she was costing him a lot of money, going on holidays when I thought they were business trips. And now she has him, it's so unfair. He pays me very little and I'm not earning very much. Our friends were all couples and he still sees them. I just feel so rotten and lonely. My flat is a dump really but I can't seem to be bothered to do anything about it. What's the point? I don't entertain now anyway. I'd be ashamed for my old friends to see what my life's become and the girls in the office are all so young.'

After working with Angela for a while she joined a club, met some people and one of the women came up to the flat when she drove Angela home one evening. Angela was so ashamed by the state of the flat that she went out the next morning and bought paint and materials and gave it an inexpensive face-lift, promising herself she would start searching for her own place the following weekend.

The pain of showing someone her flat had overcome her reluctance to make the effort to improve the situation. The problem, as she told me when she saw me a month later, was that she had now put so much effort into the place that it seemed a pity to leave, and besides, she thought, perhaps prices would come down a bit further. It was all too easy to see that unless she received another trigger of sufficient magnitude she would continue to stay where she was, put up with the travelling and, worst of all, continue to feel dissatisfied with her home.

A similar thing happened with Peter, a young doctor who had been working in a small practice for several years. He knew that for his career to continue successfully and in order to get more experience he should look for another practice or, better still, set up on his own. He had been unsatisfied with where he was and unhappy with his boss who had kept giving Peter the dull and uninteresting patients. Yet, for a long time he had done nothing. He'd kept meaning to but had rationalised that his present patients needed him and that he didn't have the time to make changes.

The final push had come when the senior partner had taken another doctor of about Peter's age into the practice. Peter had then started to look for a place of his own until a colleague had offered him temporary space in her practice. He had been in the second practice on this temporary basis for three years when he came to see me and was again feeling dissatisfied. Peter needed to motivate himself sufficiently to reach all the way to the goal he desired: his own practice.

3. Focus on the Task

Another way people motivate themselves is by focusing on the task and imagining what it would be like to do it. If you are now depressed you might, for instance, motivate yourself by imagining how it would be to sit down and write your goals. You might try to picture how you would feel doing it, what would be going through your head as you listed the goals, how the final page would look.

This works well if the task is pleasant but not if it is a dull duty or difficult task. Few people are motivated by the thought of doing the washing up, the tax figures for the end of the year, or any other task that they don't enjoy and have been postponing. After all, if the thought of doing it did motivate you, you would probably have already done it.

If you focus your attention on writing your goals and you don't like writing or being cooped up indoors, this method will do little to motivate you to do what is required to lift your depression. Some people enjoy writing their goals and their values, others find it a boring or daunting prospect. You may know what you need to do to change your situation but, focusing on the task in your mind, may realise that you will not particularly enjoy doing it.

Angela, as described earlier in the chapter, could not motivate herself to make the effort to look for a new flat. She assured herself that where she was wasn't really too bad, and that later on in the year would be a better time to look. Someone else might have been willing to make the start but, having focused mentally on the amount of time that would be spent with agents, going from flat to flat, and working through the paperwork, realised that the actual process would bore them so much that they then failed to do anything concrete.

One possible way around this situation is to reduce the task into acceptable pieces. Sometimes the task is so huge that you cannot encompass it mentally. Break it down into smaller pieces and consider accomplishing them one at a time.

One client, Robin, was a successful career woman but still lived with her parents because she could not cope with the *huge* task, as she saw it, of spending time flat-hunting, going through all the searches and legal work, decorating, carpeting and furnishing the new place, packing and moving all her possessions, buying all the bits and pieces that she would need for the kitchen and so forth. No, she said, it was all too much, it would take too much time, it was too big an upheaval, there were too many things that could go wrong. Her way around this was to break it down into chunks, and the first chunk was to simply look upon the actual flat-hunting as a fun thing to do on a Saturday, as opposed to going for a walk or going to exhibitions, both of which she enjoyed.

4. Focus on the Outcome and the Benefits

A fourth group of people motivate themselves by imagining the task completed and themselves experiencing the benefits. This is usually a successful strategy. If you can experience in advance the benefits of doing what is required it is usually a lot easier to get going.

If you know that having more friends would make you happier and you focus on the pleasure of having friends rather than the difficulties and challenges of making them, you will find it easier to go out and meet people. If you know that by living in the country, ending an unhappy relationship, changing your job or restoring a troubled friendship you will be less depressed, and you focus on the positive outcome, the steps along the way to achieving your goals will become easier.

Having reached this far in the book you will already have many different ideas and tools for making the appropriate changes. You might want to take time to make more detailed plans. At this stage do not listen to the voices inside your head telling you it is all too difficult. Just become clear on steps you can take. Then create that picture. Visualise, as clearly as you possibly can, the outcome you want.

Exercise:

Imagine the result of doing whatever it will take to get you out of your depression. For the moment, don't even think about how you will achieve this outcome. Think only of the positive outcome that will help you lift your mood and get you out of the depression.

Imagine actually being happy, content and at peace with the world. Imagine being excited, stimulated and interested in the new situation. Make the outcome so appealing that you can hardly resist it, then focus immediately on one of the tasks or exercises you must do to bring it about. Then do the task.

Mr Bennet's wife had died two years before he came to see me and since then he had seen little of his grandchildren, saying his wife had always been the family one and that he was more interested in his books really and didn't know how to talk to children. At the same time he was lonely now and wished he had made more effort to get to know them, but wasn't sure how to start, since he didn't feel really close to either of his daughters. Each time he had thought about it the effort of getting on the train and going to visit them, of wondering how he would be received, how he would behave, whether or not they would really want him, he had felt overwhelmed and had given up without doing anything.

I asked Mr Bennet to make a very clear picture in his mind of the outcome he would like.

'That's easy, I'd like them to welcome me as they did Molly when we used to go there together.'

Since he had his memory to work with the task

was relatively easy for him. I told him to make the picture as bright and as colourful as he wanted, provided that that made it more appealing. Colour, he said, helped, but when it was too bright he felt less happy. He attributed this to his enjoyment of the quiet lights of his study with its books and a general dislike for being out in the sun. So I told him to soften the lighting until the picture had maximum appeal.

'What do you hear, in this ideal scenario?'

'I can hear the children calling and laughing, the way they used to. Their gran was such fun that they were always excited when we arrived. They're not like that with me. I wish they were.'

So I encouraged him to get the sounds right.

'How will you feel when this all happens?'

'I'll feel good. I'll have the feeling I had with Molly before she died: safe and comfortable, wanted, yet not having too much expected of me.'

When Mr Bennet had fully focused on the outcome and had it clearly in his mind I told him to pick the phone up then and there and to invite himself down for the day on Sunday.

'And tell them how much you're looking forward to it,' I said.

At this I could see his face fading. 'But what if they don't really want me? I'm not much fun for them, not on my own.'

'Recreate the picture, get that firmly in place, with all the sounds and all the feelings. Now pick up the phone. Don't even stop to think about what you're doing. Get the feeling in place . . . Good. Now pick up the phone.'

Looking slightly nervous, he did as I told him

and, with promptings from me to 'Keep the happy picture in your mind', he made the call and told the daughter how much he wanted to see her.

It wasn't easy for Mr Bennet at first but in time the daughters came to understand that he loved coming as much as their mother had, even if he was quieter, and so his life changed.

This way of motivating yourself is like anchoring (see Chapter 13). You are anchoring the good feeling about the outcome of the task to the job of getting on with what you have to do now, so that what you have to do seems to be a very important and urgent thing to do. You may have a specific outcome in mind like Mr Bennet. You may have to create an imaginary outcome. This is where the last three chapters will help you. You will get further help from the next chapter on 'scripting'. Once you have written your script in detail you will always have that to refer to. Use it to reinforce this desirable goal each time you need extra motivation to do what is necessary to get there.

5. Find Things To Look Forward To

Another way of generating the motivation to make changes in your life is to create a future by using your memory line, as described in Chapter 12. If you are not able to picture your future, you have nothing to look forward to and it is no wonder that you are feeling depressed. If you read through Chapter 12 and had no future this would be a good time to create one, so go back and read the chapter again and work on creating your future. By making a future on your memory line you can start the process of creating something towards which you can work and look forward.

Combining the memory line, values elicitation, mission statements, goal setting and scripting as described in the next chapter, together with the other many and varied tools in this book, can help you to become motivated in such a way that you can make positive changes in your life.

Chapter Twenty-six

Discover Where You've Arrived

We have seen the importance of having goals, writing them down and working towards them. There is a final aspect of creating your future and lifting depression which we can consider and which you will find valuable. Before we set out on this path there is something else for you to think about, and that is your role in creating your past. If you are not ready to embrace fully the idea that you have created your life up to this point, it will not be possible for you to feel totally convinced that you can create your future, and if you cannot do this you may have to live with depression until some outside factor lifts it for you.

If you find you are still saying to yourself and to others that in the past you have been a victim of circumstances, that things happened to you, that you were the recipient of what the world, in the form of other people and circumstances, dished out to you, then you will find it difficult to create the future the way you want it. If you keep insisting to your subconscious mind that you did not have control in the past, you will find that it is unwilling to back you up in believing that you can create and control your future. If you do find your have trouble creating the future you want, you would be wise to look back to the past and examine your beliefs. This is often a challenge. Yet the exciting reward is that you will then have the capacity to create exactly the future you want.

So, back to creating the future. When you set goals you are telling your brain, and particularly your unconscious mind, where you want to go. You are setting out a path that you wish to follow. It is rather as if you have put yourself at the bottom of a mountain you wish to climb. By setting your goals, you have identified the correct mountain, you have positioned yourself at the base and now, with the peak clearly in sight and knowing that that is the summit you want to reach, you are ready to start climbing. This is much more satisfactory than wandering up and down the lower slopes of several mountains, not sure exactly which one you want to tackle, and not going anywhere. Yet it may still seem a somewhat daunting task. After all, the climbing is still ahead of you.

To make the mountain you have identified less daunting, take yourself, mentally, to the top of it and find out exactly what it is like. Look around and describe the view from there, find out what it looks like, create the internal experience of being able to see it, hear it, and feel it. Develop the feeling of having reached the peak, and discover what the experience of being up there really means to you. Make all this as real as you possibly can. Make sure that this summit has maximum appeal and if it hasn't then make the necessary adjustments. Plant this picture and this experience firmly in your mind; describe it in detail. While you are still at the top of the mountain write down everything you can see, hear, feel and otherwise experience and keep the description, the script, handy. Make yourself a commitment to read it and dwell on it at least once a day.

When you are writing goals from the bottom of the mountain you may find that you have a voice inside your head saying 'Yes, that is all very well, that is what I'd like, but it's not really possible'. The little voice may then go on to give a number of reasons why you will not achieve these goals. It may also spell out the risks you could be taking both in going for them and admitting that they are what you want – after all, what if you failed, wouldn't that be painful, wouldn't people laugh at you or feel sorry for you? These and similar thoughts can hold you back.

When you write the script from the top of the mountain, the voice has no chance to undermine your belief in your ability. It cannot tell you that what you want is impossible for you already have it – you have already climbed the mountain and reached the top; you have already demonstrated that you can create this mountain top just the way you want.

In practical terms there some specific things you must do. First choose a date in the future by which you wish to have achieved your present goals. To start with at least it is best if you keep it relatively close, as you will be wanting some feedback as to how successful you are being in this process.

For instance, if your goal is to have a new job, write: 'It is now (a date in the future that you have chosen and consider to be appropriate and desirable) and I have just started in my new job'. Then continue to describe it in as much detail as you can possibly imagine. At the bottom sign it and write, 'Script written on (today's date)'. Do the same if you want a lover, an achievement, to change part of your personality, to travel, to have a new home, an altered relationship with your family, greater spiritual peace or any other goal for which you are yearning. Since we are focusing mainly on depression, you may want to choose a goal the achieving of which would alleviate your depression.

As well as describing the mountain top, it is important that you describe the route to it. If your script includes the fact that you have a new job then describe how you got it as well. Include the fact that you answered advertisements, went to a head-hunter, talked to people in your field and so forth.

A word of warning: you cannot manipulate other people. If you are lonely, you might want a lover and desire one particular man or woman, but you cannot control them. Rather than say 'It is now (date) and (name) suddenly realised four weeks ago that she/he loves me after all', it would be better if you said 'It is now (date) and the most wonderful man/woman is in my life and loves me dearly'. Similarly with a job; rather than specify the particular company and job, you would do better to describe the ideal scenario, in as much detail as you like, but allowing for some flexibility as to the name and identity of the company. After all, if you do specify the name you could be limiting yourself. You don't know all the options and there may be a company which suits your needs and desires better than you know. If the one you want really is the best for you, your subconscious will arrange for you to get it anyway.

Write your script, describing your future but using the present tense as if you have already achieved it and the past tense to describe how you got there. You will be surprised at the power this method has and at what can happen.

I have used scripting with many people in my office and the results have been very interesting. People are usually able to be far more specific about what they want when scripting than when goal setting. It seems to be easier to describe what you already have than what you would like to have. When writing their goals from the bottom of the mountain, many people choose not to be too specific and detailed, feeling that this will limit their options. From the top, when scripting, they find it is easier to specify exactly how they want things to be. After all, they have already attained what they want and so describing it fully and in the exact detail that they require is simple.

Once you have described, in complete detail, life at the top of the mountain, live it. Read your script over and over regularly. Eat it, breathe it, sleep it, dream it, make it fully a part of yourself. You will then find yourself 'walking your script'. This is an important step along the road that will bring it into reality as your thoughts and your attitude will have a positive effect on the outcome.

> Margaret badly wanted to be an actress. When I asked her what type of actress, she was vague, saying that any sort of role would do, in any medium, and that she just wanted to act. When she started to write her script, she had to specify exactly what part she had. It turned out that she wanted to act on television and that she wanted a part in a glamorous soap that ran for a long time so she could develop the character with the story.
>
> Once she had scripted this fully, Margaret was able to act as if she had the part and, even more importantly, to focus her energies on getting the

right sort of auditions – auditions for a part that she felt she had the skills for and about which she could be truly enthusiastic. Because she was then so sure that she would get the part her nerves faded and her confidence came through. In this way she was able to have a powerful input into creating her desired outcome.

When you are writing a script it is important to specify the dates, both the date from which you are writing it – the top-of-the-mountain date – and the actual date of writing. At the top of the script put something like, 'It is now 10 August 1998', or whatever date you feel is appropriate. It can be a week, a month, a year or a decade ahead, whatever you like. You can have several scripts for different periods of time. You might want one for a few months from now and another for a year or two from now and one for a time towards the end of your life. You can also have different scripts to cover different aspects of your life, though you may prefer to integrate them. The choice is yours.

When I said this to one client she was aghast. 'I couldn't do that,' she said. 'It would be like losing my freedom, having to spend the rest of my life going down a preordained road.' She was quite happy with a script for the near future because she knew exactly what she wanted in that time. But she wasn't sure what she wanted for her life as a whole and was content to let it unfold as it would. So be it. Again, the choice is yours.

Another aspect of scripts is that you can change them. What you think you want now may not be what you want in a year or two years' time:

Veronica knew exactly what she wanted: a career in advertising. She had this fully scripted almost as soon as I suggested the idea to her. When she came back to the office she showed it to me in all its detail. She'd included the type of office she wanted to work in, the location, the sort of people she'd like to work with and the clients she'd work for. She'd also specified a partnership within three years. Within the allotted time, four months, she had her job and was well on her way. During the next two or three years she kept focusing on the partnership and was close to achieving it. Then she fell in love. Within a year she was a corporate wife, passionately wanting to have a family of at least four children. So she changed the script. You are free to do this at any time.

Be sure you write your script in sufficient detail and that you cover all aspects of the situation.

Carol wanted to get married. She was in her early thirties and had been a successful businesswoman for ten years. Now she felt it was time to marry. She scripted a gorgeous guy who would come along and sweep her off her feet. After a few months she reported that nothing was happening and no one had turned up. So I suggested she be more detailed and specific. She did this but still nothing happened, or so she said. When she showed me the script I pointed to a number of omissions: she had not stated his age, nor had she specified that he should be heterosexual and unmarried. When I pointed this out, she burst out laughing. When she thought back over the preceding months she found that several gorgeous males had indeed entered her life. Her sister had moved back into the district bringing with her her eight-year-old son. He was indeed tall (for his age), blond, good-looking, fun to be with and very loving and affectionate. She had met a couple of men she had liked but thought no more about them since they were married, and a friend with whom she usually went to the ballet had given her own ticket to a man who was gay. As Carol said, he was a wonderful companion for the evening but hardly marriage material. She then changed the script to include these important points and, some months later, she did start a serious relationship.

You might like to play scripting games with a friend. Brainstorm each other to find out what you are including in your script that you do not want. Look for the loopholes which might be present and which would weaken the strength of the script.

If you are feeling depressed now and would like to be happy, write the appropriate script. Pick a time in the future, take your mind forward to that day, and describe exactly how you feel and why. Detail the changes that have occurred in your life that have resulted in this happiness. Cover all the details and take into account your home and family, work and play, social and spiritual factors, hobbies, finances, learning, sharing, caring, goals and achievements. Make it as detailed as possible and really concentrate on what you are doing. By the time you have finished you will probably be feeling happier, certainly a lot less depressed. You can hardly focus on a time that is just the way you want it to be and not feel happy.

If you find a sad little voice insisting that it is all an illusion, that none of those wonderful things will happen to you, then you are not on the top of the mountain, you are not in the right place for writing the script, not, that is, unless at some level you want to stay depressed. You are at the bottom or hovering round the lower slopes, still facing the heights ahead. Go to the top. Sit firmly on the top of where you want to be, having achieved everything you want and need to be happy, and describe it in full detail, in the present tense.

If you still find you can't do it then you have some more thinking to do. Most people have little trouble doing this exercise. In fact it usually provides great pleasure since this is your chance to create utopia. But occasionally people do have trouble. If you do, then it could mean that you don't know where you want to go, or that you are already where you want to be and that you are deriving sufficient benefit from your depression to compensate for its negative aspects. If nothing else, consider this possibility and find out what you can learn from it. We covered this in Chapter 9 and now might be a good time for you to go back to it. It may not be easy to recognise that you are clinging to your depression or that you lack the courage to change, preferring the unhappy present to an uncertain or challenging future, but if you can come to terms with this and learn from it, you can move on.

Another possible reason for finding this process difficult is that you may still be reluctant to accept that you can create a future, reluctant to accept that you can have what you want. You may still be convinced that you are in some way bad, unworthy or undeserving. This is true only if you think it is. The moment you change that thought, it is no longer true. You may want to explore further the ideas of personal development, appreciation of self, recognition of the wonder that is you and the concept of personal responsibility for your life. This book is a start, there are many others as well as workshops, seminars and counsellors. The process of creating your life and living it to the full is an ongoing journey of self-exploration and self-realisation. It is exciting and the results are rewarding. Why choose to stay depressed, unless you want to?

Exercise:

Now it's your turn to write that script. Here to remind you are the steps:

1. Choose a date in the near future.

2. Write in the present and past tense, describing your life at this chosen date.

3. Include in this description details of things that have happened only a very short distance in the future from the day of writing, things that you absolutely know will happen. This can help to reassure your subconscious mind of the validity of the process.

4. Describe your life and yourself exactly *the way you want them to be. Don't write that you are now 'less depressed', write that you are 'very happy', assuming that that is what you want.*

5. Make the script as detailed as you possibly can and be specific. When we talked of goals I said they must be specific and measurable. The same applies to your script.

6. Do not worry if you do not know how your chosen results will be achieved, just script them.

7. Include such phrases as 'everything worked out for the best', 'it was all resolved peacefully and productively', 'everyone was satisfied' etc.

8. Sign and date the script.

9. Put it somewhere safe. (You might even like to consider where that place will be before you start writing. You want to be certain that you have somewhere absolutely private to keep the script so that you can be sure that unless you choose to share it, no one but you will read it. Then you can write it with perfect freedom and full honesty. There is little point in editing what you write in case someone reads it, or writing it with the thought of other people reading it at some time in the future. You want to be able to put your full heart into it, bare your soul and describe exactly what you want the top of your mountain to be.)

There are two important and interlocking beliefs which, as I mentioned at the beginning of the chapter, under- line scripting. If you can make these beliefs yours, you can overcome your depression and create a happy and fulfilling future for yourself.

1. Recognise that you have created your life up to this point and use this knowledge to give you the power to create your future.
2. Recognise that if the future is in your hands, so was the past. This recognition gives you the freedom to acknowledge your past as your own, to stop blaming others and to live more more fully and independently.

Think about these ideas and have fun with them.

Chapter Twenty-seven

Be Happy

Be willing to be happy. This may sound like an amazing instruction. 'That's exactly what I want,' you may be saying. 'No one likes to be depressed. I hate it, I'm miserable, I'd much rather be happy.' But would you? And if this is true why are you letting yourself be unhappy now? In truth, as we have seen already, there are many benefits to being unhappy. As well as the sympathy and the attention, there is the comfort and safety of knowing that you have little to lose. Be brave, take the risk, be willing to be happy.

It is a sad truth that the best way to motivate the majority of people is by fear of loss rather than by dangling the carrots of gain and benefit in front of them. Most people will take out insurance before they will invest in a money-making venture. They are more likely to make the effort to work harder and to do a better job when they fear the sack than when they are hoping for a rise in salary.

Pain is a great motivator: perhaps you fear the loss of painful emotions. Perhaps you are afraid that if you are happy people will expect more of you. They may expect you to give more of yourself, to share with others, to give of your time. Be willing to take that risk. You will almost certainly find that the happier you allow yourself to be, and the more that is expected of you, the more will come back to you and the more you will have to give.

We live in this wonderful world. The mere fact of being here is a miracle. Think also of all the troubles you have avoided: no matter what country you live in there are people in other countries even worse off than you are; no matter what you don't have, there are millions of people who would like to have what you do have; no matter how much you have lost, there are others who have lost more or never had as much as you still have; no matter how bad your health, there are those whose health is worse; no matter how few material possessions you have, there are those with fewer.

You have chosen just the right incarnation for yourself, for what you need, for your growth and development. Perhaps it is your mission in life to be despondent, to experience the down sides of things and the depressed range of emotions. If you are convinced of this and that you should not be happy or don't deserve to be happy, live fully in and appreciate the emotions you are experiencing.

Although I choose, most of the time, to be a happy optimist, there have been a few times in my life when things have happened that have left me feeling lost, deprived or sad. On one such occasion when a friend was commiserating with me, I had to cheer him up. I found myself saying something like, 'Don't worry, I won't feel like this for long and for the moment I am enjoying it, it is a new experience. Let me experience these emotions to the full and when I'm ready I will cheer up and move on.' He was shocked, and to this day I don't think he fully understood what I meant.

As human beings we can experience a wonderful range of emotions. To live fully it is important to experience them all, and when you do, draw deeply on the experience. Being depressed can mean that when you are happy again you will truly appreciate that experience. Nevertheless it is inappropriate for people to wallow in depression. If you are not enjoying your current emotion then change it, do whatever it takes, but change it.

If you are struggling with any of these ideas perhaps it is time to go back to the appropriate sections of this book. Or perhaps it is time to find other books on personal growth and development that can help you peel your way down to the heart of your emotions until you find the real you. If books are not enough, find a counsellor, someone who can help you. I often find with clients that just a few sessions can point them in the right direction, that a chance to discuss their ideas, after a lot of reading, can help everything to fall into place. Or perhaps a few sessions of NLP can be like the last brick in your Roman arch bridge, providing the one small stabilising factor that can hold the entire structure together.

No one has an automatic right to happiness, they must create and earn it. The wealthiest in the land can be depressed; the poorest can be happy. Those with the largest circle of friends can feel lonely; the hermit can feel content. The biggest family can have the greatest conflict; a single parent can feel the greatest closeness of family bonding. Once you have found happiness, share it. Until you have found it, fake it, share it with others and happiness will soon come back to you. Focus on what you have and, like a well nourished and much loved seed, you can grow into whatever you want to be.

Above all, take responsibility for who you are and what you are experiencing. Then, and only then, do you know, really know, that you are in control and can create your life the way you want it.

Be happy.

Index

Optimism 36
  and pessimism 95–116
  Sanguine temperament 87
Overeating, inner conflict over
    242–7, 271, 274–5

Pain strategy, in motivation
    359–63, 381
  case studies 361–3
Panic, and anchors 175
Partner, seeking 294–5
'Parts', in Transactional
    Analysis 80–1
  case study 81–3
  and inner conflict 241; case
    study 242–7, 248–9
Past
  creation of 370
  living in the 146–7
  location of 149–51
Pessimism
  of Melancholics 89–90
  and optimism 95–116
Pessimists
  case study 110–14
  change to optimism 105–16
  exercise 107–10
Phlegmatic temperament 88
Physiological creation of
    moods 57–64
Pictures *see* Visualization
Popularity 39–40
Positivism 141–2
Potential, achieving 26–7
Preferences *see* Addictions and
    preferences
Prioritisation of values, in
    decision making 262–4
Proactivity 52–6
  or reactivity 49–56

Questions, and handling grief
    224–5

Reactive depression 206–25
Reactive people 49–52
  case study 50–2
Reality 107–8, 115–16
Reincarnation 123–30
  case study 125–8
Relationships outside marriage
    21–3
Relaxation, physical, against
    depression 58–61
  case study 62–4
Religious beliefs 23–4
Responsibility, and the
    optimist/pessimist 102–3
Responsibility, personal 3
  see mainly Control
Right and wrong
  belief in self 177–82
  ethical codes 24–6
  respecting others 181–2
'Running a phrase' 43–8, 118,
    279

Sanguine temperament 87
Scripting 56, 370–80
  case studies 374–5, 376,
    376–7
  exercise 379–80
Seeking a mate 294–5
Self-belief 177–81
Senses, dominant 64–5
Severe depression 307–8
Shame and guilt 226–39
  dealing with resolved
    237–9; case study 238–9
  dealing with unresolved
    232–7; case study 234–5